"You still believing in the beautiful Light, are you?"

— Terrence Malick, *The Thin Red Line*

Wherever you turn your eyes the world can shine like transfiguration.

— Marilynne Robinson, *Gilead*

Who lit the wonder before our eyes and the wonder of our eyes?

— Abraham Joshua Heschel, *Man Is Not Alone*

The visible reminder of Invisible Light.

— T. S. Eliot, "Choruses from 'The Rock'"

BEAUTIFUL LIGHT

RELIGIOUS MEANING IN FILM

Roy M. Anker

William B. Eerdmans Publishing Company
Grand Rapids, Michigan

Wm. B. Eerdmans Publishing Co.
2140 Oak Industrial Drive NE, Grand Rapids, Michigan 49505
www.eerdmans.com

23 22 21 20 19 18 17   1 2 3 4 5 6 7

ISBN 978-0-8028-7369-9

Library of Congress Cataloging-in-Publication Data

A catalog record for this book is available from the Library of Congress

For Ellie,

again and ever.

CONTENTS

CONTENTS

ACKNOWLEDGMENTS

Many people and organizations play an invaluable role in a project of this sort. Calvin College supplied a sabbatical, and the Calvin Center for Christian Scholarship provided additional invaluable course releases. And many people have helped with conversation and comment, most notably Jon Pott, David Bratt, Carl Plantinga, Jennifer Holberg, Jane Zwart, and several who'd no doubt like to leave their names out of it. I would especially like to thank many colleagues past and present in the English Department of Calvin College. A more lively and supportive group could not be had. And once again, thanks to the remarkable Ellen and to our three splendid children and their mates, all of whom have supplied endless hospitality, encouragement, and humor.

November, 2016

THROUGH WONDER TO VENERATION

One big question shapes this book: What has film to do with "religion," or, for that matter, anything at all "religious"? Those terms are not the most precise, and especially so the latter, though scholars have been wrestling with their meanings for centuries. Still, they are the best terms we have for a particular kind of understanding of the world, especially when it comes to the possibility that there is somehow some sort of supernatural something afoot.

In merely raising that question we immediately enter what is at present vexing intellectual and experiential terrain, a fraught territory about which most everyone these days has strong opinions. To be sure, assorted religions in the West and around the globe have been around since, well, creatures achieved self-consciousness and began to wonder how humankind got here and why, mysteries to which religions have proffered a variety of more or less satisfactory responses ("answers" would be overstating the case, though that is *not* a view held by fundamentalists of all faiths). Nor has the debate disappeared, though elements of modernity have sought to banish it. On religion and religious belief in general, the militant skepticism of neo-atheists such as Bill Maher or Richard Dawkins ridicules the gullibility and hypocrisy of those who so much as consider religious questions. On the other hand, world-renowned philosophers, religious and secular alike, look askance at the puerile credulities of neo-atheists.[1]

---

1. In this regard see Terry Eagleton, luminary literary theorist, *Reason, Faith, and Revo-*

And film, what role has it in matters religious? By most accounts, the answer at present seems to be very little. Most people regard the question itself as baffling, and except for very rare occasions, it does not often occur to anyone, whether moviegoers, filmmakers, or critics.

That was not always the case. The early days of film, at least in Europe and North America, saw regular cinematic treatment of a wide array of biblical materials, though by the time sound came along that impulse had largely disappeared, save for periodic resurgences, such as the spate of "bathrobe epics" in the 1960s. First, though, with the coming of cinema came a flood of honorific cinematic portrayals of parts of the Bible, both Old and New Testaments, for which there was a ready audience. The attempt to display the sacred on the screen, as stories carried by images, seemed an exciting (and profitable) challenge.[2] Joining a long history of popular and elite representations of religious stories in books, plays, and visual art, movies seemed to provide a new and palpable immediacy to the material, as it did to many other domains of the fabled past, from Napoleon to the Wild West.

Since these early decades, however, such biblical materials have rarely been considered inviting, let alone engrossing. Nonetheless, from time to time filmmakers, for a variety of reasons, take on the formidable challenge of biblical storytelling. Late 2014 saw both Darren Aronofsky's *Noah* and Ridley Scott's *Exodus: Gods and Heroes*, both packed with gran-

---

lution: Reflections on the God Debate (New Haven: Yale University Press, 2010); eminent analytic philosopher of religion Alvin Plantinga, *Where the Conflict Really Lies: Science, Religion, and Naturalism* (New York: Oxford University Press, 2011); and philosopher (and agnostic) Thomas Nagel, *Mind and Cosmos: Why the Materialist Neo-Darwinian Conception of Nature Is Almost Certainly False* (New York: Oxford University Press, 2012).

2. See Adele Reinhartz, *Jesus of Hollywood* (New York: Oxford University Press, 2006), an excellent recent treatment. Another useful treatment is Jeffrey L. Staley and Richard Walsh, *Jesus, the Gospels, and the Cinematic Imagination* (Louisville: Westminster John Knox, 2007). Staley and Walsh provide a helpful handbook to nineteen Jesus films on DVD (from 1905 to Gibson's film in 2004). The introduction provides a set of useful inquiries both cinematic and biblical. The authors wisely include both *Monty Python's Life of Brian* (1979) and Martin Scorsese's *Last Temptation of Christ* (1988). See also, Richard C. Stern, Clayton N. Jefford, and Guerric Debona, *Savior on the Silver Screen* (New York: Paulist, 1999). In nine films spanning the history of Jesus films, the authors emphasize the rhetorical intentions in the biblical accounts and in the films, pushing a two-staged interpretive matrix. Though oriented toward those who bring Christian belief into the theaters with them, the book is useful for others in that it argues for the necessity of rigorous analysis and reflection, viewing each film through three distinct "lenses": comparative analysis between biblical and cinematic texts, the array of variables in *cinematic* representation, and viewer response.

diose effects, but neither seemed prompted by belief or devotion. Indeed, Scott's subtitle seems more fitting for the lushness of Greek epic than the Old Testament's spare narratives. These recent films seem to have more to do with the many "bathrobe epics" of the 1950s and '60s. While neither Aronofsky nor Scott did well with critics or at the box office, Mel Gibson's earnest *The Passion of the Christ* (2004), a film very much prompted by the director's own Roman Catholicism, proved remarkably successful. Though generally panned by critics secular and religious alike for its violence and its medieval theology, conservative Roman Catholics and evangelical Protestants attended in droves, making for an enormously profitable film ($30 million to make, roughly $500 million in gate).

These sorts of film, however, are hardly the whole of it, and constitute no more than a sliver of a much larger enterprise now known as "film and religion." In other words, dramas of religious leaders, whether of Moses, Jesus, or Buddha, do not constitute the only or fullest intersection of film and matters religious; to think that they do is to mistake a pond for the ocean, not only in size but also for the great variety of creatures therein. While often inviting, cinematically inventive, and moving (consider Franco Zeffirelli's lush *Jesus of Nazareth* [1977] and Pier Paolo Pasolini's stark *The Gospel According to St. Matthew* [1964]), biblical narratives are a minuscule part of a much larger tradition that has been anything but parochial or doctrinaire. Moreover, to an extent not usually recognized, major figures in the film-religion enterprise have also played crucial roles in the development of cinema as both an art form *and*, at times, a remarkable commercial success (think of Steven Spielberg's *E.T.* and the Lucas/Disney *Star Wars* "empire," lately spectacularly resuscitated and still making the ambiguities of the Force front and center).[3]

Rather, the main current of cinema within "film and religion" contains innumerable films by venerable screenwriters and directors who have grappled directly, in lastingly fresh ways, with central human concerns of doubt and belief, meaning and nihilism, despair and elation, enmity and love, and calamity and well-being. These encounters have not taken place in Pollyannaish realms of sentimental fantasy but in

---

3. Director and celebrated screenwriter Paul Schrader's master's thesis, published as *Transcendental Style in Film* (Boston: Da Capo, 1988), remains in many ways the founding text for the study of film and religion. It remains a landmark and is presently scheduled to appear in a revised edition.

sober reckonings with modernity's fearsome "darkling plain" on which humankind has struggled body and soul, perhaps never more so than in the last two centuries.

In "Dover Beach" (1867), British poet Matthew Arnold famously described the modern cultural landscape in the aftermath of the American Civil War, a slaughter whose death toll, if rendered in updated figures, would compute to roughly 10 million. No wonder that a world Arnold once regarded as "so various, so beautiful, so new" turned instead to a wasteland that afforded "neither joy, nor love, nor light, / Nor certitude, nor peace, nor help for pain." Arnold's account was but an update on the age-old problem of evil, the lamentable, unfaltering reality of suffering and death for humans and all creatures. Also in Arnold's lament is shock at the magnified capacity of "progress" for inflicting death, an appetite that would only multiply in the twentieth century's ungraspably bloody revolutions and world wars. That is indeed a forbidding landscape in which to tell any sort of religious tale that suggests goodness or a divine something-or-other in some way superintending human affairs.

In short, the grim appraisal of modern history is not the whole story but merely the scenery, so to speak, in which humans, no matter what, strive desperately to hang on to, and even relish, the seeming gift that is life.

Despite the persistent darkness of modern history in particular, and that amid supposed human progress, people still thirst and scramble hard for a realm of warmth and delight within what novelist-essayist Marilynne Robinson, in her celebrated novel *Gilead*, calls "the exquisite primary fact of existence."[4] About these appetites and longings there is little doubt on the part of anyone, whether atheistic, religious, or agnostic.

Literature, music, and film, poem after novel after song and movie, all attest to that central reality of hunger for living and its richness (look again at Ridley Scott's *Blade Runner* [1982], where even the bioengineered replicants crave more of "being"). And, as anthropologists such as Clifford Geertz explain, fast upon the heels of this appetite for being comes the pervasive quest for understanding and, if possible, meaning of some kind.[5] Then, straightaway, in this pursuit of light and

---

4. Marilynne Robinson, *Gilead* (New York: Farrar, Straus and Giroux, 2004), 190.

5. Clifford Geertz, *The Interpretation of Cultures* (New York: Basic Books, 1977); see especially his chapter entitled "Religion as a Cultural System."

the "help," for which Arnold longs, humankind enters the territory of the religious, a realm that aspires to explain and relieve humankind's psycho-tangle of fear and vexation. In sum, this tragic sense of life and of the world—indeed, as one central condition of being human—has for the length of human history given rise to religious thirsts for meaning, hope, love, harmony, and exultation. Arriving at satisfaction in any of these is no easy matter.

The matter becomes more complicated because turning religious or to "faith" does not necessarily yield easy certainty or "cure" for human ills. There is no better instance of this than the life and writing of the founding theologian of the Christian tradition, Saint Paul, who died a much persecuted Roman martyr. Throughout his long career as chief explainer of the Christian mysteries, Paul proved a stark realist, warning of titanic evils, "principalities and powers," both inner and outer, that beset humankind (Rom. 8:38). Moreover, the saint himself lamented his own moral failures: "I do not do what I want, but I do the very thing I hate" (Rom. 7:15 RSV). And for him, always there was "the dark glass" that obscures human knowledge, most especially of the divine (1 Cor. 13:12). No surprise, then, that "faith," as distinct from sure knowledge, was the defining characteristic of early Christianity because, overwhelmingly, the presence of a loving divinity was not especially evident amid the violence and chaos of the Roman Empire in the first century AD.

A Path to the Other?

Given this unchanging human predicament, much of religious inquiry and reflection begins in a posture of wonder prompted by the mystery of humankind's three big appetites: for life itself, breathing and feeling; for revelatory light of some kind and measure, light that will thin the fog of unknowing; and for human intimacy that abates the enmity of an indifferent if not actively hostile world.

The first proceeds from amazement at the fact that anything at all exists—why there is something rather than nothing, a question that lies near the center of modern philosophical existentialism. Intimately related to that question is the mystery of individual existence and consciousness. To adapt Descartes, "I wonder, therefore I am." A character in an early John Updike novel, *The Centaur* (1963), marked the beginning of the human as "when some dumb ape swung down out of a tree and *wondered* where he was."[6] Renowned twentieth-century philosopher Ludwig Wittgenstein framed the riddle differently: "Not *how* the world is, is the mystical, but *that* it is."[7] Perhaps the late philosopher and rabbi Abraham Joshua Heschel best caught the flavor of this posture of profound wonder at the mystery of being, pointedly asking, "Who lit the wonder before our eyes, and the wonder of our eyes?"[8] Or, in a more prescriptive mode, "Our goal should be to live life in radical amazement . . . get up in the morning and look at the world in a way that takes nothing for granted. Everything is phenomenal. . . . To be spiritual is to be amazed."[9]

Here, as have countless poets and composers, Heschel marks the unabated astonishment at actually being alive—breathing, moving, procreating, feeling, thinking—particularly in the complexity and seeming splendor of the empirical world and, greater still, the human capacity to apprehend it, which are all a part of Robinson's "exquisite primary fact of existence." In any case, the facts of human self-consciousness itself and the human propensity to wonder continue as central psychological and intellectual puzzles, and presently philosophers, neuroscientists, playwrights, poets, and filmmakers persist in debating what has come to be known as "the Big Problem": whether the riddle of self-awareness can ever be "explained" scientifically, and if not, where in the universe it comes from. Regardless, the one certainty is that individual humans do indeed "wonder as they wander out under the sky," as a traditional folk hymn has it.

Wonder leads to many destinations, notably both to science and to art. And very often wonder leads to awe, a more intense cognitive-affective state in which the self feels amazed or astonished by some heretofore unknown (or forgotten) reality or threshold.[10] Usually this overwhelmingness is occasioned by what humans, at least in the

6. John Updike, *The Centaur* (New York: Ballantine Books, 1996), 35 (italics mine).

7. Ludwig Wittgenstein, *Tractatus Logico-Philosophicus*, trans. Charles Kay Ogden (London: Routledge, 1922), section 6, line 44.

8. Abraham Joshua Heschel, *Man Is Not Alone: A Philosophy of Religion* (New York: Farrar, Straus and Giroux, 1951), 68.

9. Quoted in David Brooks, "Alone, Yet Not Alone," *New York Times*, January 27, 2014, http://www.nytimes.com/2014/01/28/opinion/brooks-alone-yet-not-alone.html?_r=0.

10. See Robert C. Fuller, *Wonder: From Emotion to Spirituality* (Chapel Hill: University of North Carolina Press, 2009).

West, label grandeur, especially imposing natural wonders such as the Grand Canyon, Argentina's Iguazú Falls, mountains of all sorts, and a plentitude of beautiful creatures, human and otherwise. This same mood can as well result from fresh perception of the minuscule or everyday ordinary, the surprise of the remarkable in the commonplace. Though generally skeptical of religious claims, contemporary science nonetheless displays breathtaking and incomprehensible spectacle through Hubble telescopes, but also microscopically and subatomically in quarks, microbes, and genomes. These celebrated filmmaker Terrence Malick dramatizes at length in *The Voyage of Time* documentaries (2016). So also, to leap far from science, visual art regularly provides quite another way to "see" this world—in Rembrandt's portraits, Turner's storms, Monet's light and color, van Gogh's starry night, Hopper's desolations, Picasso's Guernica, Warhol's soup cans, Lucien Freud's portraiture, and endless others, all struggling to transcribe imposing tableaux of mystery, whether splendor or horror, tranquility or carnage, delight or madness. Sometimes, indeed, everything is spectacle, imposing and ungraspable, instigating awe, voluntary or otherwise.[11]

Humankind has perennially struggled thus, sometimes in fear and trembling, to read and render the significance of awe amid the plenteous vexing riddles of existence. Sometimes the awe-struck merely transcribe; at other times they note awe and transfixing beauty as markers of divine presence. So great, as Heschel notes above, is their gorgeousness and the delight they elicit that these experiences seem quite alien and "other" from ordinary awareness and the raw, inert materiality of this world. From poets in particular there is the relish of a resplendent flame of "shining," as in nineteenth-century Jesuit poet Gerard Manley Hopkins's exultant (and fearsome) sonnet "God's Grandeur." Hopkins asserts that the world, far from bland or soddenly material, is "charged" with a sort of sensory electricity that at random moments ignites perceptual rereckoning, reappraisal, or insight that now deems the world aflame, akin to the "shining" caused by shaking tinfoil in bright sunlight.

All is not rosy, however. Horror can invert this journey. In a sonnet

---

11. For a brief and adept essay on traditional humanist understandings of the nature and value of beauty, see David Brooks, "When Beauty Strikes," *New York Times*, January 15, 2016, http://www.nytimes.com/2016/01/15/opinion/when-beauty-strikes.html.

as imposing as Hopkins's, Robert Frost's "Design" contends that visual beauty simply masks "the design of darkness to appall." In his permanently remarkable masterpiece *Moby-Dick* (1859), the young Herman Melville notes the same duality in the world: while the dazzle of the visible world suggests it was "formed in love," the invisible realms behind or below surfaces, like sharks (and white whales), occasion an abiding terror best described as "fright."[12] Frost or Darwin could not have said it better. And on the tussle goes.

Sometimes these sorts of diametrical astonishments, even simultaneously partaking of one another—whether of beauty or horror, disorienting and ineffable, often characterized by fear or elation— fast become metaphysical and very often religious experience of some sort, pointing the way to hope or despair. These seem in their surprise, strangeness, and power quite beyond natural instigation or reckoning. And this transpires in multiple domains and dimensions of human consciousness. These experiential arenas can be predominantly aesthetic, moral, relational, intellectual, romantic, carnal, psycho-emotional, or otherwise (and usually not just one of these alone but with a network of simultaneous cognitive registers). Whether epiphanies, revelations, or psycho-quirks, for the religious they suggest a causative power or agency that elicits an existential awareness or "call" that potentially alters central life commitments. Founders of major global religious traditions—Buddha (fifth century BC), Muhammad (AD 570–632), and Moses (fifteenth century BC)—all underwent these kinds of shattering experiences that redirected their lives.

It is not a surprise, then, that human experience has marked these dramatic "visions" and turnings as sacred or holy, words that, due to the insufficiencies of language, evoke more than describe. After all, how does one depict a close brush with some metaphysical Other that disorients the living conscious self? That challenge is daunting, whether one employs words, stories, or visual images. Nor are such experiences confined to the infancy or ignorance of the race. They persist among amply smart and lively moderns in literature, in the movies, in music, and elsewhere. Celtic spirituality has long talked of "the thin place," a zone of perception and experience wherein the subject senses some measure of a heretofore hidden reality, or even enters into it. This re-

---

12. Herman Melville, *Moby-Dick*, ed. Harrison Hayford and Hershel Parker, Norton Critical Edition, 2nd ed. (New York: Norton, 2002), 164.

ality is of an altogether different sort that is typically full of a ravishing sort of light, or even fire, that transfixes the deepest parts of the self and the way it has previously understood the nature of the world. In such random instances, the usual stubbornly opaque limits of perception and understanding seem to "thin" to allow insight to a wholly different but wildly "present" reality. Six brief and varied recent examples will suffice to display this elusive mode of apprehending this world.

1. In 2014, famed sociologist and best-selling author Barbara Ehrenreich, previously understood as an ardent secularist, published an unusual memoir, *Living with a Wild God*, which recounts her lifelong effort to understand an adolescent "encounter" in Lone Pine, California, a tiny town on the eastern side of the Sierras. "At some point in my predawn walk . . . the world flamed into life. . . . There were no visions, no prophetic voices . . . just this blazing everywhere. Something poured into me and I poured out into it. . . . It was a furious encounter with a living substance that was coming at me through all things at once, and one reason for the terrible wordlessness of the experience is that you cannot observe fire really closely without becoming part of it."[13] Now in her mid-seventies, Ehrenreich has ever since periodically tried to make sense of this "wild" event; she has been especially eager to find some psychophysical explanation for it and its lasting impact on her. Deeply averse to both traditional and pop spirituality, she nonetheless ends up condensing "all the chaos and mystery of the world in a palpable Other or Others" that take "form before our very eyes" and may be, in the last words of the book, "seeking us out."[14]

2. The eminent contemporary American essayist Annie Dillard has spent her career surveying the same sort of radical noetic event. In her first book, a kind of latter-day *Walden*, the Pulitzer Prize–winning *Pilgrim at Tinker Creek* (1974), Dillard recounts her lengthy search in Virginia forests for an elusive transfixing something. Finally, she encounters it, the "tree with the lights in it," not hidden away in the recesses of deep woods but in her very familiar and ordinary backyard. For a brief time, she witnesses "the backyard cedar where the mourning doves roost charged and transfigured, each cell buzzing with flame," and indeed, all seemed aflame, though the vision soon fades. In that experi-

---

13. Barbara Ehrenreich, *Living with a Wild God: A Nonbeliever's Search for the Truth about Everything* (New York: Twelve, 2014), 116.

14. Ehrenreich, *Living with a Wild God*, 237, 236.

ence, though, realizes Dillard, "I had been my whole life a bell, and never knew it until at that moment I was lifted and struck." Finally, though, it "was less like seeing than like being for the first time seen, knocked breathless by a powerful glance." Here Dillard thinks she has stumbled into the divine, or it into her, when and where she least expected it. And she is, she attests, still "spending the power."[15]

3. The same can be said for Lester Burnham (Kevin Spacey, in a best actor performance) in Sam Mendes's seriocomic *American Beauty* (1999). In a deep funk amid his "stupid little life," Lester is awakened from his lethargy when "touched by an angel," or in this case Angela Hayes (Mena Suvari), or haze, his teenaged daughter's vampish best friend. To woo her, Lester starts working out, quits his job, smokes a lot of pot, and buys a hot car, essentially reverting to an overjuiced teenager. In contrast is an actual teenager, the peculiar neighbor boy Ricky Fitts (Wes Bentley), a compulsive videographer who films everything, from dead birds to white plastic bags blowing in the wind. In contrast to Lester, Ricky deems the ordinary prosaic world worthy of deep wonder and gratitude: "Sometimes I feel there's so much beauty in the world I feel like I can't take it . . . and my heart is going to burst." Behind all that splendor, suspects Ricky, is an "incredible benevolent force." And that is something the wrong-hearted Lester, in his last moments of life, will come at last to understand as well, finally recognizing that ungraspable beauty, dazzling and abundant, lies not in a buzz and exotic sex but in the ordinary and commonplace: "Sometimes it's too much, [my] heart fills up like a balloon that's about to burst," and "joy flows through me like rain, and I can't feel anything but gratitude." In the land of awe, all seems worthy of love because the radiance of all seems infused with love by what must be a transcendent Love, a beauty so radical, intense, and rapturous that no one can take it all in, lest the heart itself "cave in" from the joy it incites in the depths of the self.

4. In fiction, no one sketches this better than Marilynne Robinson in her epistolary novel *Gilead* (2004), the winner of major literary prizes on both sides of the Atlantic. The novel consists of a memoir in letters from an aging (and dying) Protestant minister to his seven-year-old son, a strategy that John Ames hopes will allow his young son to know

15. Annie Dillard, *Pilgrim at Tinker Creek* (New York: Harper's Magazine Press, 1974), 33–34.

better his father long after he is dead and gone. Ames recounts his life and the world he sees, and a remarkable portrait it is. In a small town in Iowa in the 1950s, a markedly unlikely place and time for anything revelatory, Ames has seen it all, including, one, the death decades before of his young wife and infant son and, two, a morally dubious family history, though both his father and grandfather were clergymen. Indeed, minister and confessor that he is, Ames has witnessed ample darkness amid the living, a "lot of malice and dread and guilt, and so much loneliness, where you wouldn't really expect to find it, either."[16] Despite the ever-encroaching darkness of death, Ames remains a celebrant of the miraculousness of the everyday world of his very prosaic little town, finding in Gilead a resplendent ordinary, one that elicits steady delight and gratitude.

Though he anticipates an afterlife, he cannot imagine a more luminous realm than his present regime of wonders. He writes to his son of such splendor: "You and Tobias are hopping around in the sprinkler. The sprinkler is a magnificent invention because it exposes raindrops to sunshine. . . . Well, but you two are dancing around in your iridescent little downpour, whooping and stomping as sane people ought to do when they encounter a thing so miraculous as water" (65). Indeed, Ames has "loved . . . physical life" (69), whether in "the sweet and irrefragable daylight pouring in through the windows" of his church (177) or in the translucent calm in playing catch in the evening while smelling a distant river (242).

As for Hopkins and Dillard, Ames's world often flames into radiance "for a moment or a year or the span of a life. And then it sinks back into itself again, and to look at it no one would know it had anything to do with fire, or light" (245). For Ames, a lush extravagance abides within the mystery of being, coexistent with ample darkness, but so great is its pervasive iridescence that it seems like "transfiguration" wherein the raw materiality and dark of the world become quite "other," more in measure and different in kind, and wonder and elation ignite profound gratitude to some Other whose care has seemingly so infused all that is, and that wondrous experiential datum seems, for Robinson and others, irreducible, unconstructed, and incontrovertible. It is what it is.

5. The very same project informs the extraordinary work of con-

---

16. Robinson, *Gilead*, 6. Hereafter, page references from this work will be given in parentheses in the text.

temporary American filmmaker, writer, and director Terrence Malick. Throughout his long career, Malick has been preoccupied with chronicling the mysteries of humankind's response to an iridescent world. The defeated father (Brad Pitt) in *The Tree of Life* (2011) laments that in his lifelong drive for status and money he has missed this world's ever-present majesty and "glory." In contrast, his wife (Jessica Chastain) constantly exults in a radiant, effulgent world. As she cavorts with her three sons, her voice-over urges all to "Love everyone, every leaf, every ray of light," repeating almost verbatim the words of Dostoevsky's mystical Father Zossima in *The Brothers Karamazov* (1880). Throughout the film, Malick strives to convey wonder, awe-fullness, and glad relish for all the exquisitely simple, ordinary stuff of being alive—such as mere seeing, breathing, and swimming—laboring to evoke an experiential immediacy and gestalt with a rhapsodic stream of images, music, and only occasionally, words. In full, *The Tree of Life* pushes toward a supra-rational, embodied embrace of the splendor of living on this globe, as tragic and sorrowful as it often is. For Mrs. O'Brien—as for troubled middle-aged son Jack (Sean Penn)—that profound, inescapable enchantment and celebration point to a transcendent Other, something other and beyond that shaped this world in and for love. As much as the camera can catch or conjure, Malick celebrates the press of a radical beauty inhering in the ordinary, an efflorescent presence of Love, abiding and lambent, within the very fabric of existence. This "love" points beyond itself in a way that eludes or surpasses scientific reduction, a conclusion that Ehrenreich seems also to have reached.

6. Many more examples of the sort above abound in the works of a long list of modern and contemporary "greats," poets and novelists alike, all enrolled in this cohort of celebrants: T. S. Eliot, W. H. Auden, Wendell Berry, John Updike, Richard Wilbur, Carlos Eire, Mary Oliver, Christian Wiman, and many others. And there are, too, the remarkable displays of three of the great North American songwriters in the second half of the 20th century, namely Bob Dylan, Leonard Cohen, and Paul Simon. Especially notable are the late-life lyrics and songs of the latter two, both of whom come from Jewish upbringings. Their metaphysical restlessness and longing have been more than clear throughout their very long careers, already evident in their very first recordings. Indeed, Cohen and Simon have sketched remarkably similar topographies of religious search that seem to have arrived at resonant, even glowing affirmation, despite a world afloat in darkness personal and social. A

poet before a singer-songwriter, Cohen's "Hallelujah," with its invocation of the "Lord of Song," has become one of the most covered songs in contemporary popular music, and now in his early 80s he continues to write songs of remarkable nuance and depth that reckon with human ache for wholeness and light amid the limitless woundedness of the world. Indeed, he yearns for a relenting of the darkness "that tore the light apart" ("Come Healing," *Old Ideas* [2012]).[17] The same wrestle with divine presence continues in his most recent albums, *Popular Problems* (2014) and *You Want It Darker* (2016). And for Cohen, as for many others, the splendor of the natural world offers a token of divine care for the world ("Lullaby," *Old Ideas*). The same brokenness and hope for healing have lain near the center of Paul Simon's concerns throughout his long career. From the desperate isolation of "Mrs. Robinson" (1968) to fervent hope for rescue in a "Bridge over Troubled Water" (1970), Simon has tirelessly searched for some sort of "Graceland" (1986), a place both geographical and metaphysical where all will be received. At once reverential and playful, delicate and funny, Simon lyrics have always posed questions about beauty, evil, and human longing for love, thanksgiving, and reconciliation, what the Jewish-Christian has labelled redemption. For Simon there is always the wonder of being alive in a resplendent world of stars, rain, light, and of course, music, for "Everything about it is a love song" sung by a Creator ("Everything About It Is a Love Song," *Surprise* [2006]). That repeats in his 2014 album, *So Beautiful or So What*. So also in "Proof of Love" (*Stranger to Stranger*, 2016) wherein "a voice inside my skin" argues that life does not end with nothingness and for now bids him to "bathe beneath a waterfall of light." This late-life mystic sees angels, pilgrims, and grace just about everywhere. At present the mantle of these aging songwriters seems to have been taken up by young Sufjan Stevens, a Protestant Christian, who in his highly acclaimed *Carrie & Lowell* (2015) plunges into tangled matters of desertion and reconciliation, especially in relationship to his mother.

---

17. For an excellent recent treatment of Leonard Cohen's career and his late-life thematics, see David Remnick's "Leonard Cohen Makes It Darker," *New Yorker*, October 17, 2016, http://www.newyorker.com/magazine/2016/10/17/leonard-cohen-makes-it -darker?mbid=nl_TNY%20Template%20-%20With%20Photo%20(104)&CNDID=10245599& spMailingID=9676616&spUserID=MTMzMTc5NTQyMjQyS0&spJobID=1020932541&sp ReportId=MTAyMDkzMjU0MQS2.

The Call of the Ethical

These *exempla* of aesthetic wonder and ecstasy point to but one path of wonder. There are in fact many domains of beauty and wonder comprised of countless other appetites, experiences, rationales, and visions that prompt curiosity and wonder about the nature of the universe. Perhaps none is larger than the thirst for moral clarity and rightness of behavior, and that desire runs through individuals, societies, and cultures, whether traditional or revolutionary. In this regard, it seems indisputable that humans invariably create social and moral visions and codes. Within a seemingly limitless plethora of systems, some few have struck with such persuasive power that they seem in their purity and alterity to derive from something quite beyond human fashioning. Specifically, humankind has flourished in the wake of radiant visions of personal and relational virtue and well-being, especially in what Judaism and Christianity call shalom. These luminous eruptions of a different kind of light, this time moral/ethical, entice, inspire, ennoble, and embolden, and they have come from a diverse historical and cultural array of figures as varied as Buddha, Isaiah of the Old Testament, and Muhammad, to name but a few.

In recent history, the deeply religious social visions and nonviolent protests of civil rights leader Martin Luther King Jr. and his followers moved the conscience of generations, both in the United States and abroad, and King's brief life fundamentally changed American values and law. King imbued his Judeo-Christian ethics and devotion with the teachings and practices of Mahatma Gandhi, whose Hindu-Christian practice of nonviolent civil disobedience delivered India in 1947 from the imperial boot of England. After King came South African Nelson Mandela, whose creed of racial reconciliation began the healing of a culture long maimed by apartheid. Indeed, the fusion of moral and religious systems can exert enormous cultural power. Those northern secular liberals who, attracted by King's vision of a nonracial society, journeyed south to join civil rights protests were often surprised to witness the extent to which a deeply religious vision fueled the moral and legal crusade of King's movement.

Nor does the legacy of such exemplary people fade. The best-selling author and prominent *New York Times* columnist David Brooks has displayed at length his own thirst for goodness and moral wholeness, as shown in his recent book *The Road to Character* (2015). That quest

is made difficult in a culture adrift in its lack of ethical understanding and commitments, and in this complaint Brooks does not mimic
the glib judgmentalism of the Religious Right. Rather, he focuses on
the restless hunger for "clarity" and "meaning" among the privileged
classes generally: "many feel lost or overwhelmed. They feel a hunger
to live meaningfully, but they don't know the right questions to ask,
the right vocabulary to use, the right place to look or even if there are
ultimate answers at all." And especially "young people, raised in today's
hypercompetitive environment, are, if anything, hungrier to find ideals that will give meaning to their activities. It's true of people in all
social classes. Everyone is born with moral imagination—a need to
feel that life is in service to some good."[18] Brooks's last claim about the
universality of "moral imagination" that seeks good in life seems true
enough, though this reflex, seemingly instinctual, has led to disaster
when played upon by the twentieth century's romantic totalitarianisms
of fascism and communism.

Similarly, philosopher Susan Nieman in *Why Grow Up?* (2015) wonders at length about how we are "supposed to become free, happy and
decent people." Indeed, she argues that in the decline of traditional
religious and political sources for morality, "the right form of human
development became a philosophical problem, incorporating both psychological and political questions and giving them a normative thrust."[19]
Nieman's responses to the riddle she poses seem tepid at best.

The Strange Allure of Story

Film, though, is not philosophy or theology, for which lovers of cinema, or just plain movies, can be very glad. However, the medium has
virtually from its start wrestled with philosophical and religious concerns through the magic of its visual and aural narratives. Invariably,
in simply showing and telling stories, it has dramatized, clarified, and
mediated age-old moral and religious questions and realities. For that
matter, religious claims themselves come wrapped in remarkable nar-

18. David Brooks, "What Is Your Purpose?" *New York Times*, May 5, 2015, http://www
.nytimes.com/2015/05/05/opinion/david-brooks-what-is-your-purpose.html?_r=0.

19. Quoted in A. O. Scott, "*Why Grow Up?* By Susan Neiman," *New York Times Book Review*, June 15, 2015, http://www.nytimes.com/2015/06/21/books/review/why-grow-up-by
-susan-neiman.html.

ratives that have clearly attracted with enormous, even magical, existential and explanatory power.

Nor does the mysterious appeal of religious mythology seem in the least to fade, even amid a scientistic, cyber-tech age such as the current one. There is perhaps some irony in the fact that film, as a highly modern and technologized medium capable of stunning immediacy and cogency, has inveterately relied on very old tales and thematics to achieve its enormous global success. Add to that the tendency of films, especially in the United States, to habitually offer their own kind of "fix." The inescapable "happy ending" borders on transposing spectatorship into a religion of its own, as more than a few social critics and film scholars have observed. Indeed, that heavy dose of happy resolution often, and profitably, comes wrapped in myth-laden renderings of the way the world works and what viewers can expect from it. In short, from the multiplex to the art house, cinematic storytelling can prove deeply revelatory, probing and testing, with dexterity and even delight.

In their countless genres, films often explore the bright, dark, and gray of human experience, the same terrain so long depicted in great poems, music, scriptures, epics, novels, and plays, from Homer and Moses to Shakespeare and Cervantes, Dante and Auden, and Bach and Mozart. Unsurprisingly, in Western culture, the same core notions of meaning for human life recur over and over, perennial and inescapable, the very legacy and mantle of being human on this puzzling earth, a place both dire and splendorous, and these preoccupations do not fade away, as their constant recurrence in many varieties of film amply demonstrates.

Such has perhaps always been the case with stories, or so speculated novelist Madeleine L'Engle: "questioning of the meaning of being, and dying . . . is behind the telling of stories around tribal fires at night; behind the drawing of animals on the walls of caves; the singing of melodies of love in spring, and of the death of green in autumn. It is part of the deepest longing of the human psyche, a recurrent ache in the hearts of all."[20] L'Engle locates the appeal of storytelling in humankind's seemingly universal and insatiable appetite for understanding, delight, and meaning of some kind and measure, and nothing has so addressed these thirsts as stories. Contemporary humanity seems sim-

---

20. Madeleine L'Engle, *Walking on Water: Reflections on Faith and Art* (New York: Macmillan, 1995), 13.

ilarly preoccupied, despite its supposed secularism, with myth-laden cinematic stories that address the perennial thirsts, finding affecting existential satisfactions within pop fare, especially in the fantasies of sci-fi. Of *Star Trek* we need say little: intrepid explorers on the edges of the known world encountering Who-Knows-What wherever, whether good or evil, safe or dangerous, suprapowerful or helpless, all the while fascinated by what the next planet or system might contain. Less obvious but even more compelling, if box office means anything, have been immensely popular Hollywood films whose success resides in the filmmaker's ability to tell stories that simultaneously conceal, though barely, *and* illumine religious story.

George Lucas's original *Star Wars* trilogy (1977–1983) follows orphan Luke Skywalker's journey, or pilgrimage, from impetuous immaturity to Jedi knighthood, a posture, according to Yoda, characterized by patience, calm, veneration, and peace, all virtues repeatedly cited in the New Testament. Far from simply an eerie magnetic energy of some sort, the Force is a distinctly benign, even loving, power that embraces and supports its devotees, no more so than Obi-Wan Kenobi and Yoda and, eventually, Luke Skywalker. Both the original trilogy and the new chronological sequel, *Star Wars: The Force Awakens* (2015), rely in architecture, substance, and mood upon the Judeo-Christian metanarrative. So potent and transformative is the Force that through the lasting care and hope of Luke it effects the death's-door redemption of Darth Vader, Luke's prodigal and malign "dark side" father, who in the finale willingly sacrifices himself to save his son, for the son has saved the father, as the returned and renewed Anakin Skywalker tells his son in the last moments of his physical life. In this and in countless other ways, that first *Star Wars* trilogy offers a sterling sci-fi "pilgrim's progress" for Luke, Leia, and Han. And the new trilogy seems bent on reinvigorating that primal story of cosmic redemption.

Though George Lucas has made much of his reliance on myth and world religions, the first three films find their particular magic in a Judeo-Christian triumph of renewal and reconciliation, a metaphysical linchpin, mediated by Obi-Wan Kenobi and Yoda, that coaxes the reckless Luke from anger and impatience and restores his renegade father from the chilling allure of darkness to a realm of light whose foremost characteristic is love. The persistence in some measure of a diffuse "down-deep" appetite for these sorts of stories is more than clear in the film itself and in its record-shattering box-office triumphs.[21]

This cloaking strategy is also employed in two immensely popular "Jesus stories" in which the psycho-emotional "heft" and meaning of the Christian incarnation are deftly dramatized in gentle and fetching tragicomedy. The first of the *Superman* tales (1978), directed by Richard Donner, sought to retell in comic-book superhero form the story of the incarnation, as confessed some years afterward by screenwriter and coproducer Joseph Mankiewicz.[22] The film is soaked in biblical language, allusion, and story. We have here a hero who is "too good not to be true," as novelist Frederick Buechner put it; and director Donner, a superb cast, ingenious screenwriting, and exultant music by John Williams make it all seem so in spades.[23] The film amply displays the surprise and elation of what such an outlandish event might actually look and feel like—specifically, the arrival of a superpowerful "friend" to humankind, as Superman labels himself in answer to a befuddled Lois Lane's question about who this strange flying humanoid who just saved her life might in fact be. Moreover, this "presence" will quite literally save humankind from tragic misfortune, like lightning and earthquakes, and from malignant human evil, though grandiose Lex Luthor does not begin to rival Darth Vader in fearsomeness. The film is mostly a comic romp, one that basks and delights, as does its hero, in the improbability of its wildly hopeful premise that there is a loving supernatural hope for humankind. None of the many sequels quite measure up, as they seem to lack the high comic allure of the seriocomic élan of a buoyant tale of metaphysical rescue for the plight of humankind.

A more serious, though apparently inadvertent, take on the incarnation is Steven Spielberg's enormously successful *E.T. the Extra-Terrestrial* (1982), whose "lost boy" thematic and narrative core echoes both *Star Wars* and *Superman*. The forlorn young Elliott (Henry Thomas), whose father has run off with his secretary, encounters a strange but magical,

---

21. For a close reading of the original *Star Wars* trilogy, see chapter 8, "Tracking the Force: Meaning and Morality in the *Star Wars* Saga," in Roy Anker, *Catching Light: Looking for God in the Movies* (Grand Rapids: Eerdmans, 2004), 220–42.

22. Richard Donner and Joseph Mankiewicz, audio commentary, *Superman: The Movie* (Warner, 2000), at 15:05.

23. Frederick Buechner, *Telling the Truth: The Gospel as Tragedy, Comedy, and Fairy Tale* (San Francisco: Harper and Row, 1977), 71.

and loving, alien who willingly dies for him, rises, and then ascends in splendor, promising in his last words, while touching the boy's head with his glowing finger, that he will remain "right here" as a loving, guiding presence in the abandoned boy's life. The poignancy and hopefulness of the tale brought on more than a little wonder, delight, and even awe. Midway through the shoot screenwriter Melissa Mathison, reared and schooled in Roman Catholicism, suddenly realized that her script retold the Christ story (Spielberg's response: "Don't tell me, I'm Jewish"). Audiences, especially the adults, loved the tale of mutual rescue and reconciliation amid the sorrowful brokenness of this world. In it they glimpsed what life should be like, as well as a hopeful view of human flourishing that repairs the aching, and seemingly inescapable, ugliness of a lot of human behavior.

All these films address a central and profound human longing for a healing of being and the world—personal, relational, and otherwise— and to make that plausible and cogent they first depict, often in mythic scope, alienation and thirst. Then, amid plentiful conflicts and losses, all arrive at "fixes"—happy endings, though different from one another, all amply laden—that delineate a good deal of the substance and affect of the core of Jewish and Christian traditions. The center of it lies very specifically in the enormous hope for shalom and the reconciliation and renewal of the whole created world—among people, creatures, and the earth itself, the coming again of something like the shalom of that pacific "home" known as Eden, a realm of relational intimacy, harmony, and delight, both carnal and psycho-spiritual, a place without predation and death. Indeed, the enormous appeal and satisfactions of this sort of metastory persist.

This selfsame trajectory is transposed, dressed up, cloaked, in very different garb, in innumerable films past and present. When done well, this well-worn old stuff at the core of Western culture elicits surprise and more than a little bit of awe and deep pleasure. In this sense, the primary satisfactions of these much-loved films are religious, minus the usual trappings of that term, allowing them instead, freshly rendered, to glisten anew in fetching cogency. The "cloaking" approach is oblique. Nineteenth-century American poet Emily Dickinson suggests the effectiveness of this approach, arguing that poetry and storytelling should "Tell the truth but tell it slant." After all, says Dickinson, "Truth's superb surprise" is "Too bright for our infirm Delight," and as such is best grasped in story and metaphor. Amid the present healthy skepticism of all things religious, where old possibilities and formulations appear trite and tired, a winsome slantness may again restore a once-intense capacity to "dazzle." As always, the challenge for any filmmaker lies in finding the cinematic means that best invigorate the tale, the narrative shape and style that elicit the innumerable diverse pleasures of movie watching, including a bit of dazzle.

The comic fantasy tale, however, is not by any means the only narrative route for displaying matters religious. Some of cinema's great films present harrowing "countertales" that narrate unrelenting descents into evil, Faustian in measure, stories whose darkness leaves viewers running for cover and begging for light of any kind. Francis Ford Coppola's *Godfather* trilogy (1972–1990) traces the moral and criminal descent of young Michael Corleone (Al Pacino), though the last of the three films depicts his desperate (and failed) attempt at redemption. From the 1970s also comes Roman Polanski's *Chinatown* (1974), where jaded private detective Jakes Gittes (Jack Nicholson), a fellow who thinks he has seen the worst, runs into a depth of corruption and predation that leaves him numb and uncomprehending. In *Se7en* (1995), David Fincher created a grotesque voyeuristic tale that implicates viewers in the delights of undertaking horrific evil. All these films render a vicious reality that at first encompasses and then devours its good-guy heroes. An unrelenting evil, interior and external, culminates in a grim fatalism from which there is no light or escape. From that pit of despair, the assorted "heroes" have no recourse.

Remarkably, with such dire freight as carried by these masterworks, cinematic storytelling again proves deeply revelatory, probing and testing, with dexterity and even delight in searing depictions of intractable evil, the very sort of malignancy that major religious traditions seek to defeat. In this mode, the story sketches the complex, darksome, and very tragic "bad news" of human malignancy. Of these realities no one should be surprised, given the twentieth century's toll of civil corruption and global mass slaughter. Despite their fearsome toll, such tales remind viewers of the harsh weight of history, other people, and ourselves, and simultaneously of a universal thirst for some other "more" and better.

In Coppola's account of goodness gone lethally wrong in *The Godfather* saga, Michael Corleone first bravely aspires to virtue, emphatically not wanting anything to do with the "family business." But he abruptly reverses course in order to protect his gravely wounded father—"I'm with you now, pop"—only to end up, decades later, himself a "prince of darkness." Michael's choices, mixed in motives and disastrously flawed in execution, figurative and literal, cost Michael everything he has most loved. Appropriately enough, it seems, he dies alone, blind, and forlorn in the dust of Sicily, that place where the mafia and its devouring gangsterism had its birth. As he protests in *The Godfather Part III*, history, he himself, and no amount of penance will ever deliver him from the clutches of evil. And he hoped beyond reason, as all do, sensing something more or different, for a "joy illimited," as poet Thomas Hardy called it, of which we catch glimpses amid the seemingly omnivorous darkness of violence and death ("The Darkling Thrush"). The trajectories of these assorted protagonists, either succumbing to or devoured by evil, do not come as surprises to sober readers of biblical accounts that do not in the least mince the capacity for things moral and religious to go drastically wrong.

All these tales explore the inescapable polarities and paradoxes of human experience, the same territory forever depicted in great art. Moreover, the themes of human life, whether bright or dark, persist, despite the assertions of postmodernism that all is socially constructed and a neuroscience that sees consciousness as nothing but electrochemical delusion. Still, in the West, though some lament it, stories and much art emerge from and convey the legacies of Judaism, Christianity, and ancient Greece, attending to the full range of religious experience: suffering, petition, despair, longing, delight, community, intimacy, and joy, to name only the most central. All these compelling cinematic meditations wrestle with the possibility that this world was made in and for majesty and love—specifically, that a divine Something cares profoundly for and relishes humankind and the whole of the natural world. It is there in Homer, Job, the New Testament of the Bible, and countless heralded writers, painters, and composers thereafter.

By multiple modes and means, then, the accomplishments of the arts, cinema included, address matters of what used to be called the soul, the deepest center of being, meaning the deepest parts of a self that relish beauty, meaning, love, truth, goodness, what the father of Superman, Jor-El (Marlon Brando), identifies as "matters of the human heart," as opposed to "mere science." Tragically, the traditions of both Judaism and Christianity have lately suffered from drastic distortions and caricature at the hands of both fundamentalists and neo-atheists. Indeed, fundamentalist extremism, religious and secular, seems to infect the globe. Nonetheless, presently, as in the past, an incandescent vision of human experience contained in the Jewish and Christian metastories profoundly affects cultures and individual selves. Historically, those visions of being have shown the capacity to radically alter perception of the world in turning the self from self-concern to profound love for the exquisite goodness of creation and of all creatures therein. Such visions in behalf of love in and for all things summon all to selfless sacrifice to restore a cruelly broken world to its original condition of intimacy and exultation, that mode of being known as shalom. The possibility that the world was made in love for delight and intimacy haunts major religious visions of the world and life within it.

It is to such matters that religious tales of all sorts turn, urging and evoking wonder, amazement, gladness, thanksgiving, sorrow, reconciliation, and love. The best of modern cinema has not only recognized but also embraced the search for these facets or conditions of being alive. Both doubting and affirming, the medium has dramatized, while acknowledging inescapably murky circumstances, humanity's quest for human connection and life's meaning. This book turns to numerous representations of the breaking of various kinds of light to all sorts of people. In fresh and haunting ways, the nine films analyzed in this book track the innumerable ways such apprehensions still happen in a vast array of lives.

About This Book

In the history of cinema, efforts to make palpable and perceivable the invisible have taken innumerable forms. Sometimes amounting to a specific genre all by itself, easily the most identifiable, and probably least successful as cinema, has been the hackneyed biblical spectacle. These movies tend to record fabled notable events and figures and spend rather too much energy in making biblical miracles look empirically plausible. Even now, this stretch to bestow credibility, even with tremendous CGI budgets, seems wrongheaded or, better, wrong-hearted, attending to the least consequential aspect of religious stories.

Far more memorable (and immensely profitable) have been parables of divine presence, those stories that transpose and freshen religious content by couching it in the realities of mundane life; many of these films have seemingly caught the very wonder and longing that the big biblical spectacles have missed, namely, the mystery and dazzle of divine possibility. Surely one reason the prequels and sequels keep coming is that audiences want to know again the prospect of numinous possibility. In their "slantness," to recall Emily Dickinson, films such as *Star Wars, E.T.,* and *Superman* dramatize the way in which religious notions and experience can address the depths of the human plight, using "slantness" to convey the dynamic human consequence and affect that actions, events, searches, and visions elicit from characters.

The films analyzed in this book largely fall into another category, though they surely partake of others as well. In particular, they show the full human experiential wrestle with the possibility of religious insight and meaning—indeed, they venture a walk to the "thin places" where humanity senses the press of a wholly different reality. Clearly, those pursuits pose enormous perceptual and philosophical challenges, for people and for movies, venturing as they do into liminal borderlands between perception and reality where ordinary people (and in successful films, audiences too) run into some trace of the Mysterium, apprehending some variety of divine presence or agency. As the variety of films discussed in this book show, these sorts of occasions are innumerable and enormously varied, ranging from a mystical American soldier at Guadalcanal to a motherless blind boy in the mountains of Iran.

The films treated here belong in varying degrees to what A. O. Scott of the *New York Times* terms "a tiny and exalted tradition" in cinema that tries "to illuminate religious experience from within."[24] Such films venture into another's perception and experience thereof, and by that means, the notion goes, the numinous presence they encounter in some measure becomes palpable, whether as the still, small voice (or music) in the soul or, on rare occasion, as titanic forces, much like that phenomenal spacecraft in Spielberg's still-resplendent *Close Encounters of the Third Kind* (1977). The former is exquisitely dramatized in Kieslowski's masterful *Three Colors: Blue* (1993), a tale of a numb young widow (Juliette Binoche) who is hauled back to life by music that will not leave her alone, for her own sake and for the sake of others. Film has much to tell regular viewers, and especially stodgy religionists, about the "lived experience" of an unwieldy divine presence, namely, how the divine is apprehended.

---

24. A. O. Scott, "Between Heaven and Earth," *New York Times*, February 24, 2011, http://www.nytimes.com/2011/02/25/movies/25gods.html?_r=0.

This book follows this track through a great variety of contemporary film, from cinematic stories that are direct and simple to the experimental and highly adventurous, such as Anderson's *Magnolia* and Malick's *Thin Red Line*. Some of the films straightforwardly narrate the experience of their central characters, attending closely, as deeply as movies can, to their inmost selves, their core sorrows and joys and thirsts. We move here from the simplest and "warmest" to the harrowing. All display paths into the intimate interiors of their main characters' souls, so to speak. M. Night Shyamalan's first post–film school movie, *Wide Awake* (1998), tells the story of a grief-stricken ten-year-old pre-preppie who has lost his grandfather and wants to make sure that his dear companion is "okay." Though this description makes the film sound like gooey treacle, it is in equal parts very funny and straight-on serious, and ends movingly with a huge leap toward a complex vision of the multiple ways the divine might show up in human affairs. The same sort of thematic shapes *The Color of Paradise* (1999), by celebrated Iranian filmmaker Majid Majidi. Here another ten-year-old boy—this one blind, motherless, and a burden to his angry, harried father—searches endlessly to understand his tragic plight. He scours the sensory world for some hint or clue as to why God has so forsaken him. Sometimes Job comes in a small package.

Three films have evil in the shape of personal crime at their center. Robert Duvall's remarkable one-man show—he wrote, directed, starred in, and paid for *The Apostle* (1997)—tells the story of a tireless Holiness preacher (he belongs to an American hyper-fundamentalist group that exalts intense personal religious experience) who goes on the run after clubbing his wife's boyfriend, and for the first time reckons with himself—and others. What he discovers amid personal nothingness more than startles him and, for that matter, audiences. Adapted from Sister Helen Prejean's best-selling memoir of her work with Louisiana death-row inmates, Tim Robbins's *Dead Man Walking* (1995) provides a close look at brutal, guilty-as-hell Matthew Poncelot (Sean Penn in his greatest role), convicted of rape and double murder. Susan Sarandon won best actress for her performance as Prejean—since writing her book, a prominent death penalty opponent—who goes one-on-one with Poncelot to save his life and, yes, even his soul. It is both harrowing and wondrous in its up-close account of growth and reconciliation. Currently the favorite film of Americans, *The Shawshank Redemption* (1994) features Tim Robbins as Andy Dufresne, a fancy and very self-contained young banker convicted of the drunken murder of his wife and her golf-pro lover. It will take twenty years in prison for Dufresne to learn enough to break free, rapturously, not only from prison but also from the darker tangles of his own selfhood.

Two films feature people on the run from police. Paul Schrader's gripping *American Gigolo* tells the story of Julian Kaye (Richard Gere in his best acting ever), an upscale gigolo to the international set—until his neglect of many old "friends" sets him fleeing from a murder charge. Amazingly, amid a vortex of loss, this master of sex finds out what love really is, and is the recipient of dazzling, and unaccountable, self-sacrifice. Stranger still, in a stunning stylistic leap, is *Heaven*, a meta-physical thriller from the pen of late Polish writer-director Krzysztof Kieslowski (and his writing partner Krzysztof Piesiewicz). Shot after Kieslowski's early death in 1996, director Tom Tykwer's film casts a wondrous Cate Blanchett as Philippa, a schoolteacher-turned-bomber whose effort to kill a drug kingpin goes disastrously wrong. She and sympathetic young policeman Filippo (Giovanni Ribisi) end up on the lam in the Tuscan countryside, finding their way, implausibly but neces-sarily, to psycho-moral ascent. At once beautiful, puzzling, and haunt-ing, *Heaven* depicts just what exactly makes heaven heaven.

Two remarkably innovative films end the book. Paul Thomas An-derson's *Magnolia* (1999) swirls through the dark and sorrowful un-derbelly of TV land, linking a host of distraught, fugitive souls badly in need of healing and actual human connection. Brilliantly scored and acted, Anderson's film lays out a long lament for human egocentrism, fractiousness, and isolation. A miracle of sorts, one more than a little outlandish, does its work in jolting just about everyone to their basic humanity, and, yes, strange things do happen.

In a category by itself is the World War II film *The Thin Red Line* (1998), writer-director Terrence's Malick's first film after a twenty-year hiatus from filmmaking. With a remarkable acting ensemble and stylistic "dia-logic polyphony," Malick follows a troubled Private Witt (James Caviezel), and others, through a harrowing inland mop-up operation on the island of Guadalcanal in the South Pacific. Moving between islanders and sol-diers, Witt stumbles on "another world," as he puts it, marking his shift from nihilism to a quasi-mystical relish of the beauty and goodness of this world, including people. Full of surprise, wonder, and visual beauty, Malick's film pushes characters, like Welsh (Sean Penn), and viewers, to see the world differently, as a realm where "all things" do shine.

The films in this book all substantively deepen and expand the kinds of perceptual modes that display the world as packed with surprise, wonder, and shining, of assorted kinds of "beautiful light," even unto intimating the mysteries of some measure of divine love—in ways not usually understood or acknowledged, especially by those reductive postures that seek to disenchant the whole of the world. In their filmmaking, these diverse filmmakers find ways to deploy their own artistry to bring to the theater screen the full luster and brightness of the mystery of being.

CHAPTER ONE

"NOT ALL ANGELS HAVE WINGS"

Wonder, Light, and Love in M. Night Shyamalan's *Wide Awake*

The quest of a well-dimpled and well-heeled ten-year-old private-school boy from a very traditional family does not sound like the stuff of exciting filmmaking, especially for adults. Usually Hollywood waits till puberty to find children interesting, or at least profitable (hormones help a lot). There are kid films, of course—like *Charlotte's Web*, *Bridge to Terabithia*, the Harry Potter franchise, and yes, the Pixar many—but those films are mostly *for* the young. The odd and really happy thing about M. Night Shyamalan's *Wide Awake* (1998), his first post–film school picture, is that while it is indeed about a young boy, its writer-director pitches the boy's history very much at adults (or perhaps young adults), and it works—really well. It is at once amply poignant, terribly funny, playful, fully earnest, religiously searching, affecting, and even cogent. When all is viewed and done, the viewer departs having experienced a modestly complex, and very fetching, rendition of the sources and consequences of religious possibility and understanding. Overall, it is probably Shyamalan's best film, better even than his box-office smashes, *The Sixth Sense* (1999) and *Signs* (2002), other tales that, like *Wide Awake*, are soaked in genuine religious angst. That is hard to pull off, regardless of the protagonist's (or director's) age or circumstance.

In *Wide Awake*, the rambunctious novice Shyamalan walks a remarkably thin line between plentiful humor and dead-serious grief. The main character, ten-year-old Joshua Beal (Joseph Cross), has recently lost his beloved grandfather (Robert Loggia), who dies slowly (in flashbacks) of bone cancer. The widowed grandfather lived with Joshua's family in a sprawling Philadelphia Mainline manse. The old fellow became Joshua's best friend and chief parent, for father and mother are both amply frazzled in their physician careers. In the aftermath of the grandfather's death, Joshua misses him terribly and simultaneously wants to know that his grandfather, gone to what Shakespeare called the "undiscovered country" (*Hamlet*), is indeed all right. In a wild, cockeyed "mission," as Joshua calls it, the boy undertakes a search for palpable, sure evidence that confirms his grandfather's postmortem well-being. For Joshua, that means contacting God by any means possible. Shyamalan's stroke of genius here refracts a heavy-duty religious inquiry about immortality and divine care through the sense and perception of a precocious, though still innocent and inexperienced, ten-year-old. And here, viewers of all sorts, religious and otherwise, engage in what amounts to a simple but in many ways still sophisticated wrestle with the question of how one can "know" even some slight portion of a divine reality. That is, historically at least, the great noetic riddle of modernity and all of human life.

In addition to his inherited Roman Catholic Christianity, Josh will try more routes than a GPS device: Judaism, Hinduism, Buddhism, and even a boyish kind of sorcery. And lo, by the end, Josh comes to very big, remarkable surprises, wholly unexpected and wondrous, ones that reside in places he never ever dreamed of looking, such as right in front of him in the ordinary course of people and events. So surprising and strange are these recognitions that Josh has to run into them repeatedly before he catches their gist, and even then it takes a special assist from a bosom friend to yank around, finally, his perception of just where the holy might in fact dwell after all.

The same might be said for any viewer, because by and large hardly anyone, at least according to this film, attends to the very remarkable strangeness of the ordinary wherein Shyamalan locates a major part of the mystery of divine presence within this world. It is not too far a stretch, to borrow from Irish poet William Butler Yeats, to say that Josh finds that "Love has pitched" its "mansion" where one least expects it, smack amid the ordinary physical life of being alive in human skin.[1] Only when Josh comprehends and embraces that central paradox

---

1. William Butler Yeats, "Crazy Jane Talks with the Bishop," Poetry Foundation, accessed August 3, 2016, https://www.poetryfoundation.org/poems-and-poets/poems/detail/43295.

does he find anything at all akin to the spectacular "sign" or tangible, indisputable proof for which he has so long searched. In fact, he finds something far more profound than mere empirical proof of a supernatural reality. He comes upon not only the reality of the divine but also its core nature and meaning. At last, then, Joshua Beal comes to relish the mystery of God as manifest in consuming love, and especially, and improbably, among the very least of those all about us, a vision of meaning that his devout grandfather exhibited in all he did. In this regard, the film seems a perfect *exemplum* of Jesus's "least of these" parable of the sheep and the goats in Matthew 25. There Jesus locates his presence with the mundane and outcast—"the place of excrement," in Yeats's words—and he demands his followers go and do likewise.

To arrive there, though, Joshua must undertake a journey, pilgrim-like, a dead-serious venture that comes close to ending in despair. And though sensitive and smart beyond his years, Joshua goes about that enterprise of finding religious certainty just as any ten-year-old would—by looking for conspicuous "signs and wonders" of divine presence to confirm that God exists and, by extension, that his grandfather has found safety and even welcome in his dying. That seems a childish sort of reaction, but in fact Josh's "research," however simple and impressionistic, resembles the ways adults and philosophers undertake the same, especially amid the vast smorgasbord of religious options now contending with one another, sampling this and dabbling in that, from Buddhism to suspect movements such as Scientology. As a means of loving his grandfather still, keeping him close, Josh will attempt just about anything, try any route, worry his parents, and exhaust his sweetly concerned teachers.

Sometimes desperate people grasp at straws, hungry for any omen or portent, sign, or wonder; they take what they can get and sometimes make too much of small or plainly mistaken "clues." Confused and thirsty, just about everyone who hungers for a supernatural Something does so, and often promising routes and clues prove mistaken, empty, or just plain bogus, even within accustomed, deeply cherished avenues, such as Josh's inherited Catholicism. People languish and yearn, especially amid the desolations of tragedy and loss. For Josh's query there are no easy answers, and as he will soon find out, life is that way, full of vexing riddles and puzzles.

By the end, after a great deal of lurching about, Joshua actually does come across the sure, even miraculous "proof," present and palpable, for which he so long struggled, of his grandfather's eternal well-being. That, however, is almost anticlimax, for first Josh learns something far more necessary and profound, and that is the great dazzling surprise of his young life. That insight is likely to shape the rest of his days, and it is preparatory to and part and parcel of whatever he learns about the reality of immortality. Here Josh, perhaps like Moses, comes upon a different sort of holy ground, one that he previously did not recognize, lost as he was in an imaginary kingdom of space heroes and the like (just as adults get lost in a world of glitzy thrills and causes). Josh himself is slow to recognize what his own experience tells him about a central dimension of the reality that comes from a place Josh never thought to look. In a great metacognitive leap, belated though it is, Josh comes to recognize the dense, shining richness of ordinary life, infused with remarkable beauty and the necessity of love for life and all humankind. From that apprehension of a radical divine *caritas* infusing all things flows quite naturally the possibility of immortality as a logical extension of divine love for the entirety of the created carnal world. As such, *Wide Awake* venerates ordinary life far more than any afterlife. Very much a gift from somewhere, the "answer" is located by Josh in a place he never thought to look—the ordinary world right before him—and a stunning answer it is.

The Questions

Shyamalan lays out this story of intellectual and spiritual maturation in discrete units, helpfully supplying instructive chapter headings to make sure that viewers "get it." As the story begins, Josh is in deep funk, swallowed by the loss of his grandfather, who is, as he tells in voice-over, "his best friend." "September: The Questions" begins on the first day of the fifth grade (which is also the beginning of Fall, that time of seasonal dying), and Joshua is, as his mother says, "almost a man," though he sure does not act like it—he sleeps with plentiful "comfort objects" (stuffed animals). On this morning he is deeply sleepy, showing no relish at all for the first day of school, even falling back to sleep while brushing his teeth.

And here, as he does throughout the film, Shyamalan employs effective visual humor and surprise. Almost all the considerable gentle humor in the sequence derives from Shyamalan's visual smarts; this

strategy works extremely well in critical parts of the story where Shyamalan does more showing than telling. Some of Joshua's sleepiness is
no doubt an avoidance reaction to the august place to which he journeys
for schooling, Waldron Mercy Academy, an upper-crusty Roman Catholic school for boys, to which he goes dressed in short pants, tie, and
blue blazer. Before leaving for the first day of school, however, having
finally gotten dressed, Joshua detours to visit his grandfather's room,
where he takes time to don his grandfather's favorite flannel shirt, sit
in his rocking chair, and even suck on the old man's pipe. Here begins
the boy's retrospective voice-over narration, both sweet and pungent,
explaining that he and his grandfather "watched out for one another."
No small part of Joshua's grief derives from the fact that though the old
fellow promised that he'd never ever leave Joshua, clearly, having died,
"he lied" (4:00). That crushing truth instigates Josh's gloom.

So Josh has got some mysteries before him that inspire very good,
haunting queries, for which easy answers do not avail. In this case, the
sort of boy Joshua already is at a mere ten years of age prepares the
way for what follows. We get the first hint of this when his physician
father (Denis Leary) drops him at school. In his usual tone of long-
suffering exasperation, the dutiful doctor reminds Joshua not to ag-
gravate his teachers by asking so many questions, a habit Joshua cannot, as the next sequence will show, bring himself to relinquish. And

so it will be. In his religion class, taught by sports-loving Sister Terry (Rosie O'Donnell), wearing a baseball cap in a classroom where pictures of sports figures mix with those of saints (and no quizzes on holy days or during the playoffs), Josh sets off an intellectual riot. At one point, he interrupts Sister Terry to ask if the unbaptized, like his aunt Denise, are going to hell, just as the inane catechism workbook, *Jesus Is My Buddy*, says they are. Of course, everybody in the room knows someone who's not baptized, and pandemonium breaks out, prompting Sister Terry to announce that "No one is going to hell," after which she is saved, in a nice pun on the discussion, if not by baptism, then by the bell, telling her departing students, in full sardonic flair, that no one should "inform any of their friends, neighbors, or relatives of their impending doom" (8:20).

Given Josh's deep curiosity, a churchy setting, and the still painfully fresh loss of his grandfather, it is no small wonder that the small boy, emotionally blasted and feeling very much alone, soon comes upon the question that will shape his quest. This takes place in curious fashion in imagery that will repeat, tellingly and gorgeously, at the very end of the film. He escapes class with his buddy Dave O'Hara (Timothy Reifsnyder), and the pair walk down the august wood-lined halls of Waldron

Academy when Josh's attention fixes on lovely shafts of light pouring in one of the hall windows, a central metaphor in the biblical record. The scene clearly suggests a bent in Joshua toward the mystical, or at least attentiveness to beauty amid the ordinary (the light here is maybe foreshadowing or, in this case, fore-lighting). He stands there looking at the light in a posture of quiet wonder and amazement, an instance of unexpected, pressing beauty here leading to questions of God. So he asks Dave if he believes in God, to which Dave replies in the negative, explaining in pithy terms that "Too many bad things happen to people for no reason" (11:30). He does not mind, though, if Josh believes; after all, as he explains in a nice turn of cognitive humility, "I drink chocolate milk through my nose. What do I know?" Then, to emphasize the point, after the two boys exit, the camera lingers briefly on those shafts of light, and finally, as rarely happens in the film, the image fades not to black but to an entirely white screen.

Here, in this random meditation on light, emerges Joshua's quest, though his voice-over does admit that the idea birthing in his head is perhaps not such a good one. On the other hand, that Josh's venture is perhaps in some way blessed is suggested by that closing fade to a screen of stark white light: asking questions of beauty is a good thing, and one path to the divine. In any case, wondering at the light (or, the Light, given the scene and the question it inspires) shows young Josh's unusual aesthetic and religious sensitivity, one that melds instances of exceptional beauty with the notion of God. Clearly brainy, observant, and curious, Josh is not an ordinary kid but one already birthing an acute awareness of the strangeness and beauty of human experience. That is not a bad place to start—or end up, for that matter, as will indeed prove the case.

The dither of the new school year does little to divert Josh from either grief or curiosity. Though very undersized for his age, and against the clear warnings of his physician parents, the diminutive Joshua wants to play football because, as he tells them in a clincher, "Grandpa played football" (14:40). For Josh it seems that football promises a sure path to both his grandfather and hope. After all, as Josh later explains, "My grandpa was a really great football player. He ran for two hundred yards in one game. He believed in two things: always keep both hands on the ball, and always hold on to your faith. Faith will get you through" (16:00). Unfortunately, as Josh soon realizes, "football isn't the answer" (and neither, apparently, is religious faith), and the film comically shows exactly why with his oversized and very ill-fitting equipment, especially a helmet that falls off continually (18:45). And so comes another route, a "mission, a real mission," as opposed to football and the spaceship play fantasies imagined by Josh and friend Dave (20:00). That is, looking for God in order to talk to God "to make sure my grandpa's okay" (20:22). A useful foil, Dave asks all the hard questions, such as, in this case, "where in the world you gonna look?" (20:47). And so begins Joshua's quest, a long series of strategies, one after the other, handled by Shyamalan with both humor and dead seriousness, that Josh hopes will finally link him to the divine so he can get an answer to the question of whether his grandfather is "okay."

First off, there is a humorous take on the problem of evil. A quick look at the graphic catalogue of car wrecks and natural disasters on the evening news demonstrates that the deity will not be found there, giving some support to friend Dave's earlier counsel that there's too much evil to allow for a god who runs the world or even allows the carnage. So much for conspicuous public displays of divine presence.

Josh then attempts "knowledge by proxy," for lack of a better term. Josh searches out another conspicuous venue for God, namely, the local Roman Catholic cardinal. If anyone could speak authoritatively, he speculates, it is a religious eminence, both powerful and knowledgeable, and as a young Roman Catholic, he turns to the obvious (alas, many seekers of all kinds pursue gurus and revivalists to whom they can hand over their souls and very often, unfortunately, their brains). When Philadelphia's cardinal visits his sister's equally fancy school, located across a fence from his own, Josh escapes school, with institutional diversion supplied by Dave, so he can query the cardinal for an answer.

Josh does manage to get very close—in the restroom to which the cardinal has fled amid some sort of medical attack—but there Josh finds a man of considerable age and frailty, looking, in fact, "like somebody's grandpa" (28:18).

"I don't think God talks to him," concludes Josh (28:32). For the literal-minded ten-year-old, it simply cannot be that this man knows God or can offer answers to the big mysteries, for his very human limitations seem more than obvious. Here Josh makes the commonplace mistake of thinking power or prominence ensures knowledge or some magical charm that protects one from the inexorable diminution of very mortal flesh. Clearly, cardinals are not all-powerful and immortal superheroes. Again, decay and death make themselves known. For Josh, it seems, there is no escaping the brokenness that evil sponsors.

Here though, as is his temptation throughout, typical enough in a ten-year-old in a scientific age, Josh is tempted to trust in indisputable empirical reality, palpable evidence that will speedily and conveniently prove God's reality and presence. In this thirsty credulity, though, he's not so different from those hordes of grown-ups who wish to see in order to believe. It will take the whole film for Josh to move beyond this sort of empiricist reductionism in recognizing how God shows up in human affairs. The episode concludes with Josh recognizing, with a bit of dismay, that "this mission could take days" (28:45).

December: Looking for Signs

That Shyamalan is aware of the wrongheadedness of much of what Josh will soon test out as routes to God becomes clear in the film's second chapter, "December: The Signs." It is now a long way from September, and Josh seems no closer to any sort of answer or consolation about his grandfather's (and his own) well-being. It is no wonder, then, that in the schoolboys' obligatory monthly confession to Father Peters, Josh breaks decorum by asking, "Can we just talk?" (30:30). Peters himself seems more than a little depressed, though the film does not explain why. Perhaps it is his disappointment in not finding sufficient serious-ness among schoolboys, or, as the film strongly hints, his own sense of spiritual abandonment. With beguiling innocence, Josh comes right to the point: "You ever feel like giving up? Since it's been so long and all [and] you haven't met him? You don't even know if he's made up or not" (31:16). While Josh here uses the generic "you" to mean every-one, and does not mean Peters specifically, Peters soon takes Josh less lightly, conceding that he too at times feels the same blankness. He counsels, though, that "doubt's a part of everyone's journey, no matter what they're looking for," and he assures Josh that if he does find sure proof, Josh will be the first person he tells (31:52).

And Father Peters remembers Joshua's distress. During a choral practice, which is apparently one of Peters's duties to lead, he finds his singers, and Joshua among them, distracted and listless. He stops the singing to suggest, looking at Josh and ending with a wink, that "maybe if we all sing together with all our hearts, our voices will rise up out of this chapel, out of this building, up into the heavens. Maybe if we really sing together, God will hear us" (38:00). The choir launches into an exuberant Gloria as the camera dollies down the center aisle of the chapel to see singing boy after singing boy, fixing finally on Josh, who sings with passion and conspicuous joy, partaking for a bit in the relish of the immense promise of divine splendor and love. As a full orchestra (out of nowhere) comes in to support the singing, the screen fades not to the usual black but again to full white, a tool that seems to be Shyamalan's way of signaling the validity of a particular kind of divine presence, or a route into the beauty not of light through a window as in his previous fade to white but of light mediated through exultant music of thanksgiving.

And indeed, the audience sees, hears, and feels as much, as if God's own self has imbibed this humble musical try at adoration and exuberance, and blessed it. Here Shyamalan seems intent on situating viewers within visual and musical sequences that display beguiling, deeply moving glimpses of beauty that in the wonder elicited by their splendor and delight hint in small measure at the character of Light itself, namely, the elusive God for whom Josh searches.

The route here suggests the potency of aesthetic apprehension, though that is a strategy that is perhaps at this stage too subtle, at least for a ten-year-old, and for adults in general, to grasp or hold on to for very long. Blinkered and fumbling are we all. Still, the sequence suggests that, as poets and painters aplenty have claimed, humankind can apprehend the divine, a presence that infuses life itself, if folks simply open their eyes and become wide awake to the gorgeousness that surrounds them. For Josh this is the first sustained hint of a new sort of perceptual prism with which to see, understand, and embrace the world in which he finds himself. And that will prove Josh's own destination as he slowly comes to recognize, after lurching there and here, life itself as a glowing display of a transcendent but simultaneously immanent and pressing Love.

In his hunt for signs, Josh also looks to snow, an infrequent visitor to Philadelphia, not only as a means of getting out of school but also as a confirmation that God exists. Snow was one of the natural occurrences that his grandfather took as evidence of God's splendor. Then, too, there are the regular counseling sessions with Sister Terry, who queries Josh about his forays into Islam (praying to the east), Judaism (Hanukkah candles), and Hinduism (fasting at Thanksgiving), Josh's knowledge of such practices gleaned from the handy new, voluminous storehouse of religious information known as the Internet. Later, at a classmate's birthday party, comes Buddhism; Josh and two friends sit on the floor cross-legged with eyes closed repeating "Ommmmmm" (45:20). In the middle of that quest comes the girl from the school across the way, the same girl who helped Josh when he invaded the school in his attempt to meet the cardinal.

After all these attempts and Josh's apparent failure to find God (or simply recognize what was there already), friend Dave counsels common sense, urging Josh to stop his mission because he's "wigging, man" (48:43). After all, asks Dave, "In all this time, in all this stuff you've been doing, have you gotten one sign, any sign, to let you know there's a God?" (48:52). Dave's conclusion seems amply warranted, for "either there ain't no God, or there is a God, and he don't care you're looking for him. Either way, it's time to stop." Clearly, the outlook is not good.

And so it goes, Josh continuing to ponder and search, all the while venturing deeper into the thicket, so to speak. One evening Josh sits in his room in his grandfather's shirt and rocking chair with eyes closed and mightily petitions for a sign. Sensing that maybe "something" numinous has transpired, he runs to his parents' bedroom inquiring, as if he has recently seen *The Exorcist*, whether any mysterious supernatural-seeming occurrences, like flickering lights, wind, or "a holy vision," have come their way (49:40). Again, Josh looks for palpable displays—omens, signs, miracles, undeniable material proofs—to validate his hopes. Here, in this moment, with no such affirmatives, Josh despairs, leading to the conclusion that while his grandfather "believed in two things . . . I don't think I believe in anything at all" (51:05). Then, on the cusp of bidding farewell to his belief, Josh recalls in flashback his grandfather's certainty "that God will take care of me when I get to Him" (51:40). Josh ponders how the old fellow could be so sure, fearing still that if no one is there to take care of his grandfather, then God is simply made up. Josh recalls that snowy walk when his stricken grandfather confessed that he found proof in the beauty of the snow then lying upon the ground, a display the old fellow clearly regards through a lens of wonder, beauty, and gratitude. Young empiricist that he is, Josh offers a scientific account of snow, to which his grandfather rejoins that "there's more, much more, but maybe you're going to have find your own proof" (52:44). Beauty and awe again provide one telling factor in constructing, or confirming, belief, and this too Josh will find out, though it will take more time still for him to grasp this. It seems, then, for Shyamalan, that beauty is indeed a route, always present and significant, but whose flash of splendor a purblind humanity largely ignores.

At the very least, the scene provides a glimpse of the transcendent Love that made the world for beauty and relish, and Shyamalan shows it so largely without words and debate, amply preparing the way for the chapter that follows. The scene also signals the new path Josh will take toward wide awakeness, toward relish and gratitude for the gift of being alive in a majestic world. In what follows Josh will indeed follow his grandfather's path, savoring and acknowledging the beauty, though his referents do change, just as his grandfather had predicted Josh would have to find his own answers. The sequence prepares Josh's ultimate embrace of his grandfather's own love for the world. The close of their chat upon a bench amid the snow-covered ground provides a lovely bit of foreshadowing, as it provides warrant for what Josh must learn about the care of other people, the central part of Josh's burgeoning understanding of the nature of divine presence in the wrenchingly painful world. There on that bench his grandfather confesses that he is in fact a "little scared," and Josh says that he is too and asks if he may now cry (earlier his grandfather asked him not to, for he did not think he could handle it). For a great length of screen time, especially given how clippily this film speeds along, the camera simply watches the dying old man and the boy hold on to each other, quite literally, for dear life, the grandfather at one point passionately kissing Josh's face. The poignancy works, without being maudlin, to underline the obvious, namely, their deep, even profound, affection for one another, signaling the intimate texture of life's deepest beauty.

More so still, within the rhetoric of the film, the sequence works to emphasize a primary domain, one Josh will soon enter, more wondrous yet than the beauty of snow, light, or music, wherein the reality of God becomes blatantly, bodily manifest—if indeed one has eyes to see, if indeed one is "wide awake." With this scene as a pivot, the remainder of the film displays Josh learning to recognize an altogether different sort of revelatory splendor that soaks the world all about him. It is one he never considered, no matter how obvious, in hindsight at least. To his lasting surprise—for it profoundly alters him—Josh will find his own kind of proof, and stunning it is, though it will have to knock him on the head, or cleave his soul, four times before its rapturous, radical truth shines out.

May: The Answers

After his reverie recalling his driveway talk with his grandfather, one that began with his denial of belief, Josh rises from his chair to look out the window and sees a world swirling and dazzling with a snowfall that has already covered the ground. This is, apparently, the holy thing that earlier he sensed was afoot and about which he interrogated his family, and it is fully a wonder more complex and profound than any sort of magical-empirical proof tidily produced by this or that exotic religious practice, as nice as that would be (indeed, the whole of the film can be read as satire of the sort of blithe spiritual consumerism that characterizes much of American culture). He turns giddy with delight, clearly taking the snow for a sign from above that the world is not empty of the divine. What becomes clear, though, is that while belief is neither easy nor simple, neither is denial. With eyes wide open, awake, we might just see a world transfigured. Better still, it proves to be the very same commonplace world we daily inhabit, only now transfigured with a splendid whiteness. In short, Josh comes to fathom, at least momentarily, what the divine is all about if but given eyes to see. Josh glimpses briefly a world that is quietly but assuredly spectacular if we but wonder at it, whether in the splendor of light pouring through a hallway window passed a thousand times or, as Josh will soon come to recognize, in the splendor of other people, actual, real living beings very much like himself.

So the answers come, though it takes Josh a long while to recognize them as such, given his predilection for the palpable supernatural intervention, that big, utterly unambiguous neon light in the sky. Mostly what he gets are "hints followed by guesses," as T. S. Eliot put it,[2] that together construct a compelling sort of cogency for the soul and self, if not exactly for pure intellect, which is an elusive entity at best, even for its devoteees. In any case, hints then together shape informed guesses. What Josh comes upon is, to be sure, a tangled and varied skein, but it is a skein nonetheless. And always these hints come strange and unexpected from surprising events and sources. So different and varied are they, fixing as they do on the ordinary world and on people, that for a long time they seem random and completely disconnected. It doesn't occur to Josh, for a long while, that the "answers" he so fervently seeks lie immediately within the warm depths of his immediate human world. And none is more peculiar than the ever-strange Robert Brickman, who during class one day suddenly snatches a picture of the pope from the wall to run outdoors in the pouring rain to hold it up atop the jungle gym (Sister Terry laconically asks, "Will someone please go tell Sister Josephine that Robert's out in the rain with the Pope?" [56:24]). What Brickman means by all that, as if he himself knew, well, who knows? Perhaps it is that, whatever it is, is right there right in front of everyone in plain sight, even amid the rain.

Of course, on his mission and increasingly desperate, Josh takes Brickman's stunt as a sign of something, though he knows not what. The first clear marker toward clarity comes when the lovely young girl on whom Josh has a crush breaks ranks during a joint religious ceremony at her school to deliver to Josh a rose she carries and to inform him, with quiet assurance, that he will indeed find answers. Of course, the event itself provides the first such answer, though he does not recognize it as such. After all he has gone through, the mere fact of

2. T. S. Eliot, *The Complete Poems and Plays, 1909–1950* (New York: Harcourt, Brace, and World, 1962), 136.

empathy and encouragement within his lostness in his quest counts for something. Someone has noticed. Indeed, her gesture foreshadows Josh's increasing recognition that a good deal of the presence of God shows up in and through people and not in some dramatic revelatory miracle, though that possibility, Shyamalan being Shyamalan, is never discarded.

And, lo, immediately thereafter comes the first of these very conspicuous strangenesses, which Josh himself cannot quite understand. Occurrence number one begins with Josh waiting in the hall for his regular counseling session with Sister Terry. There he overhears the parents of his bullying nemesis, Freddie Waltman (Michael Pacienza), telling Sister Terry that they can no longer afford to send him to Waldron and have to remove him, a prospect Freddie refuses to accept. When Freddie's last day arrives, a day that Josh realizes, given Freddie's constant bullying, should be the happiest of his own young life, Josh instead feels nothing but sympathy for his longtime foe. After sweetly compassionate Sister Terry escorts Freddie, on the verge of tears, to his waiting parents' car, Josh darts from the building to chase down the Waltmans' slowly departing beat-up minivan. When Freddie slides open the door, Josh says good-bye and sticks out his hand, which the perplexed Waltman takes. They shake, and Waltman says, with due sobriety and appreciation, "Good-bye, Josh," the camera cutting, somewhat too emphatically, from the faces to the clasped hands. Waltman closes the door to put his head in his hand as the van pulls away. The reaction shot of Sister Terry, smiling approvingly on the building steps, underlines the point still further (it is a film made, at least in part, for kids, on whom minimalist subtlety is lost).

Much the same sort of thing happens in occurrence number two when Josh reckons with the misfortune of another nemesis, the overweight and friendless boy Frank. A bumbling and fawning social exile, Frank regularly throughout the film asks Josh if Josh, who's usually pleasant to the kid, will play with him. To that question, Josh always responds with "tomorrow," leading Frank to ask repeatedly, and annoyingly, "Is today tomorrow?" (57:52). On a field trip to a history museum, Frank asks yet again, and Josh explodes in response, telling Frank to just leave him alone. The strident rebuff from the only classmate to show any kindness crushes poor Frank. Then, not taking no for an answer, Frank tries to go through the turnstile together with Josh, and the mechanism jams, locking the two cheek by jowl for a full twenty minutes till a workman frees them. Josh's humiliation is added to by Frank's fear that he might "blow chunks," as boy vernacular puts it (1:04:12). Josh stays mortified and angry till he later sees Frank sitting alone and forlorn on a distant bench. To this, despite his ire, Joshua responds, inviting the morose boy to walk the museum together. "Today is tomorrow," Josh tells the boy. This time the incident stands by itself, with no commentary, camera gymnastics, or approving reaction shots from clerical bystanders.

However, just as these sorts of benign events begin to accumulate, crisis comes, severe and dramatic, and through that will emerge, with resounding clarity, occurrence number three, one that extends and clarifies the first two. In the midst of final exams, Joshua's friend Dave fails to show for a test, and Josh speculates that Dave has come down with one of his "didn't study for the exam" headaches, from which he has been suffering a lot lately. On the way home, Josh asks his mom to stop by Dave's house so Josh can see how he's doing. Josh walks into the very large, silent house, finally locating Dave in the under-stairwell storage room that is their imaginary "galactic battleship." Things are far from well, for he finds Dave half-conscious, trembling, and bleeding. Josh runs screaming out the front door, filmed in slow motion, to summon his mother physician, who sees the terror on her son's face in her rearview mirror (in a very nicely filmed sequence). All the while the voice-over informs the audience that Dave suffers from epilepsy, the signs of which are frequent headaches and blurry vision. Strangely, Josh has shown up in the nick of time to offer aid when there is no aid about, for Dave's mother is absentee and his father is no doubt off making enough money to support them and their very sizable home. In any case, Josh has again come to the rescue, this time ever so dramatically, of someone in dire need.

Still, things will get worse before they get better and Josh finally "gets it." The significance of these rescues stays murky at best, at least for a time. Instead of relief that he has rescued Dave, Josh interprets Dave's health crisis as another instance of a terrible fate befalling someone he loves, and it proves the final straw in his quest for reassurance and belief. In what becomes a kind of ritual burial of belief, Josh is found at night below a backyard tree filling with dirt a large toy dump truck, though viewers at first don't quite know what he's up to. The voice-over indicates that Josh has concluded that his grandfather was wrong and that someone "just made God up" (1:12:55), and Josh now "dumps" his quest. The emblem of that belief, soon to be literally committed to the dirt, is his grandfather's shirt.

Then, though, in the midst of Josh's burial ritual, a strange turn provides counterevidence, a fourth "occurrence," and it is perhaps the revelatory core of the film, as Josh seems at last to make sense of things as he recalls with painful relish an earlier event from the last days of his grandfather's life. The ritual burial scene dissolves into Josh's recollection in flashback of his grandfather at Josh's school track-and-field day a year earlier, at the end of the fourth-grade year. At the starting line, Joshua announces to the boy next to him that he intends to win the race for his grandfather, for the old fellow is seriously ill and will not live much longer. Midway through the race Josh stumbles and falls, and the other competitors finish while Josh remains on the ground halfway down the course. A nun is about to announce the winners when the grandfather intervenes to point out that his grandson, still lying there, has not finished the race. Thereafter, in a perfect representation of divine love, his grandfather nods and opens his arms, providing for stumbling, deflated, and sorrowful Josh the perfect, and final, destination. Josh picks himself up to run flying into those outstretched arms, crying as he hugs the mortally ill man (though it is clearly a chilly day, the dying man is conspicuously overdressed in overcoat, thick sweater, scarf, and hat).

The sequence finishes by segueing back to the tree to see the truck emptying its load of dirt into a hole that contains at its bottom his

grandfather's favorite shirt. In recalling his grandfather's display of care, however, Josh has seen his own future that is soon to arrive.

If Josh's recollection is not sufficient to complicate his growing sense of doom for his mission, another gesture of kindness brings Josh inescapably smack up against still another perplexity. Josh visits his badly battered friend Dave in the hospital (from thrashing in the seizure, his eye is blackened, his lip cut, and his arm broken). Josh announces that he has quit his mission to find God. Much to his surprise, skeptic Dave tells him to keep searching, for he has himself come to believe. Dave's rationale for belief lies in the providential riddle of why Josh happened by to rescue Dave in the very midst of his seizure. Here Dave indicates the common core in all those prior revelations: namely, a profound, surprising, and unsettling care for others, whether sad bullies or friendless outcasts. Yes, there is a warm, shining domain, the human nexus of mutuality and love, where the divine shows up and shows off in gestures of compassion and care. Much to his own surprise, Josh enacted such in his responses to bully Freddy and overweight Frank, and in doing so, Josh merely emulates the sort of care and compassion that his grandfather typically showed him, instances of which viewers see in the driveway talk and after the disastrous field-day stumble. More than that, Josh recollects his grandfather's outstretched arms, a posture that clearly mimes Shyamalan's frequent shots of a large statue of Jesus, arms outstretched, that occupies a prominent hallway location at Waldron Academy (1:22:50). The conflation of those two tableaux seems more than obvious, and especially so because the statue looms behind and above Joshua in the film's last sequence.

The crucial significance of love and care as central to human well-being amplifies enormously, needless to say, when God seems to break decisively into human brokenness, as seems to be the case when Josh, in the nick of time, visits his seizure-struck friend. The event is not so much a departure from what has gone before, one that separates the natural from the supernatural, as a fulfillment and clarification of Shyamalan's notion of a God that cares and makes God's presence and care known. For once, it seems, God intervenes decisively, as with Dave's distress. Still, that spectacular intrusion, if intrusion it is, simply extends and magnifies the very sort of agapic gesture, coming to the aid of suffering others, that Josh himself welcomed and then conveys to others. In Shyamalan's world, no matter how bizarre the events, as in *Unbreakable* and *Signs*, God is for people, meaning for the flourishing of individual people not so much for themselves but for the well-being and flourishing of others in the whole broken, ragtag mass of humankind. If Josh showing up at the right moment is a miracle, then it is a miracle that proceeds from and in behalf of human mutuality, emanating from love itself, for that indeed is the domain wherein God shows up and makes divine presence and care perceptible. If Josh had not cared, then, well, no miracle. It might be random providential luck, so to speak, but here and in *Signs*, it emerges from and serves human bonds.

Fruition

Though the film could have ended satisfactorily at this point—and perhaps should have—Shyamalan pushes his point still harder. The film's close makes this more than clear by showing just how far through the wilderness Joshua, like his biblical namesake, one also full of sorrow and doubt, has traveled in one school year. Indeed, he has, in a very real way, found something of a promised land of compassion and hope, those supreme gifts that pave the way, at least in this story, for belief. In the year-end speech Josh delivers in his oral rhetoric class, he summarizes his own transit from childhood to the threshold of adulthood. He has moved from boyish make-believe play to a very real relational world of "family, friends, and—girls" (1:18:00). Then Joshua, turning downright serious with a kind of spiritual-ethical precocity, enumerates the number and nature of those changes that mark his transit from childhood to full humanity: "Before this year, bullies were just bullies, weirdos were just weird, and daredevils weren't afraid of anything [meaning friend Dave]. Before this year, people I loved lived forever. I spent this year looking for something and wound up seeing everything around. It was like I was asleep before and finally woke up. You know what: I'm wide awake now." Wide awake, indeed, seeing for the first time the value and wonder of people with eyes of love, much like his grandfather saw the snow and saw and loved Josh, diving whole into the exultant, multifoliate wonder of being and gratitude for the world and for the others in that world.

Through the length of the speech, Josh has on his face a pensive, faraway look, and the speech as a whole plays well, winning huge smiles from his new friend Frank and an approving warm smile from the otherwise very serious Sister Sophia (Camryn Manheim). The clarity and passion of Josh's reflection prove deeply rousing, for the boy has grabbed on to the everlasting mystery of the centrality and holiness of love. And Josh experiences love as both holy and mysterious. Having arrived there, he receives, it seems, a final gift, a glowing reassurance that the love he has grasped and enacted continues on through the whole of this life and into another.

In *Wide Awake*'s closing sequence, that mystery expands into a liminal-mystical magic land that inducts Josh into a further, final realm of "wide awakeness." Sister Terry has sent him into the hall to look for an absent classmate (in fact, Sister Terry has miscounted; no one is absent). There Josh encounters the small blond boy who has shown up regularly on the periphery throughout the story, though this is the first time Josh actually talks to him, informing him that he's missing the class picture. The boy, smaller still than Josh, reports that he's not in Josh's class, news that surprises Josh and prompts him to ask the fellow's name. The response that follows is strange indeed. "This is the first time you're seeing me, isn't it?" Not at all, insists Josh, for he sees him all the time: "You're always around, always smiling, and you're always watching me" (1:21:50). Still the small kid pushes the matter: "But this is the first time you've *really* seen me," he says, in effect asking Josh to stretch his newfound wide awakeness further still.

There the conversation would end if not for the boy's cryptic declaration, with a dead-serious intense stare on his face, that "You don't have to worry, he's happy now." Josh thinks he means Dave, but the boy replies that he does not mean David. A little spooked, Josh turns to rejoin his class, and then the answer dawns in a flash that "You mean Grandpa?" but, alas, when Josh turns, the boy is no longer there. After a few seconds of stunned perplexity, Josh breaks into a broad laughing smile as he gets some idea of what the small kid has told him and just who the small kid really is (whatever he is). Indeed, the voice-over, echoing the film's "I believe in . . . ," informs viewers of the plain fact that "not all angels have wings" (1:22:56). Not only has his grandfather entered some sort of paradisaical life, but his grandfather also takes special pleasure, happiness, in the fact that Josh has found his own "proof" of divine care for the world, which is the very fact that there is transcendent care.

The last shot retreats from Josh to take in once again the golden light pouring through the hall windows, bathing the scene in quiet but arresting visual splendor, mimicking, in fact, the sort of light and color that floods a Monet sunset of haystacks in a snowfield. As befits reve-latory appearances of the divine, light drenches the hallway, shaft upon shaft of light pouring in. This is, after all, exactly the same spot from which earlier in the film Josh first noticed the beauty of the light pour-ing in the window, presenting him for the first time with some thirst for a numinous reality, either for beauty or for the divine itself, as if the two can be yanked apart.

It is this same light, in fact, that seems to have instigated his quest for certainty. And if there be any doubt as to what Shyamalan is up to, at the far end of the long hallway stands, looming immediately above Josh, the statue of shepherd Jesus, lit candles adorning his feet, seem-ing to bestow on Josh an ample dose of divine embrace and blessing. He stands there in a perpetual gesture of compassion and love that reiter-ates the welcome his grandfather extended to Josh when he stumbled. That very posture is an apt representation of the "answer" to Josh's metaphysical quest for certainty. The primary, central arena of divine presence and display lies not in spectacular, palpable signs and wonders but in reconciliation and love. That sort of presence suggests God first made the world, and now remakes it toward relational wholeness, and in Shyamalan's world it is a deep-down wondrous process. That light of love infuses the mundane and ordinary, transfiguring everything for those "wide awake" to the press of its reality. And, remarkably, even small, grandfatherless boys can see, imbibe, and manifest that selfsame light, however unexpected, just as angels do, winged and otherwise.

CHAPTER TWO

AND THE BLIND SHALL SEE

Grasping the Radiance of Being in *The Color of Paradise*

It is a remarkable sight, one that is not easily forgotten, both for what it depicts and, strangely, given the predicament of its central figure, for its visual dazzle. After all, its subject is a small, very conspicuously sightless boy (as is actor Mohsen Ramezani offscreen), who squats by the side of a mountain stream, hands in the water, feeling its flow and the rocks beneath, trying to discern in their random placement, by means of Arabic Braille, a message of some sort.

He takes the streambed, and nature generally, for a cipher—a kind of hidden providential puzzle—that holds within the answer to the riddle of why he cannot see. Not often do we find ten-year-old seekers after divine intent, and this young fellow fervently searches everywhere by every available means to grab the slightest clue of any sort (on the likelihood of children searching for God, see as well the discussion in the previous chapter of M. Night Shyamalan's *Wide Awake*, a story that in some respects parallels director Majid Majidi's tale). Moreover, beyond his blindness, though to some extent because of it, his life has not been kind but rather one hard blow after another. Yes, even small blind boys can query the perennial hard question of human suffering and divine justice.

Trouble has been plentiful. Obviously, blindness is an incalculable deprivation for anyone, but perhaps for young Mohammad, extraordinarily acutely attuned to the wonder and splendor of being alive, it is a doubly sore loss. This is made poignantly obvious from the splendid

49

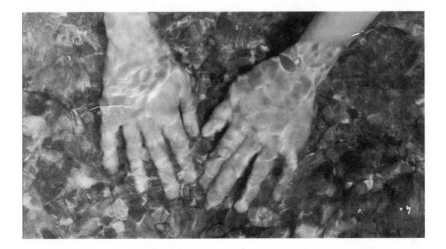

performance by Ramezani, his sightless eyes nakedly displayed in the film, as is the blindness of his classmates in the school for the blind that he attends in Tehran.

Also missing from his life is his mother, who died some years before. This loss is compensated to some extent by the deep affection of two sisters, one younger and one older, and a kindly grandmother (Salameh Feyzi), who live in a small mountain village. As loving and kind as they are, a good deal of trouble comes from his hard-pressed father, an angry, self-pitying man (Hossein Mahjoub) who feels deeply his own ill luck—widowed, lonely, and poor—with three children to raise, including a blind son, and his elderly mother to support. Most of all, he does not know what to do with his son, especially now that he has a chance for a new wife, spinster though she is. He fears that the burden of caring for Mohammad will scare off his prospective bride. Sighted though he is, he does not really see, or even seem to want to.

Just how desperate this father is—we never learn his name—becomes clear right at the start. The film opens with Mohammad in class on the last day of the school year at his boarding school for the blind in Tehran. It seems a lovely place, a quiet, verdant oasis full of caring, devoted teachers. While parents flock to bring home their children for summer vacation, Mohammad's father arrives hours late, leaving Mohammad, alone and deserted, the last child to be picked up. Worse still, as soon as he does arrive, the father begs the school administrator to keep his son for the summer, something the school is not equipped to do. Only with the utmost effort does this morose and grudging father muster any welcome or compassion for his son. Rather, his biggest concern in Tehran is to buy fancy gifts for the family of that prospective bride (a reverse dowry). Nor does his grumpy demeanor change on their long journey home by bus, by horseback, and finally on foot, as the pair travel through the lush mountain landscape of Iran (it is on this trip that Mohammad tries to read the stones in the stream). Days after arriving the father takes Mohammad, without even asking or informing him, to a far-distant young carpenter, who is himself blind, to live as an apprentice. The boy's grandmother so objects to this arrangement that she leaves her son's house, thus creating a local scandal that will have its own costs.

Through all this, Mohammad grieves acutely his blindness and his lost parent and, remarkably, he also searches and searches—streams, birdsong, plants, scripture, prayer, lament, wind and storm—for some trace of divine care. The wonder infused in all these quests Majidi lovingly displays on the screen, over and over again. In all of them, Mohammad does sense some measure and kinds of benign presence that press ever mysteriously upon humankind with hints of numinous splendor and power. Still, despite this presence (or is it Presence?), Mohammad's blindness thrusts him, over and over, into a long, sorrowful exile, first from school, then from his father and family, and then even from the carpenter mentor.

Given who Mohammad is—a bright boy of remarkable religious sensitivity, full of both sorrow and glad wonder, two signal poles of human experience—the title plays as cruelly ironic, for he has no access to either color or paradise. This double deficit is made especially vexing by Majidi's setting Mohammad's home within a resplendent mountain landscape, one that the director takes care to display in all its varied gorgeousness, from vivid fields of flowers and rippling streams to alpine storms. So fetching is Majidi's visual feast that *New York Times* reviewer Stephen Holden called the film an "explicitly religious" and even "visionary experience of the natural world."[1] The particular effectiveness of the film, making Mohammad's fate more poignant still, lies in the

---

1. Stephen Holden, "A Spiritual Vision Imbues the Trials of a Blind Boy," *New York Times*, September 25, 1999, http://www.nytimes.com/movie/review?res=9F00E3DB1339F936 A1575AC0A96F958260.

fact that viewers do see and know the very colors of the luminous visual paradise for which the boy so longs. Mohammad, though, is much acquainted with grief, and he seems a lot more like Job than Peter Pan or even Huck Finn, a fellow who had hardships of his own.

By the film's end, however, the title's seemingly inscrutable implications for Mohammad come startlingly clear, miraculously and very literally, in a moment of breathtaking luminosity. At last, light comes to Mohammad to repair his losses in blindness and exile in new life and welcome—a place, in short, of divine compassion for a sorely wounded, sorrowing humanity. Happily, this surprising climax, rather than sentimental or sensational, seems a logical extension of all viewers have seen of the splendorous character of the natural world. Mohammad's search for a shred of divine compassion finds completion as transcendent light finally, at last, touches him. He has striven throughout to touch in order to see, and now he knows what it is to be seen—by his own father for the first time and then also by unsurpassable divine light.

The film's conclusion argues that the wildness of the love displayed in the ravishing beauty of the landscape is the same that erupts in the end to embrace father and son in reconciliation and new life. The love present in the lavish divine gift of natural beauty also contrives, as in a dance, to transfigure the multiple forms of Mohammad's despair. In short, the last scene makes overt another dimension of all that Mohammad has throughout sensed and beheld in awe and gratitude, and the significance of the slight blind boy who senses and knows erupts unequivocally (when it comes to displays of the holy, critics generally much prefer the equivocal and ambiguous, even when it runs counter to what the story has anticipated from the start). Much like Carl Theodor Dreyer's *Ordet* (1955), those seemingly unable to see and really know, at least by ordinary standards, are those who see and know the most. Indeed, the last and least are first. In what is perhaps the oldest trope there is, from Oedipus to Isaiah, running through both Hebrew and Greek culture and also apparently Islam, the blind often come to see far better than the sighted.

In sum, the shock of the unexpected turn in the conclusion emerges from the conspicuous visual thematic Majidi has labored to develop throughout the film. The remarkable Majidi ends with a bracing divine presence that heals the thirsty, aching woundedness that has engulfed Mohammad and, still more, his callous, purblind father. Throughout, the world of nature and people has transfixed young Mohammad, and the blind boy searches with touch and hearing, transfixed and in delight, for clues to the inmost nature of the achingly ambiguous world in which he finds himself. In this lies the genius of the film's heart and soul. The viewers throughout hope for better, given what they see, and ultimately the miracle of the ending emerges from the same divine well as the aesthetic delight they have savored throughout. Having seen or somehow sensed the great beauty, the conclusion comes with no great surprise or implausibility. It is Majidi's cinematic ingenuity that effectively hauls viewers, arduous trip though it is, into the selfsame mystery of yearning, awe, splendor, love, and new life.

"Seeing" the Way Home

The story arrests viewers right from the start: a room full of blind children identifying by ear their lost cassette audiotapes as their teacher inserts each into a portable tape player. Soon after, another teacher dictates sentences about the warmth of the bright sun that the students write in Braille: "The sun brightens the earth. The sun warms the earth while shining on it during the day. The sunny days are warm and bright" (3:29). There is here more than a little incongruity between the text and the task—the sightless zealously copying out descriptions that extol something they cannot see but whose warmth they can nonetheless access, a trope for the story as a whole. For these students the text has a troubling "yes but" quality that will become front and center in Mohammad's own life. The scene continues for a long while until the boys leave for their large dormitory room of stacked bunk beds where they gather their possessions before departing for summer vacation. Mohammad takes special care with the bright trinkets he has gotten for his sisters and grandmother, stuff his teacher kiddingly labels junk but Mohammad claims are "souvenirs" (5:20). Even here the bright red barrettes contrast with the drab, cool palette of the school's interior. There is a rich, resplendent world the audience relishes to which these children have no access, a tension that repeats throughout and steadily adds to the story's poignancy.

The scene then moves outdoors to the lushly shaded entry lane of the school's grounds where viewers soon have a lengthy, close, and largely silent look at the story's protagonist. In the natural and colorful setting, students await their parents. (In outdoor scenes, Majidi seems to go out of his way to saturate his colors, and especially so in natural settings; in stark contrast, interiors seem drab and dim.) Long after all have left, Mohammad sits alone, anxious, sad, and scared, for his father has yet to arrive to take him home for the summer. It is here, while he lingers, that viewers have that long look at the character of the seemingly abandoned boy. In the midst of his own disappointment, Mohammad hears amid the trees bordering the lane a fallen hatchling fussing loudly—and also the hungry mewing of an approaching cat. Knowing well enough what that means, the boy "hears" and feels his way into the thicket to locate the fallen bird. Then, with great difficulty, the bird tucked into his shirt pocket, Mohammad climbs the tree from which the bird has fallen, restoring the lost creature to its nest, a gesture he greatly enjoys as he smilingly allows the birds to nibble his fingers. The whole sequence—the bird's plight paralleling Mohammad's own circumstance and hope for rescue—would play as old-style "heart-of-gold" sentimentality about children and the disabled if it were not so well done. The scene offers as well a lengthy exposure to Mohammad's extreme sensitivity to life and its manifold wonders, especially its beauty in sound and texture. And it deftly, wordlessly, initiates a convincing portrait of a remarkable soul, full of caring and delight, fast on its way to maturity, albeit a painful one.

With patience and vividness, Majidi slowly builds the case for Mohammad's uniqueness. He hears and feels, literally, what no one else does, usually animals, and delights in them, as shown amply with his relish of birdsong. On the bus homeward, while his father sleeps, Mohammad's hand rides the wind outside the bus window. When his father wakes, Mohammad wants to know what sort of landscape they are traveling through, and when they turn to walking, he eagerly runs on ahead down the paths in the fields they cross. Later, with Mohammad on horseback, the two ascend the steep mountains, full of woodpeckers and birds, a visually stunning landscape whose splendor Mohammad cannot see but somehow senses and knows, primarily through touch and hearing. As they rest streamside, Mohammad, on his haunches, splashes his hands in the flowing water and feels the pebbles on the streambed, whispering aloud the Braille letters they randomly shape. Who knows by what random sequence they might disclose some hint of divine reality and presence, a prospect for which the thirsty boy yearns.

The same spontaneous relish replays when he arrives home. He excitedly yells from the horse as he hears the distinctive soundscape of his village. His brightly clothed sisters come running, and he proceeds to feel their faces, commenting on how they've grown. They soon deliver him to his "granny," who works the fields above the village. He clumsily hides behind a tree as she watches, full of compassion and love, as is evident by her body language and the look upon her face.

The two then tour the landscape: trees, wheat fields, flowers, corn. Mohammad wants to know it all and imbibes through touch and hearing the whole romp of savor and connectedness. And Majidi's camera shows all of that for what it is, the earth and people full of splendor and welcome. The setting and photography are fully lovely, making this more of a romp than a tour, and for one of the few times in the film, Majidi hauls in Western-style music, strings and harp in particular, to rhapsodize the sequence's exultant pictorial and emotional richness. Similar scenes soon follow with Mohammad, dressed in his own bright red shirt and straw hat, walking a hillside of pink flowers, and after that a huge field of red poppy and yellow flowers, as his grandmother and sister pick bouquets for the making of clothing dyes. All seems idyllic, pastoral, and even Edenic, but most of all, the slow, extended montage is plausible, compelling, cogent, and affecting.

Strangely, while viewers easily see the gorgeousness of the above, or so they should, as Majidi hopes, blind Mohammad seems as well to "get it," relishing and exulting in response far more than any sighted character. He is, in fact, a kind of guide, schooling both family and viewers in how to perceive, absorb, and savor. Reviewer Stephen Holden rightly calls attention to the "ecstatic sensuousness" that pervades the film, and this seems to be what Mohammad "gets," despite his perceptual limits. This rapturous vision of a world densely charged with beauty, and tacitly miraculous and infused by divine Love, from family to birdsong and wind, assumes in its glowing immanence a measure of transcendent ontological heft and, in so doing, prepares the way and anticipates the film's startling ending. Indeed, here the shining—the aesthetic blitz, that "ecstatic sensuousness," of the natural world as well as the human capacity to apprehend it—carries immense metaphysical weight. Majidi constructs a magical sort of fittingness in meshing or melding object and subject, offering great aesthetic cogency in the witness of the sensorium.

And always, amid those regular ecstasies, Mohammad listens and touches, counts and spells. Though he cannot see, he seems fully to sense the splendor of that world amid his other senses, primarily touch and hearing. Through his hands, he searches, it seems, for some unambiguous verbal confirmation of his sense of the world, "reading" with his fingers the nodes on a head of wheat or the branches on a flower

stalk. And he insists to his grandmother that the distant woodpeckers talk to each other with their knockings (and given what science has recently discovered about birds, Mohammad is very likely very right in his claims about birds communicating). With birdsong, it seems that Mohammad repeatedly tries to decipher what message it might have for him, and he counts the taps in a way that parallels the writing in Braille that opens the film. Always he strives to hear some hidden reality or meaning, perhaps what is intrinsically an indecipherable or inscrutable excess or surfeit of splendor that lies beyond speech and remains, ultimately, unnameable. Something, though, some elusive but palpable presence, the boy senses—in body as much as soul or, more aptly, through the body to the soul. Indeed, Mohammad seems to roam the borderlands, the "thin places," between the profane and the sacred. For him, some numinous Something or Another seems poised to show Itself, lurking about, on the liminal fringes, just beyond the lights, so to speak, only to flit off, much like the butterfly his sister catches and puts in his hand (41:16). Body language and behavior tell the tale, though viewers may be taken aback by the acute sensitivities of so young a person—or anyone, for that matter. Viewers stand in awe of the boy's awe, for Mohammad's behavior and the world in which he exults, here so very lushly rendered, speak volumes of adoration and gratitude.

At the very least, Majidi offers a master class in what philosophers are coming to recognize as embodied perception, a mode of knowing that for some has at least as much cogency as the privileged epistemic domain of empirical reason. For Mohammad, the realm of beauty he senses, though he is foreclosed from much of its immediacy, bears, potentially at least, meaning and truth, however elusive those prove in their precise message or import. It is Presence "irrefragable," in novelist Marilynne Robinson's word, inescapable and even immanent, though it remains ever mysterious and elusive.[2] Sensibly, having apprehended this numinous pressure on his awareness and being duly enticed, Mohammad desires to achieve intimacy, relational immediacy and fullness, insight that imparts the exact "color" of the divine, itself Paradise, despite the blindness that proscribes a vital means of experiencing the divine care manifest in the lavish display of the natural world.

For this particular blind boy, sensing divine presence pushes the limits of mundane knowing—the dark glass the Christian tradition acknowledges—and amid his personal turmoil about his blindness and his conflict with his father, Mohammad embraces a persistent, even heroic, posture of deep relish and gratitude, which is a pretty good place for a sightless ten-year-old. And all of this, in a measure rare in films, envelops the viewer, for the viewer can see and sense what Mohammad cannot—and does what in response? It is an elegant construction that prods audience self-reflection: If this small boy, deprived of seeing the dazzle displayed on the screen, exults so, then why not also the viewer who, obviously enough, *does* see the fullness of the splendor in that lambent display? That such beauty and delight can exist at all, even for this little boy, sightless and only half-grown—well, that interrogates, uncomfortably, the self-absorption and skepticism of those possessed of their senses who see nothing at all. While the world shines for the boy, luminous though not visible, for the well-sighted viewer, shining bursts to outright flame, bright, enthralling, and even ravishing, or well it should.

Darkness Complete

In general, though, darkness increasingly befalls Mohammad, and oddly enough, that serves to highlight, in the literal meaning of the

---

2. Marilynne Robinson, *Gilead* (New York: Farrar, Straus and Giroux, 2004), 177.

word, the role, value, and meaning of light. Tragically, the storm that looms from the start of the film, specifically the malevolence of Mohammad's father, breaks out just as Mohammad adapts to village life. His return has been very happy. He has even attended the village school where he reads, to the amazement of all, teacher included, from his Braille text. When he is at home and feeling almost "normal," his father strikes. Without giving Mohammad any choice in his fate, he hauls him from home for a bus ride to a distant blind carpenter with whom he'll live and from whom he'll learn a trade. As this prospect settles on Mohammad, he vainly tries to run from his father, having not the least idea of where he is, and he begs only to go back home. That is to no avail, however, though the father is clearly troubled by what he feels he must do. The carpenter himself is kindly enough, and he lives in a lovely woodland setting, full of birdsong and wind, and next to a pond full of geese Mohammad comes to enjoy.

His new mentor interrupts a tour of his workshop and grounds when he detects that Mohammad is quietly crying, the boy's tears falling on the carpenter's hand. Though he enjoins the boy to be a man, for men do not cry, Mohammad weeps still and explains through his tears the source of his sorrow, citing the isolation his blindness has imposed on him, even thinking that his grandmother consented to this cruelty by his father: "Nobody loves me. Not even Granny. They all run away from me because I'm blind. If I could see, I'd go to the local school with other children, but now I have to go to the school for the blind on the other side of the world" (56:55).

Still, amid this litany of sorrow, Mohammad recalls the counsel of one of his teachers at his boarding school. The core of the comment seems to have imbued him with immense hopefulness and has shaped his urgent search for divine presence: "Our teacher says that God loves the blind more because they can't see, but I told him if it was so, then He wouldn't make us blind so that we can't see Him. He answered, 'God is not visible.' He is everywhere. You can feel Him. You see Him through your fingertips. Now I reach out everywhere for God till the day that my hand touches Him and tell Him everything, even all the secrets of my heart" (1:00:45). An eloquent but desperate speech, wonderfully delivered by this young actor, this confession—more a heart song or psalm, actually—hauls viewers into the full depths of his brokenness and sorrow but also into the logic that informs his relish and search for beauty amid his besetting quest. It is not much consolation for the be-reft Mohammad that his new teacher simply endorses this view—"Your teacher is right"—and he gets up and feels his way away, leaving the boy to himself.

And then, immediately following, as if to validate Mohammad's hope, Majidi goes out of his way cinematically, letting images and sounds dive into the viewer, to underscore and affirm Mohammad's sense of reality as fraught with meaning in the common stuff of nature. Majidi cuts to a vertical shot looking down on the desolate boy, and then follows with a panorama of the mountains with clouds hanging low between the tops. Viewers hear again the portentous tapping of woodpeckers, followed by thunder, wind, and the eerie, long cry of an unknown mountain bird (1:02:05). The sequence re-iterates Mohammad's sense of the world as dense with mysterious divine presence, and goes a long way to make cogent his fetching metaview, literal and figurative, of this world and beyond. While the precise meaning of the sequence remains indeterminate, as are all such visual displays, the cinematic whole once again conjures a numinous sort of mystery that, on the one hand, weighs upon his soul and, on the other, infuses it—mind, imagination, and emo-tion—with the possibility of a dense, "thick" immersion into the experience of the pressing but inscrutable majesty of the palpable world in which we find ourselves. Somehow sacred Mystery seems afoot in the setting wherein this small boy, and audience too, enact their lives.

The camera follows Mohammad's father on his homeward journey through pouring rain. Amid the darkening day, the chilly soaking seems a fitting judgment on his callousness. That, though, is just the start of his ill fortune, for his decision to rid himself of Mohammad leads to a series of personal disasters. As he arrives home amid the downpour, a soaked blanket draped over his head for cover, his mother stands on the porch with a satchel, ready to leave his household in disapproval of his treatment of Mohammad. "Only this way remains to me," she says as she heads into the downpour to find an uncertain refuge else-where (1:03:02). And here, like his son in the preceding sequence, the father recites the calamities with which life has pelted him. And though he weeps like his son, the father's tears emerge not from disappoint-ment but from anger, indicting in bitter, self-pitying complaint first his mother and then her God:

You want to spite me . . . I did it for his own good. . . . What have I done wrong to be stuck with taking care of a blind child for the rest of my life? Who will look after me when I am old and weak? Why doesn't that great God of yours help me out of this misery? Why should I be grateful to Him? For the things I don't have? For my miseries? For a blind child? For the wife I have lost? I've put up with it for five solid years. . . . That's who I am, a poor and miserable man. I lost my father so early I can hardly remember him! Who helps me? Who cares for me? Go. Go wherever you like. (1:03:05)

This scene ends, as did the scene with Mohammad, with the camera looking down on a desolate figure, this time on the solitary, weeping father standing in the rain, which could as well be the universe's tears for the plight of ordinary humanity. The cinematic agility of Majidi allows him to get by with what could readily play as hokum. As unlikable a character as the father is in his persistent turmoil, this eruption of feeling hauls viewers, even this late in the film, into at least some provisional sympathy for just how lost and mournful he has become. Father and son alike know the dregs of woe amid the more wrenching sorrows of being alive.

"Granny" does leave, departing into self-exile, till her son soon thereafter realizes his potential loss of "face" and rides out to beg her to come home. But it is too late, for days later the tender old woman dies from what is presumably exposure in the cold mountain rain. Her dying is briefly but touchingly rendered. We see her hands on her prayer beads as she recites prayers, much as we have seen Mohammad "reading" aloud the nodes on wheat stalks in his effort to "see" God through his fingers. When her son asks if it would cheer her to bring Mohammad home, for she sits with tears in her eyes, she simply replies that she is more worried about him than Mohammad, after which the camera slowly approaches to dwell on the worry and self-accusation on the distraught father's face (1:07:40).

Her dying is slow, as all the while her son prepares his home for his new bride by re-mudding and painting its exterior. And then, in a wonderfully haunting and wordless long sequence, we see the grandmother's last moments, moments that seem, unaccountably, to be sensed and mysteriously shared by her absent grandson (1:12:03). Wind and cloud move among the mountains in the early morning, and again

61

woodpeckers, seemingly responding to each other, sound along the slopes. Then comes again the haunting call of a bird heard throughout the film. Mohammad, dressed in his red shirt, sits up to listen closely, as light shines on his face. For a half-minute of film time, Majidi freezes the camera to stare at clouds swirling through the mountains as that mysterious bird peals its song. In such moments the world seems fraught with meaning, mysterious though those meanings stubbornly remain.

Toward the closing of this tableau, Mohammad's grandmother lies in her bed hearing the same wind and the same birdcall. The sound bridge unites the grandmother and the grandson in their perception of the beauty of the world, for as she listens the camera approaches and she smiles in deep pleasure as the light on her face brightens, a perceptible external sign of her inward delight, just in case, it seems, some might miss the significance of her delight. From there the camera for another twenty seconds returns to the mountainscape and the thick swirl of clouds, from which emerges and remains briefly the face of Mohammad, who seems to have sensed his grandmother's death.

In the aftermath of her dying, the son's bride-to-be attends the grandmother's funeral, scowling the whole time at her weeping fiancé, who soon learns, when the family returns all the bride gifts, that the marriage is off; they have recoiled at the prospect of marrying even an old maid to such a wretch as he. It is no doubt a rude moral shock to the grown man, who is both a son and a father, for immediately after his mother's funeral he goes to retrieve Mohammad from his forlorn apprenticeship. Upon arriving at the carpenter's home, though, his resolve is not strong; having second thoughts, he chases after the bus that has just left him off. Retrieve Mohammad he does, however. Still, their journey home is grudging, as he yanks Mohammad along through puddles and rain. Once in the forest, amid approaching storm and billows of fog and mist, and Mohammad now upon a horse, the father seems to lose his way, appropriately enough, and when the pair cross a rushing mountain river on a rickety wooden bridge, the bridge collapses, the horse and Mohammad falling in the stream. Mohammad flails in a seething, roiling cascade, one whose peril mirrors the texture of his treatment by his always angry father.

Mohammad's plight thrusts the ultimate choice straight into the father's soul: Try to rescue his son—or not? For an eternal twenty seconds the father simply watches, his face full of indecision. First he runs the bank screaming the boy's name, for the first time in the film sounding like he cares, and only then plunges into the rapids in a desperate and most certainly futile attempt to save the boy's life at the risk of losing his own. Majidi captures well the peril involved, often using subjective camera shots from within the stream itself. At one point the father manages to pull himself up on a tree limb that hangs just above the water, but when he sees his son's shoe caught in brush nearby he lets go, determined now to find his son at all costs. Eventually he disappears in the wild water, and we see him no more. Almost.

Light

The nature that Mohammad (and his grandmother) so relished as a habitation of God has swallowed him up, as it did his grandmother, who, in effect, also died by water (having caught chill in a large puddle into which she had fallen). The duality only adds to the mystery, not only inscrutable but also plainly brutal. The story's beautifully filmed last sequence transpires on the shore of the sea into which the moun-

tain stream empties. As seabirds loudly call, echoing the haunting
mountain birds, the camera looks down on gentle waves lapping the
shore where lies Mohammad's father. Typically for this film, the calls
of birds portend significant events and questions. Here they summon
the man to wakefulness, a hard-won state after the pummeling of his
long, desperate ride down the rapids. It is, in fact, a wonder that he
survived. Only slowly does he recall how he got there, and then he
thinks of Mohammad, whose body he sees fifty yards down the beach.
He painfully raises himself to run stiffly to cradle Mohammad in his
arms, loudly sobbing on and on. The camera cuts to a large and loud
flock of seabirds, and then back to the weeping father, and then again
to the sky, to many ducks noisily making their way. In an inversion of
the camera's usual perspective, the film's last shot looks down from
high above on the father's back hunched over the seemingly dead child
he has enfolded in his arms.

As the camera very slowly descends, waves lap, and suddenly sounding again is the eerie mountain bird we've heard at pivotal moments,
especially in the blissful death of the grandmother. The camera finally
rests in close-up on Mohammad's limp hand as it stretches out from his
father's embrace. The bird sounds yet again, and light, as if transcen-

dent love itself, seems to transfuse the limp hand to glowing. Orchestral music sounds, and Mohammad soon moves his now glowing hand, slowly turning palm upward to cradle and gather light. The screen goes black as music plays and credits roll, and so ends the film.

The ending has, as might be expected, drawn more than a little controversy, many critics thinking it discards plausibility to mar an otherwise poignant film. The complaints perhaps suggest a critical failure to see what Majidi so plainly shows throughout the many journeys of the film. After all, the splendor displayed throughout the film in the liminal zones of natural majesty and the tender love of family simply leaps further to achieve a sort of logical culmination. To put it another way, the miraculous accessible even to sightless Mohammad, and even more so to viewers, here flames into visibility. Some sort of presence has been afoot from the start, and at the close it rather suddenly but not unexpectedly flares full. The warmth and brightness of the sun, emblems of divine love, as detailed in the first words of the film, prove sufficient to restore life to the blind boy—and also, remarkably, to the father, though now in full realization of his love for his blind son, incubus though he has been. It is the father, and not his blind son, who finally sees, restored by the depths of his love. Clearly, there is more than one sort of blindness. The last frames extend motifs present throughout: birds calling, the warmth of the sun, the waves of the sea, and the search for the embrace of another. Finally, in his recognition of love, the father loves his son to life again. Love in its fullness has broken in, for the father has at long last actually "seen" his son.

It is not difficult to argue that the divine that so infuses an efflorescent sensuous world of mountains and flowers with an enveloping splendor intimates the press of a transcendent love that might also revive the small boy in the same manner now that, implausibly, his own angry father's love at long last cradles him. For those who've seen the film fully and duly attended to the tale, in which prime agents are not just characters but motifs of landscape, birds, and even climate, this denouement, while startling, and about which some critics have complained, seems merely a logical manifestation of the power so amply displayed throughout. Perhaps what is objectionable, morally and dramatically, is that this should *not* happen, so cogent and affecting is the perceptual and symbolic richness of Majidi's story. Indeed, the implicit question of the narrative, very present without being in the least tendentious or argumentative, rather starkly addresses the viewer: How can the sighted *not* see what the blind boy grasps by mere touch and hearing?

Throughout, Majidi seems less interested in argument than in display, letting the images and metaphors speak and elicit what they will. In this regard, splendid filmmaker that he is, Majidi pulls off the hardest task there is for cinema. He renders Mohammad's experience with such remarkable fullness and immediacy that it simply envelops viewers, and they too perhaps sense (and also see) in the splendor of the palpable ordinary, all of what Mohammad knows by touch, sound, and soul. Limited though he is, young Mohammad knows the "color" of love manifest in this iridescent paradise in which he lives, knowing realms and kingdoms far beyond the grasp of his resentful, self-concerned father. All along he has searched, seeking a final, decisive clue to the nature of the world in which he has found himself, a small blind boy adrift without parents, his mother dead and his father hostile. And at the last, there breaks out, for viewer and father alike, a relational awe, or even rapture, that emanates from the very majesty of the created world, including nature and people alike, and all this resounds with the moral and religious character of the universe.

CHAPTER THREE

THE EDUCATION OF A
ONE-MAN PREACHING MACHINE

The Realization of Love in *The Apostle*

The telling moment in Robert Duvall's *The Apostle* comes well into the movie and is one of the quietest moments in the film. The broken-down, murdering preacher Euliss F. "Sonny" Dewey, appropriately alone and in the dark, leans backward against the hood of a car to stare at a tiny, very dilapidated church in a Louisiana backwater, the humble building very far from the hype and glitz of the noisy stage from whence he fled. Indeed, the building and the man seem mirror images of one another. Now, though, "a vagrant and a wanderer," a latter-day close cousin of Cain, (Gen. 4:13 NEB) in jealousy killing a man over a woman, Dewey stares at the empty church, for once in his life still and motionless, and almost wordless, and he quietly laughs in pleasure and gratitude.

His voice is virtually a whisper, an unusual mode for a man who typically shouts and stomps aplenty, and not just in the pulpit histrionics of his Protestant Holiness tradition. It is indeed a signal moment, and a forecast of the unusual man Sonny Dewey is about to become. At this moment, he's deep into the fabled dark valley of the shadow of death. A fugitive murderer facing decades in prison, bereft of the fame and adulation he's always relished, he nonetheless now quietly gives thanks and petitions blessing for the barely inhabitable building and the tiny ragtag flock of worshipers he's likely to have in an obscure little backwater congregation. That's a remarkable posture, especially for this lifelong man of the cloth, forty years a preacher saving souls for God and also, so it seems, very much for himself—and all the while himself

profoundly in need of redemption, meaning in this case an existential embrace of not ego and success but the dictates of Christian love.

Saved and a preacher since a child he may have been, but, as writer-producer-director-star Robert Duvall shows in this stunning, much-lauded one-man saga, redeemed he is not (what the old Calvinist tradition called sanctified, meaning a state of spiritual and moral maturity). Thanks to Duvall's deft work in all these roles, viewers from the very start suspect that Sonny Dewey, flamboyant preaching machine though he be, is badly in need, though he knows it not, of a whole lot of what he's trying to dispense to others. Finally, to his great surprise, and also the viewers', this central dimension of what Sonny calls "Holy Ghost power" will envelop him in ways he never before imagined. And Sonny will transit, following upon his gauntlet of severe knocks, to a different, more deeply Christian mode of being, what critic David Denby aptly describes as a "period of grace."[1]

What is most notable about Duvall's Dewey is his very ambiguity, a vexing mix of zeal and sordidness, as much prodigal as saint. On the one hand, Sonny is clearly not the usual Hollywood stereotype of revivalist preacher as buffoon or huckster, as displayed in a host of notable treatments of revivalists as con men, such as *Elmer Gantry*

1. David Denby, "The Gospel Truth," *New York Magazine*, January 12, 1998, http://nymag.com/nymetro/movies/reviews/1975/.

(1960), *Marjoe* (1972), or *Leap of Faith* (1992). Still, while sincere in his beliefs, Sonny Dewey is by no means a paragon of purity or insight, no cardboard saint, no Bing Crosby (*The Bells of St. Mary's* [1945]) Holy Roller. For most North American viewers, this ambiguous "mixed-bag" preacher mystifies from start to finish, especially because American cinema has never before seen anything remotely like him (European cinema has in the early work of Bergman and Bresson a rich history of searing religious ambiguity). In fact, the eminent A. O. Scott of the *New York Times* goes so far as to see Duvall's Sonny as "rich, fascinating, and nuanced a portrayal of a single individual as you'll ever see."[2] So rare is it that, in a 2011 review of *Of Gods and Men*, Scott placed *The Apostle* within "a tiny and exalted tradition" of films "that try to illuminate religious experience from within."[3] To its lasting detriment, American culture seems either to deify or demonize clergy, save perhaps for literary exceptions in the work of Hawthorne, Melville, and Updike, all of whom arduously chased down the tangled churnings of

---

2. Critics' Picks, with A. O. Scott, TimesVideo (*New York Times*), December 28, 2009, http://www.nytimes.com/video/movies/1247466297226/critics-picks-the-apostle.html.

3. A. O. Scott, "Between Heaven and Earth," *New York Times*, February 24, 2011, http://www.nytimes.com/2011/02/25/movies/25gods.html?_r=0. In something of a surprise, *The Apostle* received a loud chorus of praise from a wide array of prominent reviewers. David Denby in *New York Magazine* called it the "best movie ever made about a man of God," because of its honesty and its moral ambiguity (Denby, "The Gospel Truth"). In a thrall of praise, Lisa Schwarzbaum in *Entertainment Weekly* found the film "fearless and fascinating," an "unusual, unhurried tour de force—a seamless match of strong artistic vision and physical performance" (Schwarzbaum, "The Apostle," *Entertainment Weekly*, December 19, 1997, http://www.ew.com/article/1997/12/19/apostle). Emanuel Levy in *Variety* wrote about it as follows: "Beautifully detailed and deftly structured, every scene in *The Apostle* logically leads to the next one, each elaborating on the central theme of religious redemption" (Levy, "Review: The Apostle,'" *Variety*, September 10, 1997, http://variety.com/1997/film/reviews/the-apostle-2-1117340103/). If anything, regard for the film has only increased over time. From England and in hindsight, *TimeOut: London* reviewer Geoff Andrew regards the film "a thrilling, insightful, uncommonly honest study of religious experience" ("The Apostle," June 24, 2006, http://www.timeout.com/london/film/the-apostle-1997).Despite this chorus of critical praise, the film did not do well in the Academy Awards. Only Duvall the actor was nominated, losing out to Jack Nicholson's scenery-chewing performance in *As Good as It Gets* (alas, Jack had never gotten the best actor award, and Duvall already had one for *Tender Mercies*). The film did not lose money, however. It cost approximately $5 million of Duvall's own money to make, and according to the Internet Movie Database, box office exceeded $20 million, giving Duvall a hefty profit, especially given its minimal advertising budget. Duvall did undertake extensive personal publicity, availing himself for interviews ranging from Pat Robertson's *700 Club* to the scholarly *Journal of Religion and Film*.

souls after God, or Whatever, amid abundant human darkness inside and out.

Whatever sins and demons Sonny Dewey carries in himself, these are not the sorts that trouble most viewers, especially of the sophisticated film-buff variety. Rather, it is the flip side of Sonny, meaning the character of his religious belief, and in particular the intensely evangelical posture of Sonny's "God thing." Sonny believes, all right, the whole unscientific business, and for him genuine, heartfelt belief means a stark hyperevangelical heaven-or-hell take on the world. That is true from the first seconds of the film to the very end. Sonny most certainly believes, and feeling called to preach, he heartily preaches up a vision of exultant roaring grace, and always in the name of "Jee-suss," which for him is a pretty constant invocation in pulpit and out. For many viewers, then, especially for tame evangelicals and still tamer mainline believers of all types—Christian, Jewish, and even agnostic—this is the central problematic in the film as a whole: what to make, either culturally or religiously, of all of Sonny Dewey's hyperkinetic shouting, stomping, cavorting, and whooping, heaven-bent for glory, rolling and soaring in exultant "Holy Ghost power." What is this, anyway—scam, inspiration, revelation, fireworks, entertainment, trip, delusion, rant, or some potent, deeply messy mix of all? (Duvall, in his director commentary, characterizes Holiness worship style as a variety of "spiritual entertainment" [4:50].) And further, throughout the world of trouble Sonny makes for himself and others, he never wavers, even as he thereafter trudges through a dark valley of death and despair.

That interpretive challenge is acute indeed, for one of the great accomplishments of the film is that Duvall displays with plausibility, respect, and, yes, even relish a problematic, marginalized mode of religious apprehension or, in the language of our time, an idiosyncratic spirituality that hordes of Christians worldwide embrace and still other hordes, religious and secular, openly disdain. Duvall's audio commentary makes clear his "respect" and great affection for not only Sonny but also the entire Holiness tradition (*Commentary* 2:45).[4]

---

4. What exactly Robert Duvall thinks of his protagonist and the tradition from which he hails is not entirely clear. He does regard the preaching traditions of the Holiness tradition as a "true American art form" (*Commentary* 14:45), and he clearly thinks that Sonny does come to be "reborn" (*Commentary* 12:50). He clearly understands the idiosyncrasies of the tradition that separate it from almost all the rest of Christendom insofar as the tradition allows for "one-to-one dialogue with God and Jesus Christ" as opposed to other Christian

The very notion of labeling the Holiness tradition—the likes of Sonny and his followers—a spirituality, as does Duvall, makes more than a few cultured believers gasp and despisers scoff. Very intentionally, Duvall has set out to give the tradition "its due," as he has put it, thus challenging prevailing intellectualist notions about the relation of genuine faith and its expression to the usually arbitrary, and elitist, presumptions of a religious taste culture, specifically the notion that the higher the liturgy, music, and theology, the purer and "righter" the faith, both intellectually and spiritually (*Commentary* 2:30). That indeed is a very tough agenda, and it is front and center in the story Duvall sets out to tell. What finally comes to Sonny—or he to it—smacks him, and viewers, with much surprise and even shock. And that is why we find him quietly elated and grateful leaning upon the hood of that good-ol'-boy hot rod. Light does come, and sometimes especially so, amid the darkness. Which perhaps makes all that inner travail good for something.

Sonny—That Most Flawed Preacher

It is clear, then, that Duvall's film is very much a character study of a man in perpetual motion, and there's hardly a scene where Sonny Dewey is not front and center. From the film's very beginning, Sonny Dewey seems very, very far from a perfect vessel for divine grace, and Duvall calculatingly problematizes Dewey, and this becomes the film's chief narrative hook. In big conspicuous ways Sonny is very impressive. For one, he has enormous, even ferocious, energy in behalf of his cause of bringing people to personal confrontation with the reality of personal evil and the necessity of personal faith in a loving God as displayed in the person of Jesus, who forgives sin and promises eternal life.

In the film's first sequence, for example, Sonny and his mother (June Carter Cash) come upon a horrendous four-car accident. A few police are there, but ambulances have yet to arrive. Sonny pulls over, grabs

---

traditions that see the divine as at least somewhat more remote, at least through a dark glass (1 Cor. 13:12), if not much removed (*Commentary* 16:50). Nonetheless, Duvall allows for "intuitions and premonitions" (*Commentary* 18:20) that, as the film makes clear, may or may not be trustworthy indications of divine reality.

his Bible, skirts the police, and runs to a distant car lodged in the weeds of an empty field. There Sonny finds a badly injured young couple, the woman unconscious and the young man awake but unable to move and barely able to talk. Sonny first petitions for a miracle, his hands raised in supplication, and he gently but forthrightly urges the boy, blood oozing from an ear and clearly facing death, to embrace Christ for comfort and salvation (evangelical Christianity firmly believes that only faith in Jesus's power to forgive sin will deliver one to heaven). During the last portion of the talk with the boy, a policeman arrives to shoo Sonny from the scene. Tenacious, head inserted in the car window, Sonny continues to reassure the boy while simultaneously kicking backward to keep a policeman at bay.

It would all be funny if were not quite so serious, but of such go-for-broke mettle is Sonny, this man who violates law and taste to care more about souls and eternity than law officers. As he tells the openly skeptical cop, he'd "rather die today and go to heaven than live to be a hundred and go to hell" (7:50). Strange though it seems to tamer folks, given how he sees the world, this is exactly what Sonny should be doing, for his success with the couple determines not only their mortal but also their eternal fate. As if to make that very point, minutes later, as Sonny and his mother drive from the accident scene, director Duvall cuts very briefly to the accident with a close-up glimpse of the hand of the young woman, who has thus far seemed more dead than alive, and, lo, the injured woman now tightens her grasp on the man's arm, amply

signifying the possibility that a miracle has resulted directly from Sonny's prayer for healing (*Commentary* 9:48). As for Sonny, when he returns to his car, he proudly announces to his mother that they've "made news in heaven today," though one is uncertain whether Sonny celebrates more the salvation of the young man or his own role in accomplishing it (8:35). As they drive off, mother and son exultantly break into song, the now raspy but wonderfully expressive voice of the aging June Carter Cash belting out the tuneful "Victory Is Mine."

This, though, is Sonny, a complex mix of God zeal and self-regard. Surely, he loves God and loves to preach, which he does with great intensity and pleasure. In the director's commentary on the DVD, Duvall continually reiterates the sincerity and authenticity of Sonny's belief, especially the remarkable notion that one can have constant spiritual exchange with God himself, likening it to Roman Catholic adoration of the saints (16:50).

Unfortunately, there is a rather nasty snake amid the zeal and piety, and that is the possibility that what Sonny most loves in the midst of his devotion is himself, namely, not so much God as his own deep sense of special calling, of somehow being God's special agent. As Charles Taylor puts it, Sonny "appears to need to exalt himself almost as much as he does God."[5] Sonny has been a revivalist since age twelve, and his besetting error is, simply put, a stalwart and deep pride in calling. It is rank old ego; he fully relishes the idea of being God's fair-haired boy, a status he pursues with fervor, so much so that his conviction breeds a good deal of moral blindness, raising the question of whether he really "gets" the Jesus he so fervently pushes and preaches. For him, Jesus heals and saves, and Jesus is full of power to save, power that God, and specifically the Holy Spirit, inevitably imparts in some measure to the very special Sonny. It does not seem, however, that Sonny's theology, or his sense of the complexity of self or world, stretches much further than that. In this film Sonny will have more than a few surprises, but he first has to lose his arrogance and everything else. Eventually, on the run and exiled, there will come ample surprise and wonder at the depths and cogency of what he has heretofore overlooked.

From the first scenes, we run into more indications of Sonny's inordinate pleasure in doing what he deems God's work. First off, there

5. Charles Taylor, "The Apostle," *Salon*, February 2, 1998, http://www.salon.com/1998/02/02/apostle/.

is that nettlesome, even inordinate, satisfaction of making "news in heaven today," as he tells his mother when he returns to the car. Sonny takes his role seriously, as well he should, but very often the whole ethos of preaching and revival becomes more about him as vessel, especially in a religious realm that emphasizes charisma and special gifts in ministry. Evangelical Protestants tend to exalt superstar preachers as unique vessels of God, much as Roman Catholics exalt saints and popes. For Sonny, then, much depends on performance and, as Duvall calls it, the "showmanship" that is the art form in the heart of the Holiness preaching tradition wherein worshipers sometimes "celebrate the spectacle more than the substance" (*Commentary* 13:23). Sometimes Sonny's preaching outruns the purposes of venerating God and spills over into entertainment, though it remains in some way spiritual; despite the "theatrical," says Duvall, the preaching retains a "spiritual substance" (*Commentary* 13:38). Indeed, evangelical preaching tends to emphasize faith, hope, and divine forgiveness, all helpful anodynes in the messiness of living.

While Sonny finds due and proper satisfaction in pursuing his calling, Sonny just loves to be loved. He believes all, he preaches all, and sensualist of the spirit that he is, he loves particularly the power, trappings, and rush of being God's special agent. In some ways Dewey might be compared to Graham Greene's whiskey priest in *The Power and the Glory*, a novel that explores the frequent gaping disparity between personal morality and pastoral efficacy.

That's clear even before the film's first glimpse of the man himself. Before viewers see Sonny preaching, they see the big preacher's car that he drives, a fancy Chrysler sedan, and it sports, appropriately enough, as the camera twice displays in close-up, a vanity plate—SONNY—telling volumes about his character and fate (13:28). And then there's the public look of the man, meaning his costuming, which declares him to be very much a platform dandy. In his first preaching gig, one of revival-tent tag-team preaching, he sports a natty double-breasted light gray suit while all the other male preachers are soberly dressed in plain style and dark colors (15:03); in his second preaching appearance, he again stands out, this time in a three-piece white suit, two-toned dress shirt, purple tie, and matching pocket handkerchief (15:33). And when he crashes the service in his own church after being deposed, he shows up in that same white suit wearing a pink shirt with a pinker tie and, in theatrics abundant, even sunglasses (28:51).

Whether this is wholly ego-driven or merely an inescapable part of what the calling demands—that his work requires that he display bold charisma—is rather beside the point, for Sonny clearly loves the trip. He preaches long and hard on a host of topics that fix on evil and the devil, but he never quite makes its potential connection to the worm of self-love—until much later, that is, when he gets the ego-stuffing drubbed out of him. In short, Sonny lets flourish the incipient egotism that resides in much Protestant preaching, and especially in revivalism, for it construes that so much of the "spirit" happening here and now depends on a particular preacher's capability in becoming a conduit for divine grace. If in Roman Catholicism the sacraments serve this function, in much of Protestantism preaching is, as one wag put it, the only sacrament, the only churchly means by which God shows up and does God's thing. Prayer and Bible reading also provide routes to God, but the public, corporate side of evangelicalism seems to function as if preaching were the only means by which grace entices worshipers.

Moreover, spiritual pride is not the only sort of allure toward which Sonny is bent, for Sonny is well acquainted with multiple paths of destruction, and in those lie more conspicuous and eventually very public stumbles. Just as his thirst for a demonstrative Sonny-loving God abounds, so do his more carnal appetites for adoration, particularly in his outsized sexual appetite, even though he has a fetching co-pastor wife, Jessie (the late Farrah Fawcett), and two lovely children. As becomes clear in his conversation with Jessie after he discovers her infidelity, Sonny has his own troubling history, one that he regards rather lightly.

Shared intimacy with God seems to slide all-too-easily into decidedly more carnal sorts of shared intimacy. He belittles Jessie's concern about, as he puts it, his "wandering eye and wicked, wicked ways" (22:31); he later loudly admits to God that he is "a once-in-a-while womanizer" (26:27). He ascribes this "wandering bug" to his love for evangelization, an admission that in a more introspective man might instigate serious scrutiny of his motives and his profession (22:38). Jessie herself is fully aware of this history and points that out to him when he threatens to make a fuss in their church about her extramarital conduct. Still, for a man whose wife has just cheated on him with a man of a very different sort, meaning a sensitive "puny-assed youth minister," Sonny is rather calm about her specific carnal straying, probably from the knowledge that he really has, given his own history, little grounds for complaint against his wife (20:50). What seems to goad him most is the offense to his pride—that his wife would wander and with whom she would wander. In lots of ways, then, Sonny cuts himself a good deal of moral slack, even suggesting that his womanizing is an inevitable and permissible spillover of the intense soul-wrestlings of the revival circuit. He just doesn't seem to get it, his ego-thirst skewing his moral perception.

Nor is this Sonny's biggest problem, as Jessie shows right off. Riddling the mix still further, the flip side of his excitable promulgation of his version of God, is Sonny's very human volatility. Sonny is by no means a tame fellow, especially in his inability to control eruptions of anger that quickly turn violent. That temper first comes to a boil when out of the blue it dawns on Sonny one night that his wife is having an affair with the church's youth minister. This recognition dawns while Sonny travels the revival circuit, and Sonny dashes home to find his suspicions confirmed. He finds, one, his own house empty and, two, the refusal of the youth minister to answer his door. Surprising though it may seem, Sonny bothered to grab his handgun from his bedside table, and as he sits in his car in the youth minister's driveway, he contemplates using it, though finally the clear declaration in the Ten Commandments against murder deters him. What he does do, though, is to leave a terrifying calling card. He throws a baseball through the front upstairs bedroom window, amply mortifying both Jessie and her lover. It is not a surprise, then, that the drunken, cuckolded preacher will later, after amply cursing the youth minister to his face, swing a bat that murders the mild-mannered fellow, lecher though he is.

That this volatility is not simply an occasional eruption when under stress but part of a steady current of anger and meanness deep in Sonny comes clear in a brilliant interchange between the characters, a scene wonderfully constructed by Duvall and played splendidly by Duvall and Fawcett. Indeed, most of what the scene tells viewers, as with the film as a whole, comes through acting and gesture rather than words. Here it becomes clear that whatever Sonny is, or has been, plainly scares his wife, who shrinks and skitters as they sit on opposite ends of a couch. Looming throughout the whole sequence, and barely contained, is Sonny's threat of physical violence toward his wife, a power he rather enjoys and even teases her with at one point (20:27). That reality is more than obvious, given the fact that Sonny has apparently begun their talk by laying a handgun on the coffee table in front of the couch on which

Jessie sits, and she takes the first opportunity she can to pick up the gun and empty it of bullets. Apparently, she has no doubt that he is very capable of extreme violence.

Throughout their heart-to-heart, Jessie continually fidgets, always trying to keep a safe distance from Sonny, who seems to hover over her with occasional feints in her direction, from which she reflexively recoils. The measure of her jumpiness has less to do with dislike of being touched by Sonny than with fear of him coercing her physically. During their discussion, he expresses his love for her, which she acknowledges, but he also takes her arm to try to force her to her knees so they can pray together. Resistant, Jessie complains that her "knees are worn out with praying" (22:24). She simply wants out, sensing the futility of endless and long-since-senseless rounds of petition for change that yield no change. God, she says, has given her leave to leave, though Sonny cannot believe *his* God would be telling her something he does not tell Sonny. Here Sonny's own personal take on God in these tangled marital matters seems an extension of his own taste for power that has apparently dominated the relationship since before they were married. The dissonance in their relationship and their belief is contained in Sonny's last comment to Jessie as he rises and leaves the room: "God help you, because you're gonna need it" (23:19). Tellingly, Sonny has both begun and ended their talk about reconciliation with threats of retribution and physical violence.

Letting the scene speak volumes about Sonny, Duvall does not spend much time on what happens next, trusting that what we've seen of Sonny thus far pretty much makes inevitable the mournful events that follow. First, Sonny spends the night at his mother's house loudly contending with God about the fate the divine has apparently bestowed on Sonny, and Sonny's stance throughout is once again more than revelatory. Oddly, amid his mystification at the disasters that have befallen him, losing wife, family, and church, it never occurs to Sonny that he might have had some role in effecting the disasters. Instead, he seems to assume that his lifelong chumminess with God—"I've always called you Jesus, and you call me Sonny"—somehow gives him a free pass on bad consequences (26:40). For God's obvious favor toward him, as a child delivered from death and a preacher since age twelve, gets him off the moral hook, even though in the course of his rant he acknowledges, though hardly confesses or repents, being a womanizer. And all the while downstairs in her own bed is Sonny's mother, proudly relishing her son's rantings, though they keep the neighbors awake. The scene makes more than clear from whom Sonny derived his sense of special exemption and privilege, and it plainly was not God.

Desperate and confused, Sonny crashes the raucous Sunday morning service of his thriving church—or rather, his former church, for he has been with the machinations of Jessie deposed, though for reasons unexplained. In the midst of the ecstatic singing, he parades about in that white suit, pink tie, and sunglasses waving a hundred-dollar bill. However, he soon concludes that he has not received the sort of rousing welcome from the congregation that he had hoped for. Having lost his wife, kids, and church, Sonny takes to drink and then shows up drunk at his son's ball game, whereupon he dispatches the youth minister with a bat. Guilty as sin, undeniably so, now prodigal, criminal, and fugitive, Sonny hits the road in his fancy car, taking back roads to God knows where (he stops at empty crossroads to kneel in prayer for God's direction). What happens then is the Big Problematic in the film: preacher Sonny gets redeemed. Or does he not?

On the Road to Glory

Bereft of wife, children, home, and church, and now suddenly deeply shaken by the extremity of his deed, and a fugitive, alone and vulnerable, wandering and wondering, the overwound Sonny slowly winds down, ending up quiet and still at ground zero of his being. First, necessity forces him to get rid of those very conspicuous emblems of himself, the fancy car and vanity plate, and he does that decisively. He quite literally sinks them both in a rural pond, Duvall the director allowing the camera, as the car settles to its watery grave, to dwell in close-up on that plate, a fitting visual farewell to all that Sonny has been. At the same time, the watery burial prefigures the Sonny who will rise from a similar pond to signal what Sonny newly understands and indeed proves to be, as seen in deeds and attitudes, in authentic rebirth. For now, though, out in the boondocks and on foot, the strut and hustle of this man who was always perpetually running, a fellow of seemingly inexhaustible energy who could barely constrain himself to simply walk, wearies and fades. Slower and slower he goes, as if the fire of life and belief slowly ebbs from him.

At the nadir of his life comes the redemption part, though some viewers have had a hard time seeing the transit Sonny undergoes. First, high-stepping Sonny ends up bereft, sweat-soaked, and dusty on the shore of a rural lake, begging a one-legged black fisherman (William Atlas Cole, himself a Holiness preacher who never goes to movies) for a place to stay for a couple of days. And so Sonny ends up in this poor man's pup tent, at last dead still, flat on his back and fasting, and he proceeds for days to shrive his spirit, repenting and petitioning. There, for once still and quiet, in a kind of divine irony, Sonny travels further than he has in all his journeys on the revival circuit, for he reckons, seemingly for the first time, with his own deep darkness and essential nothingness (this descent parallels those of Julian in Schrader's *American Gigolo* and Andy Dufresne in Darabont's *Shawshank Redemption*). Sonny simply lies there in his tent Bible-reading and praying, a process that parallels the moral sorrow of Jessie, whose prayers and readings from the Bible provide the voice-over text for Sonny's own inner searching.

It is a deft, efficient touch by director Duvall, one that smoothly displays the depth of moral and religious seriousness in the Holiness tradition in which he sets the film. Yes, revivalism often seems to provide more spectacle than substance, as Duvall readily admits, but when things get tough, earnestness serves to sober and refocus.

The introspection ends when Sonny immerses himself in the lake to baptize himself into new being with, tellingly, a new name, "Apostle E. F.," though this renaming can also be seen as a stratagem to give himself a much-needed alias. The old Sonny is gone, or so it seems. It has taken a lot—mainly Sonny's own flagrant crime and his inestimable losses—to get Sonny's attention. All of that has blown his cover, even to himself, and finally, it seems, he might wise up in coming to know just what he has missed in all his decades of preaching about grace, namely, notions of gratitude and love for the less fortunate "least of these," which, amazingly, he understands now includes himself. Before this he'd been more than willing to save their souls, but not much else. Such seems the toll of an intense pietistic experientialism that can encourage spiritual narcissism.

Throughout Sonny's brief lakeside sojourn, his host wisely sleeps with a shotgun by his side, having no idea who this vagrant white fellow is. In an apt way that neither Sonny nor viewers recognize, this old, soft-spoken, and very unspectacular fellow who accommodates this peculiar white man, offering him his backyard, shelter, food, and drink, points the direction, spiritually and practically, Sonny himself will go. In their first encounter, this man is humility and gentleness incarnate, a posture that even brash Sonny himself will adopt. Moreover, as we find out when Sonny moves on, he provides Sonny with a ministerial contact, his cousin in a small Louisiana town, who will perhaps guide him to return anew to ministry. From his refuge on the lake, Sonny sets out again to arrive, in very curious fashion, in a small Louisiana bayou town where he will labor to restore a defunct Holiness church and congregation. It is there, in contrition and humility, that Sonny truly begins to find for the first time holistic fullness to holiness.

What is significant here, and proves bothersome for conventionally religious people of all sorts, is that in his transformation Sonny continues to believe and do the same old religious stuff he has his whole life. In personality and style, he remains very much the same fellow, bumptious and a little wild, and, more curious still, there is in this story of change no repudiation of the central currents of his past, meaning his preaching, theology, or spiritual style. That kind of change would for some viewers make liking the film a lot easier, thinking that the genuineness of Sonny's change should appear in an embrace of a proper theological tradition, like Lutheranism or Calvinism, and most of all, some higher "worship style," something from what Sonny dubs the "frozen chosen" (1:07:03).

What gets changed here is Sonny, and the resources of this theological tradition, as threadbare as many would think them, suffice to effect a profound change, albeit one that takes a while to clarify in Sonny and for viewers. What is clear, though, is that Sonny does stumble into something new and different; he is able now to confess both guilt and gratitude, if only to his best friend and mentor, the Reverend Blackwell (John Beasley). There is new self-knowledge and love; he knows that his work in this obscure little church is the "best thing I've ever done in my life thus far" (1:48:25).

Slowly Sonny himself develops, meaning he slowly transmutes into a new substance, a different and "fuller" person, especially as he takes on the empathy and compassion of the Jesus he vaunted. That happens not in a sudden, blinding Damascus road blitz or with angels flitting about, as both Hollywood and Sonny usually render it, but it comes clear bit by bit, incrementally, both to Sonny and to the audience. Most of those markers on a new path are not so much articulated as shown, which is altogether proper in drama (as in all this world's religious traditions, actually). In other words, Sonny does not change doctrines or taste cultures theologically or religiously. He is, first and last, a Southern Holiness preacher, and that he will remain even through an arresting final sequence that plays beneath the end credits. Rather, he reckons, finally, with his own nothingness—only to fill it with gratitude and heartfelt love for his own calling and, the most conspicuous shift, the least of these who will become his congregation. He has loved God and himself aplenty, and now he will discover a new passion for the *full* humanity and well-being of his congregants.

The marks of this alteration are numerous. First, shriving himself in that pup tent, Sonny repents of his crime but also of his life in general, soon admitting to God and himself that his zeal and virtue have "zigzagged off course"—in fact, "more zagging than zigging" (45:14). Indeed, Sonny comes to recognize the messiness in his own life, that much in his life has been deeply mistaken, as first indicated in that lakeside voice-over read by his wife and then by Sonny himself as he makes his way to Bayou Boutte. He earlier conceded that the human creature in general, including himself, is a "mutt," a sort of half-lovable mongrel but nothing too nasty, especially Sonny himself (26:08). Thus

81

far he's been able to deny the seriousness of his flaws, but not any longer. With the clarifying reality of his own murderous heart and deed staring him smack in the face, he's plain scared, for his inmost self has caught up with him, and so apparently has the judgment of "his" God. Now a new sense of essential wrongness pervades his soul, taking the shine off his habitual "me-and-you-Jesus" egotism and bravado. Sonny turns repentant and humble. This is nowhere more evident than in his attitude toward his cheating wife: at first he rages against her, but after a while he forgives her and sincerely prays for her well-being. His own clear wrongness and brokenness bring him to forgive hers as well. He puts her, quite literally, back in the picture. Having initially torn her out of a snapshot of his family, he eventually tapes her back into the photo (1:17:05).

Further, Sonny's manner softens, not so much in his preaching, although there is subtle change there too, but more in his "relational style." Personally, and in his address to God, he is quieter, and with others too, he is gentler and more patient, especially as he gathers a new congregation that consists of the lowly and outcast of all sorts, black and white together, an interracial mix that has historical roots in the Holiness tradition. Their church—and not so much Sonny's—he aptly names, displayed in bright lights, One Way Road to Heaven. There Sonny reconciles spatting ladies, and in worship he relishes the cacophony of an old man spluttering on a battered trumpet and little kids whacking at toy guitars, a marked contrast to the fancy, pumped-up electric bands of his Fort Worth church.

If before Sonny seemed a locomotive whose tracks were people that he ran right over in the name of Jesus, this "Apostle" comes to display a restless tender love for his people and his work. The new preacher runs, just like the old one, but now he runs from homes of the poor after he anonymously drops off food at their front doors (1:25:48). This new posture results, as preacher Apostle confesses, from having known both abandonment and the grace of charity amid his dire exile. The old Sonny, we sense, did *not* do much good without making sure that God and other people knew about it. The new Sonny is humble and, partly because of that newfound meekness, deeply grateful for every little thing (1:16:35). Now able to recognize the messiness in himself, he more readily sympathizes with the mess in others. As the perceptive David Denby, now of the *New Yorker*, has put it, and as what follows makes more than clear, Sonny now "rounds up isolated and demoralized people and forges them into a community."[6] Indeed, the new Sonny leaves behind his itinerant preaching-machine routine in order to dwell instead with and among his people.

Some small changes are especially telling. Sonny goes from gaudy attire—white suits and pink ties—to bland dark suits and ties, an ample indication of new self-effacement. And there are no more fancy cars in which to sport about; he now happily rides with other people, including his cheerful last ride with the state police where he chats with the arresting officer about the model of car that is carrying him away to trial and prison. Or he drives a borrowed car or a notably unsplendorous tubby old church bus he has labored to repair.

More than that, in a nice symbolic echo, instead of living off of his congregation, Sonny now supports himself and his new church by fixing things (auto mechanic) and serving up sustenance (as an ice-cream vendor and short-order cook). As a mechanic, he tends to vehicles to make them (and their owners) run better, which is especially the case with timid, fumbling Sam (Walton Goggins), the young man he's moved in with (and on whose couch he happily sleeps

6. Denby, "The Gospel Truth."

each night—again, a marked contrast to his comfortable Fort Worth house).

The most conspicuous instance of Sonny's new self comes in the oft-mentioned encounter with the racist in the bulldozer (Billy Bob Thornton), who wants to flatten Sonny's interracial country church. When the fellow shows up with his machine during a church picnic, Sonny quietly stands up to him (the first time the intruder disrupts a service Sonny punches him out) and forgives and loves him into repentance and into the congregation. Admittedly, this sounds like the old hokey melodrama of revivalism, but here it works. The odd thing here is that somehow Duvall shifts the focus of the event from the actors to the baffling strangeness of the event itself, and even the most skeptical viewer departs the sequence wowed and hushed. Here the wonder and surprise Sonny feels about his newfound being echo in the viewer. Here, as Lisa Schwarzbaum puts it, "sinner disarms sinner."[7] Incredulity gives way to plausibility, a "perhaps maybe," at the very least.

Nor is Sonny the same bully he once was, especially with women, but also with people in general. That is not to say that he has become a sensitive new-age guy, but neither does he any longer coerce and dominate, as was clear in his relationship with Jessie. Sonny can now hear "no" and still respect the person who says it. He comes to know Toosie (Miranda Richardson), who works in the radio station where Sonny advertises his church, and that relationship slowly grows. However, when Toosie finally reconciles with her estranged husband, Sonny abruptly removes himself from her life, likely seeing in her restored family what he himself wrecked in his own, and now misses.

Perhaps the most affecting moments in Sonny's transit have to do with his meager new congregation. In his first service only nine people show up, including children, but the new Apostle relishes the occasion and quite sincerely cajoles them into mutual warmth and festive gratitude. All this seems to fulfill Sonny's quiet hope that the church will flourish, and it grows markedly in just a month's time. And in the film's closing sequence, in roaring Holiness preaching style, he bids an aching, fervent farewell to the congregation, finally leaving via Sam all his earthly goods to the tiny church. Again, all this contrasts mightily with the prosperity, showiness, factiousness, and pride in the Fort Worth church in which Sonny paraded like a bantam rooster. Back there, he

7. Schwarzbaum, "The Apostle."

flashed money to celebrate himself; in Bayou Boutte, he gives all quietly, not letting the left hand know what the right is doing (2:08:10).

What this all amounts to is that, an exile in a backwater town, Sonny has come to know a notably fuller measure of himself and divine compassion and for what purposes he preached in the first place. He no longer runs for Jesus or success in soul counting but for something different and more, so much so that he ultimately chooses to run no more, and he tranquilly meets his punishment at the film's end. Redemption here has had a slow, hard take, for Sonny is a hard case within his shell of pious egotism. Some fundamentalists have complained that Sonny shows no repentance, apparently because he does not engage in the histrionic breast-beating repentance and dramatic turnaround that predominate in that religious style and taste culture. That repentance and redemption do occur, however, clear and certain in countless manifold ways, including a last-minute confession to his fellow pastor, the Reverend Blackwell, is inescapable. Sonny-cum-Apostle has by happenstance and also apparently divine care journeyed, however haltingly, into a fuller realization of the Love that lies at the core of the message and God that he zealously preached but faintly grasped. There are the shedding of evildoing and a loss of self-exaltation, and in a newfound wholeness of soul, Sonny is never so free and "together" as when he heads off to jail. The language Sonny touted so loudly seems now, to no one's surprise more than his own, actually to apply—redeemed. And Sonny himself knows it, telling the Reverend Blackwell that "being here may be the best thing I've ever done in my life so far" (1:48:23).

The shape and direction of Sonny's "one way road" are best suggested by high church poet T. S. Eliot in his *Four Quartets*; his words pertain as well to Holiness preachers as to elitist Anglicans. Eliot understands Christian maturation as a "lifetime's death in love."[8] For Sonny the Holiness preacher, as for Eliot the poet, both would-be pilgrims, that ever-elusive destination demands going a way different from one's natural inclination and ends in transformation into a markedly different creature immersed in gratitude and self-giving. Eliot's journey repeats the one charted by the much-lauded Saint Paul, Christianity's first theologian and himself a convert from a militant anti-Christian Judaism: "This is my prayer, that your love may grow ever richer and richer in

---

8. T. S. Eliot, *The Complete Poems and Plays, 1909–1950* (New York: Harcourt, Brace, and World, 1965), 136, 143.

knowledge and insight of every kind, and thus may bring you the gift of true discrimination" (Phil. 1:9–10 NEB). Better still, in the rhapsodic language of Paul's hymn in 1 Corinthians 13, Sonny moves on from his pivotal lakeside recognition of his essential nothingness toward an embrace of love for all things. No matter his success and preaching and his passionate faith, he has at last come to love, and in that indeed is much cause for stomping and shouting. To Robert Duvall's enormous credit, he accomplishes far more than simply making Sonny's suspect world credible and palatable. That in itself is no small accomplishment, for Duvall has managed, in A. O. Scott's words, to "illuminate religious experience from within."[9] More than that even, Duvall succeeds in making Sonny's "one way road" a path both enticing and luminous, a path that imbues its earnest pilgrims with love and delight in the supreme gift of divine *caritas* for a befuddled and very broken world where even, and perhaps especially, the preachers can get it all wrong.

9. Scott, "Between Heaven and Earth."

CHAPTER FOUR

LOVE'S PURE LIGHT

Moral Light and Reconciliation in *Dead Man Walking*

The camera looks at him through the bars of a cell that seem to define his short hell-bent life. He sits alone in a white T-shirt in bright white light against a starkly white cement-block wall. Macho-pretty to the very end, he still brandishes pompadour, sculpted sideburns, mustache, and goatee, the model of tough-guy bravado or, as *Time*'s Richard Schickel put it, "inchoate rage tempered."[1] Only now, mere minutes from execution, director Tim Robbins shows quite another Matthew Poncelot (Sean Penn), slumping small and frightened against that blank jailhouse wall, as chilling a portrait of aloneness as there is in contemporary American film, matching even the desolations of Coppola's Michael Corleone (Al Pacino) at the close of *The Godfather Part II* and of his Harry Caul (Gene Hackman) in *The Conversation*. And well he should feel so. This is no saint incognito wrongly convicted but a guilty-as-hell rapist and murderer who's self-deluded and vicious and never wins much sympathy from anyone around him or, for that matter, from viewers. Even the most eloquent reviewers were hard put to find words bad enough to describe the depth of Poncelot's evil: Brian Johnson in *Maclean's* called him "a selfish, snickering racist"; Terrence Rafferty in the *New Yorker* judged him "a proud, fearless working-class loser"; and for Owen Gleiberman in

---

1. Richard Schickel, "The Executioner's Song," *Time*, January 8, 1996, 33.

Entertainment Weekly, he was "an arrogant young white-supremacist thug . . . a scuzz."[2]

Unlike in nearly every death-row film ever made, Poncelot will get what's coming to him, at least according to the state of Louisiana and the federal courts. All legal appeals exhausted, he will receive no last-minute reprieve from the needle (the two inmates on whom the story is based died in the electric chair, but filmmakers thought that too gruesome to depict realistically). In just half an hour, he will be dead. Amazingly, though, in these few remaining minutes of life, Poncelot, at long last, by means of some mysterious current that courses through the heart of the film, finally fesses up. Against all odds for this woe-be-fallen creature, deliverance does at last and surely come, full of its own peculiar kind of shock and awe: admission, remorse, forgiveness, absolution, and ultimately, reconciliation not only with God and himself but also, incredibly, with those trying to kill him. And then, finally, amid these "honest tears," shows forth, in the deft language of Terrence Rafferty, "a luminous, abandoned joy,"[3] for against all odds, and wondrously, Poncelot has found his way to a wholly new mode of being. And that elation follows Poncelot to his death, tempering his anger, fear, and grief, into the unimaginable territory of reconciliation. There's hardly a sequence like it anywhere in film.

Still, as dramatic as this death-row conversion plays out, it is by no means the surprising last-minute, skin-of-the-teeth, save-my-soul *deus ex machina* conversion that sentimental Christianity adores. To the contrary, the single piece of the Bible that best captures the action of *Dead Man Walking* is Jesus's renowned parable of the lost sheep, a story that remains amply strange because of the improbable measure of unfathomable, tireless caring it displays, something both rare and wholly unexpected (Luke 15:1–7). The long, hard labor of retrieving one so utterly lost is under way from the start and concludes in that white cell in the last minutes of life. In short, in Tim Robbins's adaptation of Helen Prejean's best-selling book, that protracted soul-wrestle consti-tutes the imaginative and dramatic mainspring of the story.

2. Brian D. Johnson, "Murderous States," *Maclean's*, January 22, 1996, 62; Terrence Raf-ferty, "Amazing Grace," *New Yorker*, January 8, 1996, 68–72; Owen Gleiberman, "Dead Man Walking," *Entertainment Weekly*, January 19, 1996, http://www.ew.com/article/1996/01/19/dead-man-walking; see also, David Denby, *New York Magazine*, January 8, 1996, 47; David Ansen, "The Killer and the Nun," *Newsweek*, January 22, 1996, 47.

3. Rafferty, "Amazing Grace," 68.

Yes, controversial aspects of capital punishment do indeed loom large and provide the high-stakes setting for the tale. Ultimately, though, the most surprising thing about Robbins's film is not that *Dead Man Walking*, against all popular expectation, stays neutral on the death penalty (if anything, the film seems to support execution). The bigger surprise, overlooked at release amid the controversy over death-penalty politics, lies in the dramatic mainspring of the film, namely, Robbins's plausible, psychologically complex, and cogent chronicle of a multifoliate richness within Christian redemption. Robbins's notion of religious conversion leaps far beyond the self-concern of simply being "saved," meaning the rescue of one's soul from eternal hellfire, which woefully shrinks and distorts what the biblical story means by salvation. Here, of all places, Light happens, bringing one woebegone hell-raiser into the precincts of divine love, of all unlikely places for a (just) confessed murderer.

What Robbins puts up on the screen is strikingly clear, and it is just about the hardest thing in the world for cinema to pull off. That is, put simply, the credible, though ever-mysterious, transit of an individual person—though the film makes "soul" seem a better term—from a vicious, self-wrought perdition to a radically different sense that his life, as foul as it has been, is ultimately encompassed, body and soul, by divine love for the purposes of bringing one "loser" to love all that is. In his very last moments, Poncelot sheds his desperately constructed identity as jaunty punk racist-rapist-killer to become—surprise, for himself and viewers—"a son of God," as Sister Helen Prejean (Susan Sarandon), both provocateur and Beatrice for this journey, names him, just as she herself is a daughter of God (1:36:30). In Robbins's hands, this journey not only seems propitious but also seems, oddly, metaphysically sensible, necessary, and inescapable, the only possible fix for the dire evil that contorts Poncelot and survivors. That seems so because, given the evil Poncelot is, only something so radical as the transcendent love the intrepid Prejean insistently pushes into view could prove sufficient to retrieve so lamentable a self as his. Indeed, at film's end, a wordless, achingly beautiful closing sequence, Robbins inducts all viewers, willy-nilly, into the selfsame arduous journey toward a holy domain of loving reconciliation. The logic therein seems inexorable and indispensable, and the film becomes "a hypnotic struggle for his soul."[4]

4. Schickel, "The Executioner's Song," 33.

The film crisply tracks Poncelot's pilgrim's progress, stage by stage. With patient psychological realism, writer-director Robbins lays out bit by bit an entirely plausible, and ever-so-logical, process by which Poncelot arrives at repentance, love, and reconciliation. In visit after visit, the insistent, gentle prodding of Sister Helen Prejean pushes Poncelot to ever-clearer recognitions of his own deep wrongness. Gritty but unassuming persistence shows what the warm heart of love looks like, the subtext for which abounds in the writing of Saint Paul (1 Cor. 13:4–7 and Gal. 5:22–23, to name but two sources). Nor is this sentimental in the least, because Prejean does indeed prod Poncelot, not only on matters of belief and "feeling," but ever more relentlessly on the deeply moral questions with which they are inextricably entwined, at least in the Judeo-Christian religious traditions of the West. First, Prejean goes after the sexism of his macho "games" and then his nasty racism and finally his pervasive moral evasion that scapegoats everyone for his own crimes. By the end, the purity and depth of care shown by this sisterly hound of heaven jostle him to confess his horrific crimes—kidnapping, rape, and murder—but also to recognize the reality of a Love, manifested through Prejean, he has heretofore never seen or even dreamed of. Poncelot himself is amazed, as is Prejean, and well they should be, given his encrusted pretense.

The evidence of the reality of the Mystery that smacks Poncelot full force in the depths of his own "lived experience" shows up straightaway clear and palpable in a changed demeanor. Suddenly the braggadocio disappears, exposing the fearful kid that deep-down he has always been. With inescapable execution pressing upon him, what he at long last recognizes, thanks to the ministrations of his loving mentor, is not obliteration or damnation but, as Prejean tells him, God's own "face of love," for which she is but a proxy, the conduit for Love's pure light (1:41:53). Knowing now his own nothingness, a condition he shares with all humanity, and, at the same time, indispensably, with that loving face, he can finally admit the truth of his crimes—that he, Poncelot himself, and not just his sidekick, in drug-fueled laughter and high spirits did terrify, rape, and murder. This grown child finally gets it—not what he knew all along, that he raped and murdered—but that only love can pay for the vicious caprice that killed the dead and, in very real terms, the still living survivors, something the film makes achingly clear in its regular display of the grief-ravaged families of the slain. So finally, amid tears and relief, Poncelot admits aloud—actually confesses—and repents his viciousness. Oddly, and perhaps this is the genius of Robbins's film, nothing Poncelot has ever done seems so necessary and pressing as these few simple words. In fact, hardly any literary document anywhere makes the central Jewish and Christian notions of transgression, guilt, forgiveness, and reconciliation so cogent, exigent, and clamorous as does this scene. Ultimately, it seems that nothing on earth or in human imagination, save perhaps for Dante or Dostoevsky, could conceive of so vital and necessary a passage as what these few minutes of screen time capture.

As surprising as this turn is, it is not in the end so improbable, for Poncelot in his unusual confessor has run across one very tough, albeit ever-kindly, advocate. And his end, at least for her, is no great surprise. After all, Poncelot's confession of responsibility and pursuit of forgiveness constitute the very destination toward which spiritual adviser Prejean has for long gently but insistently pushed Poncelot. Even though the story goes on for another twenty minutes, following Poncelot through his execution to his grave, this is the effectual climax of *Dead Man Walking*, Robbins's version of Prejean's well-known memoir of her work with death-row inmates in Angola, Louisiana. Through her good offices, Poncelot does indeed arrive at an actual, full-blown Christian redemption—for that is, purely and simply, what it is—and in that moment he for the first time finds his true identity, not as a posturing young tough, but as, in Prejean's words of absolution, "a Son of God," a status, he admits, that he had never ever imagined for himself. As such, Poncelot confesses, embraces sorrow for the death of others and his own death, and also, amazingly, especially for him, forgives those who seek his death—in short, to be the love he never knew. Mysteriously, and yet seemingly inexorably, a radical Something has by means of Prejean's kind and relentless but also hard-nosed love retrieved the repugnant Poncelot from all the monstrous wrongs—murder, racism, misogyny, machoism, hatred, arrogance, and just about every violent attitude imaginable—and turned him into quite something else. Here flashes beauty that is moral and, for lack of a better term, spiritual, one that seemingly transmutes the ever-strange depths of individual self-conception.

The sequence is all the more affecting for Robbins's resolute understatement—no trumpets, mush music, swooping cameras, heavens opening, lightning bolts, or strobing lights—just that chilled, cowering, sorrowful young man stumbling in the little time he has left toward forgiveness and meaning for his ill-wrought existence. Instead of apocalyptic fireworks, Robbins emphasizes the human nexus by which this happens: Poncelot himself, magnificently played by Penn, and Prejean, his only friend and spiritual adviser, the role for which Sarandon deservedly won the Best Actress Academy Award. As subdued and steadfastly plain as she is, Prejean is nonetheless, for Poncelot, light of God itself, lovingly dogging him the whole way, simultaneously welcoming and prodding, the agent provocateur and guide for his path toward recognition, honesty, confession, redemption, and final death's-door realization of newfound humanity, of what he should have been all along if only circumstances, life itself, had been different. In this, Robbins forges an acute and remarkably stringent psychological and religious realism that makes the unimaginable rebirth of Poncelot entirely likely, given what has befallen him—the plain and plainspoken nun that has come his way.

Getting to Know You (and Everybody Else)

The world in which Helen Prejean finds herself on Louisiana's death row is not one she ever imagined when she became that increasingly rare creature, a Roman Catholic nun. Indeed, all of this is more than Prejean herself bargained for. At the film's start, she lives and works in the St. Thomas housing projects, where she teaches adult literacy classes. She encounters Poncelot simply because a friend who works with prisoners asks her to write him. From pen pal she soon moves, responding to pleas of loneliness, to visitor, and so begins the brief but intense relationship that culminates with Prejean becoming his official spiritual adviser and deep (and only) friend.

This is not an easy process for these alien characters, and Robbins resolutely refuses to prettify or elide its false starts and lasting tension. After all, Poncelot comes from poor, working-class white people who are stuck forever, it seems, on the lowest rungs of economic and social ladders they cannot even locate. Theirs is a hard life, full of toil, futility, and hard living that is both protest and salve. Poncelot's father taught him to drink heavily at age fourteen, and from there he incorporates drugs soft and hard, heavy doses of a virulent racism, and fierce pride. To be sure, he's unlike any person Prejean, from an upper-middle-class, staunchly Roman Catholic Baton Rouge family, has ever run across.

One of the great accomplishments of the film is to display, both dramatically and cinematically, the slow flourishing of the bonds of peace, an unlikely and gracious fabric of trust and caring, between two disparate souls, a murderer and a nun.

Robbins cuts right to the chase, deftly compacting preliminary exposition, the film's backstory, to move quickly to the real stuff of the film. Five minutes in, Prejean is making her first visit to the notorious Angola prison. Before that, though, audiences glimpse the contours of Prejean's life by means of home-video flashbacks of her confirmation and then her entrance into the novitiate and finally her life as a resident adult literacy teacher in the projects. This culminates with her drive to the prison for her first encounter with Poncelot, as a voice-over of Poncelot reads his first letter to her. The entrance into the prison is forbidding, full of guards and endless doors of bars clanging off hard surfaces, and it is not auspicious for the sort of work she will undertake within its walls. In one of the film's few lurches toward symbolism, the large metal crucifix Prejean wears about her neck sets off the metal detector through which she must pass. In the alarm and the camera's brief close-up on the cross, the film quietly suggests that the cross is fundamentally alien to the violent world Prejean is about to enter.

At the end of her long journey into the prison's interior, Prejean meets Poncelot, whose posture is an odd mix of appreciation, macho swagger, and petition. Poncelot seems more than a little chagrined that at this stage in his life he has to turn to a nun for friendship. While one part of him appreciates the gesture, another takes it as an insult, and he goads her to determine what she is made of. First, flaunting his racism, he takes a swipe at the people and the projects where she lives; after that it's her superior social class, as he contrasts her family's relative wealth with his own impoverished background. Prejean ignores his first salvos but then ventures that they have something in common in that they both live with the poor, he on death row and she in the projects. Through this first conversation, Robbins deploys standard shot/reverse-shot procedure, since in the visitors' room the two are separated by a sturdy black mesh wire screen. Mostly the camera stays on Prejean's side, viewing her unobstructedly, but peers through the screen to give Poncelot an ominous pall. Only toward the end of this first conversation, as Poncelot extends some measure of trust, does Robbins shoot both in the same manner—close to the screen as light reflects off of it, giving it a kind of luminous sheen.

Clearly, in this first meeting some distance has been traveled. Poncelot has assayed this nun, and the judgment is positive, as indicated by his parting gestures: he trusts her with a valued copy of his self-authored appeal so that she might place it with a sympathetic lawyer, and then he actually expresses admiration for her: "You didn't come here to kiss my ass and preach all that hellfire and brimstone crap. I respect that. You're all right. You got guts. You live in a neighborhood where every n—— has a gun" (13:05). And so ends their first meeting.

Between visits to the prison, Robbins gives the rest of the story, so to speak, but no more than necessary to make the film work as narrative. He supplies an ample quantity of information about the dubiousness of the death penalty but refrains from making the film propagandistic. What he does supply, as with his treatment of the victims' parents, seems to be there to depict the darkly tangled human drama that is life itself. The audience learns the truth of Poncelot's viciousness when Prejean reviews police files and watches television news stories about his approaching execution. This unpleasant information then smacks up against Prejean's (and our) compassion when in a late evening call Poncelot pleads with her for help—"You're all I got"—now that the governor has set his execution for eleven days hence. And in comes the crusty but kind old lawyer, Hilton Barber (Robert Prosky), whose avocation is warring against the death penalty and giving help to the condemned. His realism about the gross dysfunction, even futility, of the jurisprudence "system" makes his dedication all the more admirable. The badness of the men he defends seems only to increase his idealism.

And then there are the families. Prejean visits Poncelot's mother Lucille (Roberta Maxwell), a hardscrabble, old-before-her-time widow, at once both tearful and embittered. Toward her misbegotten son she is both protective and angry, for he has, after all, savaged what good she has tried to do for her family (Poncelot has four younger brothers). A first glimpse of the justly furious family of the raped and murdered young woman comes during the television news story on Poncelot's execution. And last we observe Prejean's own family as they sit around a well-appointed dining table discussing her new charitable work with death-row inmates. With this they are generally not pleased, thinking that while she may indeed be large-hearted, she may also be empty-headed in assessing the social utility of this new work. While serious in their doubts, they remain always fond and supportive in a world that lies a universe from the one that produced a Poncelot.

The Come-On

Just how far this warm family is from prison and Poncelot comes starkly clear in the next scene, which is Prejean's briefly treated second visit to the inmate. Poncelot reminisces about his life, fondly recalling how his father took his then fourteen-year-old son to a bar, where the two got "drunk as a couple of coots" (25:45). The recollection of the male initiation ritual seems to push Poncelot into full-blown macho posturing to the extent that he attempts to flirt with Prejean. Making bold, he asks her why she's a nun, which she ascribes to "good luck," just as his criminal life looks like "bad luck" (26:09). Undeterred, he asks if she misses "having a man," a question to which Prejean does not respond, after which he only pushes further (26:17). She avers that she has many friends, male and female alike, with whom she has a depth of intimacy, a word onto which Poncelot grabs, suggesting, amid his best leer and "snicker," as the shooting script puts it, that they have intimacy now. Visibly displeased, Prejean abruptly changes the subject to her visit with Poncelot's mother. Still, clearly relishing his sense of male sexual power, and with the camera filling the screen with his leer, Poncelot ignores her ploy to again push the sexual: "I like being alone with you. You're looking real good to me" (27:01). This is more than enough, and Prejean quietly but dead-seriously yanks him back to the reality of his circumstance: "Look at you. Death is breathing down your neck and here you are, playing your lil' Matt-on-the-make-games. I'm not here for your amusement, Matt, so have some respect" (27:04). Being who he is, though, Poncelot still doesn't get it, thinking she's referring to respect for her profession when she in fact has a larger, more fundamental truth in mind: "Because I'm a person . . . and we all deserve respect" (27:10).

This exchange makes emphatic the stratagem of quiet truth-telling that Prejean patiently but rigorously deploys throughout her brief but intense relationship with Poncelot. She did this in their first meeting when Poncelot tried to indict her social background and current work among the poor, and she will do it again when he parades his racism, his moral evasiveness, and, most tellingly, his struggles to reckon with his own lostness. She simply will not back off; she is as tough and persistent as any military drill instructor. In Prejean and the unsentimental love she displays, Poncelot has more than met his match.

And so has Prejean—just about—for she has entered a world that is strange, alien, and amply intimidating. The point is smoothly driven home at Poncelot's pardon board hearing. Lawyer Hilton Barber makes a desperate plea for the board to spare Poncelot's life, schooling them (and viewers) on why only the poor inhabit death row, the inhumanity of even lethal injection, and the notion of the death penalty itself.[5] Whatever sympathy Barber elicits from viewers, the district attorney defuses in citing the completeness of Poncelot's appeals, the impact on the victims' families, and finally, the barbarity of Poncelot's crime, first raping and stabbing (seventeen times) Hope Percy and then shooting Walter Delacroix in the head twice. All the while the camera surveys the bystanders: Poncelot's mother, whose uncontrollable sobbing ended her testimony at the hearing, and, of course, the angry, impatient families who want Poncelot's life. The board rejects the clemency appeal, and on his way out of the hearing room Poncelot, still full of swagger, asks Prejean to serve as his spiritual adviser for his last six days of life—"It looks

---

5. As Prejean reports in her book, the Louisiana Pardon Board was a creation of four-term governor Edwin Edwards, who himself would later serve eight years in prison for corruption. The members of the board were all political appointees, meant to keep Edwards from the political liabilities of having to make death-penalty decisions, and several of them were receiving bribes for pardons.

like you're all I got, sis. . . . Ride along into the sunset with me" (34:36). More than "a tough road," as Barber names it, the pair commence a journey to the terrain of desolation and death (35:08).

Every bit as forbidding is the crucible of pain into which Prejean will be more or less abducted. While the board deliberates in private, Prejean is accosted by Earl Delacroix (the splendid Raymond J. Barry), the father of the murdered boy, who as a proud Catholic angrily indicts Prejean for her selective compassion: "How can you sit by Matt Poncelet's side without ever having come to visit me and my wife or the Percys to hear our side? How can you spend all your time worrying about Poncelet and not think that maybe we needed you, too?" (32:12). Rather befuddled, Prejean offers formulaic responses, finally giving her phone number in case the families want her to visit, and this time it is she who is brought up short. "Me call you? Think about that, Sister. Think about how arrogant that is" (32:12). And if that were not enough, *The Shooting Script* adds the term "self-righteous" to describe Prejean's behavior.[6] Clearly, Poncelot is not the only one with a lot to learn about respect, though Prejean will prove far more teachable.

And thus begins Prejean's second journey in the story. The first goes inward into the depths: into her own soul and mind as she confronts the realities of death row and the darkness of Matt Poncelet. The second journey, the one initiated by Delacroix, is outward, beckoning her to recognize and weep for those inconsolable people whose lives were so ambushed by evil that it seems as if the demonic had with relish thrust a hand from the recesses of hell to torture and kill the innocent and rake with sorrow and rage the survivors who loved the dead more than life itself. Their own lives shatter, and hatred and vengeance provide the only means thereafter for holding them together.

Chastened, Prejean ventures to see both the Delacroix and the Percy families, just as she has faithfully attended to Poncelot. An honest and gentle man, Earl Delacroix greets Prejean with hostility but appreciates her courage and honesty in coming to see him, and they soon warm to each other. Amid the disarray of the living room, for the couple is separating, as do many couples who have lost a child, Delacroix quietly talks of his marriage and his son, his only child. Robbins films the sequence in tender, delicate fashion, shooting the two actors in subdued, warm light as they sit quietly across from one another leaning in to hear each

6. Tim Robbins, *Dead Man Walking: The Shooting Script* (New York: Newmarket, 1997), 55.

other's words. As their conversation draws to a close, the camera slowly retreats to a two-shot, framing the two, simultaneously emphasizing their togetherness and their aloneness; they are small figures trying to reach toward trust and healing amid the wrenching vale of evil and tears that constitutes so much of human life.

The subsequent visit to the Percys does not go at all well, a fact that Robbins again dramatizes visually by never putting Prejean and the Percys together in the same frame. The Percys do welcome her, and they tell in minute, wrenching detail the story of daughter Hope's disappearance and death, tears falling throughout, but all the while they have the mistaken impression that Prejean's visit means that she has abandoned Poncelot and has embraced their demand for his execution. When she tells them otherwise, the meeting ends abruptly, though she tries to explain, invoking Christ's love for all people, the motive for her care for Poncelot. For Clyde Percy (R. Lee Ermey), evidence suggests that Poncelot lacks a soul, for his crime shows him to be less than an animal. After all, and a telling point it is, animals do not rape and murder their own kind.

The Adviser

In between these visits that acquaint her and viewers with the victims' families, Prejean again visits Poncelot, the man who caused all this unfathomable woe, and hereafter the focus remains rather tightly on Poncelot. On this visit, Prejean goes as Poncelot's official spiritual adviser to accompany him through what will very likely be the last week of his life. To this, she brings the same honesty and guts that prompted her visits with Delacroix and the Percys.

The old-school priest in the prison, Father Farley (Scott Wilson), tries to warn her off, mentioning her supposed gender liability, her inexperience, and her obligation to save Poncelot's soul by simply getting him to receive the sacraments. Prejean takes all this seriously enough, as we've seen in the rebuke of Poncelot's come-on, and the audience soon sees exactly how seriously she deems the task of soul saving, though not by the means or end the priest suggests. Indeed, while she shows herself to be very much in the hunt for Poncelot's soul, her interpretation of salvation differs markedly from Chaplain Farley's constricted notions of grace by sacrament.

In Farley's hidebound traditionalist theology, salvific efficacy inheres in partaking of the Eucharist, the sacramental ritual wherein lies access to salvation; in this view, it is the sacrament that does the work of salvation, delivering the soul to eternal life. As the rest of her relationship with Poncelot makes clear, Prejean pours radically different meaning into traditional language about saving souls, and it in effect differs not at all from her goals in meeting with the parents. Prejean pushes Poncelot toward personal appropriation of all that the Eucharist itself constitutes: confession, meaning the admission of responsibility; repentance, the experience of remorse for one's offenses; and the purpose and fruition of the process, reconciliation—between Poncelot and the parents of those he killed and, of course, between Poncelot and God, who is the source and impetus for this ineluctable itinerary into the divine heart of love. It is this transit that increasingly becomes the focus of *Dead Man Walking* in Prejean's passage with Poncelot, but also, along the way, with Earl Delacroix. For Prejean, all journeys end before the face of a God whose love envelops a suffering world.

In her first visit to Poncelot as his spiritual adviser, Prejean shows two marked changes—she starts asking him questions, hard ones, and she begins to probe whatever religious or moral sensitivity he might have, a capacity he has not exhibited previously. Her first question opens the door: "Do you ever read the Bible?" Poncelot replies that he "ain't much of a Bible reader but I pick it up and read it sometimes" (41:20). Prejean pushes the matter further by quoting W. C. Fields's explanation of why he read the Bible, namely, that he was "lookin' for a loophole" (41:45). Poncelot doesn't get the allusion, never having heard of W. C. Fields. She explains; he laughs, and proclaims, "I ain't looking for no loophole," and abruptly changes the subject to who will be killed next, meaning himself, since the state has just executed an African American (41:51). Here again his virulent racism flares in his wish that "they clean that thing [the execution gurney] before they put me on it" (42:17). As she did with his earlier attempts at flirtation, only now with alacrity, Prejean goes after Poncelot's loathing, of which scapegoating composes the major part. In particular, Poncelot dislikes the way African Americans seem to brandish victimhood and dislike work. She catches him in his ill logic, first, when he admits to admiring Martin Luther King ("he kicked the white man's butt") and, second, by saying it's simply lazy people he dislikes, whether white or black (43:29).

Things get worse for Poncelot when he appears in a television interview during which he praises Hitler and white supremacy. Afterward, Prejean straight out chastises him, essentially echoing the portrait of Poncelot given by Clyde Percy: "You're a fool. Don't you see how easy you're making it for them to kill you? You're coming off as a crazed animal, a Nazi terrorist mad dog, someone that's not even human that deserves to die" (55:56). Poncelot goes huffy in response, giving her leave to leave if she wishes. She refuses but takes the occasion, since the topic is just exactly who he is anyway, his deepest sense of self, to ask if "you ever think about those kids" and the suffering he and his cohort inflicted on the families (56:24). Again, Poncelot dodges the question, saying, first, that it's hard to have sympathy for people who are trying to kill him and, second, that he is innocent of the crimes.

That the relationship between Poncelot and Prejean has by now changed is made more than clear by Robbins's marked shift in his visual scheme, specifically the story's movement to the second of the four stages of relationship between Poncelot and Prejean. Robbins captures the markedly increased measure of trust between the two by now placing them for the first time in the same frame. Instead of the shot/reverse-shot scheme he has employed thus far, one that usually looks at Poncelot through the barrier, whether mesh screen or glass, he now employs a "cheat shot" by filming the pair from the side, placing the camera where the separating wall would be. The effect of this is to stress by visual means that these two have achieved a kind of parity; they are just two human beings wrestling with the dire fate that awaits one of

them. So they chat, but they also dispute and sulk, as compatriots only can. The new camera position, though it "cheats" in its plausibility, dramatically catches the two as they lean toward one another in their effort to hear and speak, something that prison has effectively obstructed but is now surpassed by the urgency of their souls.

In their next meeting Prejean returns to the subject of reading the Bible to push Poncelot toward a crucial recognition of his own moral shortfalls by highlighting the wildness of the radical love manifested in the person of Jesus. "You read anything in that Bible about Jesus?" (1:03:54). Says Poncelot glibly, "Holy man, did good, in heaven, praise Jesus" (1:04:01). Here Prejean labors to replace his picture of Jesus as namby-pamby innocuous. First, she links Jesus's predicament in facing death with Poncelot's, and in response to Poncelot's assertion of his own manly superiority to "one of those turn the other cheek guys," Prejean asserts the risk and danger in loving others: "His love changed things, Matt. People that nobody cared about, prostitutes, beggars, the poor, finally had someone that respected them, loved them, made them realize their own worth. They had dignity and were becoming powerful, and that made the guys at the top so nervous they went and killed Jesus" (1:04:36). Narcissist that he is, Poncelot reads Jesus's dangerousness and execution in terms of his own fate—"Kinda like me, huh?" (1:05:00). Prejean quietly but emphatically disabuses him of that notion, suggesting that the two are in fact polar opposites: "No,

Matt, no. Not at all like you. Jesus changed it with his love. You watched while two kids were murdered" (1:05:04). Altogether, her words in the scene constitute her most directly apologetical statement, and present a moral standard (and judgment) as clearly and candidly as any Poncelot had probably ever heard. It's the beginning of the hard push that will save his soul, not just to get him safely to heaven, but to initiate him, the murderer, into a transformative moral and spiritual realm. Poncelot, in typical fashion, squirms and asks again to change the subject, though it is clear by what follows that the question has begun to churn in the depths of his soul.

In between visits, Prejean has to make funeral arrangements for Poncelot (he doesn't want to be buried by the prison at the prison, and he doesn't want to burden his mother with wake planning), deal with hostility from her neighbors for befriending the vehemently racist Poncelot, and attend a victims' support group meeting with Earl Delacroix. She talks to the guards who work on the execution team about their work ("just part of the job"), and, unhappily, receives another lecture from the prison priest on the urgency of saving Poncelot's soul, during which she faints from, it seems, lack of food. All in all, it's a harrowing trip, more than enough to deal with for anyone counseling a badly frightened man who sees certain death fast approaching.

For the next-to-final stage in Poncelot's journey, Robbins moves to a third, and wonderfully ingenious, visual scheme. While the camera looks over Prejean's or Poncelot's shoulder, the image of the other reflects in the thick glass that separates them, in effect placing the two side by side; this is a two-shot, allowing viewers to take in the reactions of both at once. In simplest terms, the strategy goes a long way, quite literally, toward doubling the emotional freight the film conveys.

That freight clearly skyrockets as the remaining minutes of Poncelot's life tick away. That the pressure has mounted is made clear the next day when Poncelot erupts before Prejean because she was not allowed to continue her visit after her faint. She finds a distraught inmate who's had to face his own deep loneliness, so much so that he asks her if she ever gets lonely. Her honest answer is that on Sunday afternoons when she hears families playing together she feels much the fool for having chosen a life of solitariness. He misses most the sex, to which she responds, again with a full measure of honesty, "Well, Matt, let's face it. If I had a husband and family, chances are I'd be with them this afternoon, instead of sitting here visiting with you" (1:10:51).

And then, perhaps for the first time in the story, save for his eruption about her absence, viewers see a measure of Poncelot's humanness, confessing a very unmacho appreciation to, of all people, a nun: "I'm glad you're here" (1:11:05). As if that were too much, he quickly reverts to his fear of looking weak: "I ain't gonna let 'em break me. I just pray God he holds up my legs on that last walk . . . that countdown gets to ya." Amid the fear that is now spilling over into pure terror, he goes so far as to regret his "stupid mouth" in his interview comments on race and terrorism (1:11:32).

Home Free?

Amid growing distress and shrinking time, Prejean again turns the talk toward the Bible, and to this Poncelot readily, even proudly, responds, declaring that religiously he's now "home free." "I appreciate you trying to save me, but me and God got all things squared away. I know Jesus died on the cross for us, and I know he's gonna be there to take care of me when I appear before God on Judgment Day" (1:12:58). Prejean is more than a little perplexed, and also duly alarmed, by this statement because it hardly comports with her notion of the demands and genuine fullness of redemption. What Poncelot propounds is a notion of salvation that resembles what Farley and many Protestant evangelicals have in mind. Tellingly, in response Prejean employs the word "redemption" as opposed to "salvation," which often consists of a desperate grasp to save one's soul from hell's suffering just in case all the Jesus-as-God talk should prove true after all. "Matt, redemption is not some kind of free admission ticket that you get because Jesus paid the price. You've got to participate in your own redemption; you've got some work to do. I think maybe you should look at the Gospel of John, chapter eight, where Jesus said, 'You shall know the truth, and the truth shall make you free.'" "I'll check that out," he replies. "I like that, 'the truth shall make you free'" (1:13:09).

Here, benighted as he is, Poncelot grabs on to the notion of truth and his impending lie detector test, implying that if he passes that, not only will all know he's innocent but God will too. Again, Prejean plays his truth monitor, pushing Poncelot not toward the easy reassurance of "believe and be saved" but toward the hard task of reckoning with his own genuine responsibility. "Matt, if you do die, as your friend I want to help you die with dignity. I can't see how you can do that unless you start to own up to the part you played in Walter and Hope's death" (1:13:44).

And that, more or less, tells the tale, posing the final wrestle for Poncelot's mortal life, the question that hangs over his last few living minutes. On that last day, his family comes, mother and three brothers, and they together struggle through a long, awkward farewell, much of it taken over by silence, but all desperately trying to act as if things were normal and just fine and Matt's imminent death was not more than a long vacation. During the visit, for five full minutes of screen time, Poncelot plays and preens as the family bad boy, half-happy scoundrel, and loving big brother. As painful as this sequence plays, it diverts attention from questions of truth and guilt, but only for a brief time, for after the visit word comes that the results of a lie detector test have proven inconclusive, given the stress of his fast approaching death. It is within the context of responsibility, with a little more than three hours of life left, and with Poncelot now located in a cell adjoining the death chamber, that Prejean wants again to "talk about that night" and what actually happened. Poncelot, genuinely rattled now, simply says he doesn't want to talk about it, though two hours later he is roaming his cell, ranting, "pissed off" at the dead kids being in the woods that night, at his buddy for getting him in the woods that night, and mostly at the parents who want him dead and whom he wants to denounce in his last words (1:27:22).

Prejean calls him on his hatred, dramatizing how angry the parents must feel, getting Poncelot to admit that he would do worse than they if one of his children was murdered. This death's-door combat between the two also plays out in the visual scheme of shot/reverse-shot to which Robbins now returns. Gone is the quiet cordiality of the side-by-side mirror shot of Poncelot's last days. This is the final hard transit from life to death, from moral obliviousness to culpability and redemption. Appropriately, Poncelot is throughout framed by bars and pitted against the cold stark white of the cement-block walls of his cell. Prejean, in contrast, sits and leans forward to the bars, beseeching, imploring, sallying to find some cranny in the facade of belligerent denial.

In fact, Prejean queries Poncelot with the ferocity of a tough-minded interrogator, only this time the goal is not legal but moral and redemptive. She insistently strips away his stratagems of denial. Alas, it wasn't the drugs, for he'd been harassing couples in the woods for weeks and months before the fatal night. Or was it idol worship of his buddy Fatella that prompted Poncelot to impress him with his cruelty? Poncelot squirms and evades, claiming ignorance of what happened, finally blaming Fatella for going psycho (in fact, as the intercut enactments of the crime show, Poncelot was the primary instigator). And then, with as much intensity as Prejean musters anywhere in the film, she rattles off the list of his scapegoats: "you blame him, you blame the government, you blame drugs, you blame blacks, you blame the Percys, you blame the kids for being there; what about Matthew Poncelot, where's he in this story; what is he, just an innocent, a victim?" (1:28:25). Finally the goading touches some vestigial nerve, and he sneers back, defiant and swaggering, that he "ain't no victim." The momentum of the dispute breaks when the warden enters to inform Poncelot that his application to the federal Fifth Circuit Appeals Court has failed. With that news Poncelot is hauled away for preparation for execution. Prejean retreats to the women's restroom, and there we see her desperate pleas to God for strength to persevere through the next hours.

Love's Pure Light

We next see Poncelot cowering in the corner of his cell, dressed now in that white T-shirt and jeans, his tattoo-laden arms exposed ("you're gonna think I'm a bad person" [1:31:22]), and chains on his ankles and wrists and his pant leg torn to give the execution crew access to his leg. Stripped naked—"tragic nakedness," to borrow a phrase from Frederick Buechner[7]—or at least deprived of his usual costuming, Poncelot loses his macho preening, and for once he looks shaken and wounded, perceptibly shrinking into himself.

This new physical vulnerability, even more than the denial of his appeal, seems to drive him to recognize the certainty of execution and that he too is vulnerable and frail. After a tearful telephone farewell to his family, he recounts to Prejean what he told his mother, namely, that it was his fault for following Fatella, the hell-bent pal he admired and wished to outdo in being "tough as hell" (1:34:38). With that admission as catalyst, Poncelot at last arrives at the end of his days-long journey

7. Frederick Buechner, *Telling the Truth: The Gospel as Tragedy, Comedy, and Fairy Tale* (San Francisco: Harper, 1977), 33.

into himself, his first and final confession of the heinous wrong he has done, admitting to Prejean, "That boy, Walter . . ." "What?" she injects amid Poncelot's long pause. "I killed him," and he then admits also to raping Hope Percy (1:35:20). As the child he is, he responds to her questions amid tears with incongruously polite "yes, ma'ams," even to the question of "taking responsibility for both of their deaths" (1:36:01).

It is, frankly, one of the most arresting sequences ever put on film—full of fear, sorrow, and longing, a realistic microscopic portrayal of one approaching execution and, oddly, the death's-door discovery of his own humanity, conscience, soul, or whatever term encompasses the deep springs of his being. And it is all ever so beautifully filmed and acted, without histrionics or sentiment, Penn especially seeming to utterly vacate himself to enter the tangled darkness of the man's soul.

And upon contrition does begin, albeit very unexpectedly, that startling, marvel-filled transit called redemption. Admittedly, given what viewers have thus far seen of Poncelot—a resolutely vicious brand of self-infatuation—this is not a likely turn. But when it does happen, it nonetheless plays as plausible, cogent, and even necessary, as both invitation and demand, a moral and spiritual nexus that is strangely but sensibly woven into the deepest fabric of human reality. If the film purposefully does not answer questions about the rightness of the death penalty, its dramatic logic does nonetheless emphatically go after bigger game still: that matters of guilt and confession are not arbitrarily imposed on humankind but are themselves intrinsic to the human creature, emanating from the depths of humanness as crucial and inescapable human psychic demands that are as much an appetite as those for food or sleep. The same can be said for what follows, for nothing else on the earth seems so fitting and necessary. Ultimately, spiritual and moral reprieve indeed prepares the way for new birth, "true shelter" for his tragic nakedness, as Buechner names it, that here looks to be something markedly more important than saving Poncelot's mortal life, such as it was. The old Christian metanarrative here seems to play out as the only plausible recourse to his upside-down life history.

Nor does the turning stop here. After this comes the good end that Prejean enjoins Poncelot to pursue, which for him constitutes a remarkable leap into the fullness of redemption. Having received and at last comprehended authentic love, he can now muster some for others, despite the manifold terrors of the execution that fast approaches. He can thank Prejean for loving him in a way that far surpasses the tawdry notions of carnality with which he began their relationship, and he can also offer contrition and penance to the parents of the children he slew. Part and parcel with this, there is in Poncelot even a variety of gladness. In that cold, harshly lit cell, a sizable measure of the warm light of divine love, for which Prejean is the conduit, has engulfed him. Robbins's visual scheme emphasizes this pointedly: while Poncelot is fully lit against a stark, empty whiteness, and himself in his white T-shirt a part of that whiteness, Prejean has always over her left shoulder a splotch of glowing red-orange something, its source never entirely clear. It is not, to be sure, a halo or any such clumsy announcement of sanctity, but it does provide a sort of atmospheric penumbra of warmth such as is typically associated with light and care. It is fitting finally to call it what it is—the pure light of divine care for benighted humankind.

In Robbins's portraiture of Poncelot, there is from start to finish the sense that what this craven man most needs is exactly what comes his way—and it is a rare thing to find in cinema—a plausible, cogent display of the miracle of holy love, usually called divine grace, though here it surely doesn't come as the spectacle or neon light in the sky that most folks, including earnest religious people, expect and even desire. Rather, more sensational still, what mercy comes his way arrives from, of all people, a mild-mannered middle-aged nun, seemingly unexceptional in every way, whose quiet but relentlessly hard-nosed ministrations finally deliver Poncelot from the delusions of his own darkest self into a redemption wherein he perceives that Love, at once transcendent and urgently this-worldly, forgives even his deeds. Prejean's labor of love blooms fully at last, though it has throughout most often seemed, given Poncelot's resolutely impenetrable macho-shell, altogether futile. Her love accomplished in Poncelot's confession, remorse, deliverance, and gratitude, Prejean amid amazed tears pronounces for Poncelot—cold, quivering child that he is, and a contemporary thief on the cross in a modern techno-Golgotha—a sort of absolution, that his sins are forgiven and he is, even the likes of him, God's new creature, the child of a loving Father, as is the whole of humanity: "There are spaces of sorrow only God can touch. You did a terrible thing . . . a terrible thing, but you have a dignity now. Nobody can take that from you. You are a son of God, Matthew Poncelot" (1:36:18).

The shock is that Prejean's words bestow on this cruel, almost entirely unsympathetic man the same measure of love as that received by saints, something within the divine economy that he has always had but for his failure to recognize its constant, all-encompassing reality. All of that comes clear enough when he volunteers to Prejean, having now finally seen the real thing, "You know I never had no real love my-self. . . . Who ever figured that I'd have to die to find love. . . . Thank you for loving me" (1:37:03). Prejean then agrees to sing, unmusical though she is, choosing a hymn about crossing "deep waters," an apt image for what lies ahead. For his final "dead man" walk, she follows Poncelot down the hall to the death chamber, hand on his shoulder while reading from his Bible. In his last mortal words Poncelot protests his killing by the state but also asks forgiveness from Earl Delacroix and expresses hope his death will bring peace to the Percys.

Last Reckoning

Just as the moral spiritual contest is resolved, the film unexpectedly seems to turn back upon itself, departing contrition and forgiveness to inspect the ugly mechanics and morality of execution. In one sense this seems fitting and right, the completion of the story of Poncelot's last days and the culmination of the wish of the still distraught parents. What follows provides another calculus to assess Poncelot's deeds and the rightness of the death penalty.

For the most part, the execution sequence is predictable, including just what viewers might expect, and to which Robbins gives due atten-tion: the belting of the body to the gurney, the insertion of IV needles that will allow for the intravenous supply of the lethal chemicals, the last words, the flipping of the switches that begin death's flow, and Poncelot's effort to look at Prejean, "the face of love," in the witnesses' gallery as the state does "this thing" called execution (1:41:58). The ges-ture concludes a long journey Poncelot would not have traveled if not for that "face of love" that has so painstakingly built up between them the bonds of peace, an unlikely fabric of trust and caring between the predator and, of all people, that mild-mannered sister of mercy.

Then, much to the audience's surprise, through the long, painstak-ingly observed death sequence, Robbins begins to violate the narra-tive realism he has thus far so carefully constructed. The effect of this deviation is startling in the extreme. Through the whole length of the execution, in blatant authorial intrusion that tries to invoke a wholly different calculus of justice, Robbins cuts to scenes of the rapes and murders by Fatella and Poncelot. We've seen already this cinematic practice of cutting away to images of the crime as expressions of Prejean's attempts to understand the full measure of Poncelot's guilt, especially as his story diverges from the account given by his criminal file. Now, though, the moral economy propounded in this account computes very differently from the one transacted between Poncelot and Prejean in the minutes before his dead man's walk to the execution room.

Robbins's somber series of crosscuts between the dying Poncelot and the phases of the crime suggests a kind of equivalency—that here, in strictly human terms, justice is in fact being done. This impression is confirmed when in the very last shot of the execution sequence Robbins inserts a two-shot of the two dead teens, looking very much alive but expressionless, peering down on one cause of their completely horrific end. This is, to say the least, an unexpected and strange overlay in a film that has thus far featured unflinching psychological and religious realism. Regardless, the effect of the sequence, especially in its use of the down-looking camera, sheer verticality, is to argue in forcefully cogent terms that Poncelot has gotten by some transcendent justice exactly what is coming to him: an eye for an eye. A terrible loss has been compensated, and a severe but necessary justice has finally been accomplished. The graphic display of the rapes and murders of two young people rouses the demand for justice, which in this instance seems to be the amply fitting loss of Poncelot's own life.

All in all, the sequence stands in radical contrast to Sister Helen Prejean's distinctly Christian computation of guilt and punishment from which flows her opposition to the death penalty, and it is this emphasis that has, rightly so, the last word in the film. It is, after all, her story and her views of the death penalty and Christian mercy that inform the source material. Fittingly, then, the conclusion moves quite beyond the question of the morality of capital punishment to suggest that what is most important is the kind of work that Prejean undertook with Poncelot and that, in effect, every single viewer should embrace. It is, indeed, that important.

The segue into that argument comes at Poncelot's graveside committal, where Prejean spies Earl Delacroix observing from a distance. She afterward approaches him, and during their conversation he confesses his own incapacity to forgive and that he has still, even after the death of Poncelot, "a lot of hate" (1:52:24). The sequence is made all the more effective because Delacroix, as wonderfully underplayed by Raymond J. Barry, is a quiet, serious, thoughtful, and tender Roman Catholic. Prejean suggests that perhaps they can work on that "hate" together. From that discussion the camera cuts, in the film's last scene, to a small white rural church that it slowly approaches. Amid the piercing notes of Eddie Vedder's electric guitar, the camera slowly approaches a side window through which we see Prejean and Delacroix together in the otherwise empty church kneeling in prayer. After a brief glimpse of the pair, the camera retreats to the music and lyrics of Bruce Springsteen's song written for the film. The suggestion seems to be that capital punishment as revenge or satisfaction does little to quell the riot of anger and hatred that consumes the hearts of survivors, and from there but one route to resolution exists, and that is the path of reconciliation, the same one taken by their brother Poncelot in his last minutes.

In the intensity of its narrative and thematic focus, Robbins's superb film excels as a searching treatment of the morality of the death penalty and, probably in ways unanticipated by Robbins, as a cogent rendition of the ferocity of Christian love. In that sense, *Dead Man Walking* the movie offers as incisive, searching, and poignant a delineation of the Christian sense of the world as is found on film. A hymn stanza catches it perfectly: "This is love come to light, / now is fear put to flight, / God defeats darkest night."[8] *Dead Man Walking* is unique in its achievement: a wrenching, and also joyous, dramatization of this wonder of compassion—in traditional terms, the reality of love and grace, meaning unimaginable, unfathomable divine care for this tear-sodden earth—that lies at the core of the Judeo-Christian story. Simply put, the great surprise and wonder here are that divine love goes even, and especially, to the damnedest places—utterly dire hellholes, like morgues and death row—to heal wrong and brokenness, the pall that soaks the globe. That this sort of thing happens, as is so transparently the case with Prejean and Poncelot, is the deepest core and primary evidence for love as the metaphysical fabric of the universe. It shows forth in the film version of *Dead Man Walking* because the central narrative so deftly displays the thematic skein of a very radical love that labors to retrieve one of life's least likely candidates for redemption.

Indeed, a good deal of the power of Robbins's film lies in its completely plausible and thoroughly unflattering portrait of Poncelot, for he is until virtually the very end just plain odious and repugnant, a person who really does seem to love doing cruelty to make himself feel better. We know enough of his background to understand how he turned out as he did, but the film never in the least excuses his crimes because of that background, which is the sociological indulgence

8. Fred Kahn, "Down to Earth as a Dove" (Carol Stream, IL: Hope, 1968).

frequently bestowed by liberal Hollywood politicos. As such, the film smashes usual sentimental expectations about the nature of evil, asserting instead Poncelot's very human freedom to make evil choices. As sobering as that portrait is, Robbins simultaneously sets forth a remarkably full-fleshed version of hope, namely, a redemption that is not so much getting a ticket to a scot-free cushy afterlife but finding a new *raison* and manner of being in both life and death. This is nothing new, for it is the pilgrimage specified for all people by traditional Christian theology, though that vision has been badly distorted by the privatism of twentieth-century American revivalism.[9]

The radical nature of this pilgrim transit—informed by a divine economy that transcends human grasp and means—is first to last what the film and Prejean seem fixed upon. Remarkably, the film displays the nature and means of an outrageous God who works outrageously to transform the worst of criminals. And a very great surprise it is. After all, that divine caring goes even to places like Angola's death row and even to the likes of Poncelot, the prodigal lost-sheep rapist and murderer. The criminal and the state's sanitized techno-Golgotha together make a strange venue for love to show up to do its work. Albeit quiet and unspectacular, this is a love that at its core, in its persistence and in its sheer gratuitousness, is breathtakingly wild and plangent. And the story here merely echoes a long and tangled biblical history in which light and love come to a very messed-up humankind, such as Abraham the liar and David the murderer, and on it goes. With Helen Prejean its unassuming handmaiden—who in her resolve and compassion is herself, embodied and present, "Love's pure light," as the carol "Silent Night" puts it—love chases down the prodigal, lost, and late-coming schmuck, and it does fundamentally change how he views himself, others, and what life is for. Light and love come, and he embraces them, plain and simple, in the realm of the self, where "the meanings are," as Emily Dickinson puts it. And best of all, the audience comes to see Poncelot as God sees him, glimpsing in that moment, as does Poncelot himself, a startling and wondrous numinous transcendent gaze that is light of an outrageous holy Love.

9. In a recent collection of essays, *The Givenness of Things: Essays* (New York: Farrar, Straus and Giroux, 2015), 102–7, internationally celebrated novelist Marilynne Robinson, herself a dedicated Calvinist, lays out a scathing indictment of contemporary American evangelicalism as reprobate and bound for hell for its sorrowful neglect of the biblical record on pressing and tragic social crises.

CHAPTER FIVE

WHEN HOPE BREAKS OUT

Love and Redemption in *The Shawshank Redemption*

Most everybody has seen *The Shawshank Redemption* (1994) at least once, and it now, remarkably, resides at the very top of the Internet Movie Database's user-voted list of best films (it did poorly at the box office in theatrical release). It is indeed a truly memorable prison tale full of scenes and images that surprise and move profoundly, and viewers eagerly reference them with delight and considerable passion to explain why they so love the film. There is little question that writer-director Frank Darabont brought vibrancy and depth to Stephen King's rather drab novella, *Rita Hayworth and Shawshank Redemption* (1982).

Much of that vibrancy and depth comes in quiet but dazzling sequences where Darabont deftly melds words and images. An early example comes in a scene where inmates at the prison tar an aging roof. In a simple but eloquent voice-over, one just short of doxology, the film's narrator, Red (Morgan Freeman), praises the pleasures of beer and sunshine. Meanwhile, the camera surveys the inmates' silent contentment as golden sunlight bathes their tired bodies and battered souls. Freeman's soft, melodic voice, Darabont's words, and Roger Deakins's camera together haul viewers into the very same relish and quiet elation enjoyed by the crew. Take one away, and the sequence goes flat. The same three elements shape as well protagonist Andy Dufresne's (Tim Robbins) stunt of piping Mozart through the prison's loudspeaker system. Clearly, Andy himself exults in the music and his prank, and the prisoners in the yard do as well, transfixed and looking upward, arriving as close to a beatific communion of awe and longing as is likely possible within Shawshank's walls. The camera again surveys Mozart's exultant listeners while Red adds his lyrical take on exactly what those "cons" were feeling and thinking.

So good is Darabont that he sometimes shuns words altogether, letting pictures do the talking, as well they should in movies (to be sure, a lot of words usually prepare the way for the wordless). Nothing in the film surpasses the dazzling, even transfigurative, emergence of Andy from the sewer pipe by which he has escaped Shawshank's massive stone walls: he spills into the stream amid pouring rain and crushing thunder, and flashes of lightning, all working, it seems, to shear off the layers of filth and darkness from his two decades in Shawshank prison. In ecstasy he raises his arms to the sky to welcome cleansing, freedom, and the fulfillment of hope. There's hardly anything like it in film, save perhaps George Bailey's run through the snow-covered streets of Bedford Falls following his return to life after a brief glimpse of hell in Frank Capra's *It's a Wonderful Life* (1946). Wonder, awe, gratitude, and elation—all seem to envelop Dufresne. And in what little we see of him post-escape, he seems to waltz his way into freedom and wholeness.

All these sequences are fully remarkable, without question, and they are glowing, mythic moments in the history of popular cinema. Still, the scene that best explains the shape and meaning of *Shawshank*, and adds depth and complexity to these iconic scenes, has received hardly any attention, even from those who have recognized the heavy dose of religion in the film. Nor do viewers usually remember it, for it is easy to glide over. That brief sequence in fact explains the very strangeness in the title of the film—redemption—a term that has perplexed innumerable critics. More than a few have wondered in print just where in the film is the redemption so prominent in the title.

It is there, though, in plain sight. Immediately prior to his escape, Dufresne emerges from two straight months in "the hole," isolation in complete darkness to which prisoners are consigned at the whim of a satanic warden who's fond of quoting the Bible on judgment and damnation. Dufresne ends up there because, after nineteen years in prison, he has run across another inmate who can identify his wife's murderer. That news not only quickly gets the informant murdered by the warden but also lands Dufresne in the hole for merely suggesting that, being innocent, he should get out of Shawshank prison. Unfortunately, Dufresne has made himself indispensable as bookkeeper and investment manager of Warden Norton's (Bob Gunton) corrupt but immensely lucrative penal management practices.

After those two long months, looking wan and spent, Andy quietly announces to his good friend Red, another lifer in for murder, that he did indeed kill his wife—if not literally, then, for sure, emotionally (1:41:33). In explanation, Andy blames his own habitual self-enclosure, meaning his temperamental distance and impersonality, a posture that drove his wife into the arms of a country-club golf pro and the tryst wherein an intruder murders them both. In this regard, Shawshank, this hell of a penitentiary, has proven a purgatory for the shriving of Andy Dufresne's guilty soul, though it took him decades to recognize his own culpability. And given the depth of his obliviousness, it does indeed take all that time and suffering to expose to him a fundamental flaw in his being, namely, the full measure of his own self-contentment and insularity in not recognizing his wife's relational needs. With Andy, though he adored his wife, his own autonomy and self-enclosure equipped him with a superb set of blinders. Amid his own comfortable sense of self-sufficiency, he failed to realize the emotional needs of others. His crime was inadvertent, one of omission, but it proved lethal, both relationally and mortally.

That is not to say that Andy Dufresne is not a remarkable, even splendid, man in just about every way—smart, brave, beauty loving, resilient, grateful, hopeful, respectful, and kindly. Still, in some profound and mysterious way, Dufresne has, while possessing these many admirable traits, lacked human warmth and connection. Self-contained and independent, he has happily lived removed from deep connection with others in what Nathaniel Hawthorne long ago called "the magnetic chain of humanity."[1] Instead, Andy habitually ascribes his murder conviction to a fearsome "storm" of bad luck that has blighted his life (1:42:45). That may be so, but there is a sense in which that explanation entirely misses the mark—and that from so smart and learned a man as Dufresne.

It is in Darabont's scheme that Dufresne's "time" was, given his coldness, a necessary penitential regimen that would bring Dufresne, after much suffering, to an unexpected inner place where he at once recognizes his own transgression and the depth of a new, mature agapic posture, *caritas*, that he learns to bestow on his friend Red. That seems to be the reading that the actors themselves grasped, or at least Morgan Freeman, a fellow who admits to a belief in "Providence" and possesses "deep faith."[2] In a documentary on the making and meaning of the film, Freeman even suggests that prison was the best thing that ever happened to Andy Dufresne.[3]

What is sure, however, is that finally, and paradoxically, two months in utter darkness, an apt image of his own moral state, have shown Andy the "light" or truth of his own darkness. It takes the darkness to recognize light. Having arrived at this juncture of recognition, sorrow, and remorse, having in fact served the dire time necessary to come upon that light, Andy Dufresne escapes two days later, to quote the Gospel of Matthew, "the land of death's dark shadow" that is Shawshank—and the human condition of which it is an expansive symbol (4:16 REB). From there, as Red's narration recounts and we watch, Dufresne travels, possessed of a new fullness of being, to Zihuatanejo, Mexico, a magical land of sun, freedom, and no memory, a land that,

---

1. Nathaniel Hawthorne, "Ethan Brand—a Chapter from an Abortive Romance" (1852).

2. "Morgan Freeman Takes You Through the Wormhole,'" *Talk of the Nation*, National Public Radio, June 1, 2010.

3. "Hope Springs Eternal: A Look Back at *The Shawshank Redemption*" (Warner Brothers, 2004): 15:30. The documentary can be found on the "Special Features" disc of the 2004 tenth anniversary special edition of the film.

like Paradise itself, has wiped away suffering and tears. And it is there, the way paved by Andy, that Red joins him, two friends together sharing their days in sunlight and comradeship.

What King and Darabont have supplied, then, in *The Shawshank Redemption*, unaware though Darabont at least seems to be, is the narrative structure of the classical Christian meta-scheme of redemption: guilt, contrition, and new birth from egoism into love. Much of the power derives precisely from Darabont's deployment of a wonderfully apt symbolic universe to capture the power of this central mythic transit. That scene in the creek, for example, not only rapturously marks Andy's liberation from the unremitting darkness of Shawshank, but it is even more so a ritual baptism in which light, water, and rain wash him clean of what Red calls the "shitty pipe" through which he crawled to new life. He emerges from the stream not only free but also whole, doing justice in exposing Warden Norton, but more than that, renewed and loving, delivered from hell to a radiant kingdom of relish, gratitude, and love.

His dream is to become "welcome" itself, a concierge, a host, taking in strangers in his small hotel on the blue Pacific. If Andy and Red have not quite found the new Jerusalem, what they have made constitutes a close approximation of prelapsarian Eden, a land of delight without enmity or strife and without tears. To be sure, Andy here savors the same deep natural goodness of being alive that he exalted in the memorable scenes in Shawshank, namely, the rooftop beers for his crewmates and the playing of Mozart for the beleaguered denizens of the prison. In the end, though, he achieves a new fullness of being in liberation from his own darkness and into the precincts of human love. That's a pretty good place to end up—and a necessary one. First, though, comes a blind pilgrim's path. Andy's habitual aesthetic relish of the exquisite goodness of ordinary life, as seen in his love for rocks and Mozart, expands to a new fullness of being as he comes to revere and relish similar needs and enjoyments in others.

Death's Dark Shadow

Surely a good deal of the unsettling power of *The Shawshank Redemption* derives from its relentlessly graphic treatment of predatory, mutilating evil in all its ugliest manifestations—institutional, social, sexual, and personal. Darabont stacks up a mountainous cascade of enmity that in one way or another swallows anyone who walks through the gates of Shawshank, whether as prisoner or as guard. The varieties, power, and depth of evil frolic so intensely that evil seems the first and final reality that encompasses human experience. This Darabont renders, with the particular help of cinematographer Roger Deakins, in setting, sound, lighting, action, language, and everything in between. The place itself, like one of the principalities and powers run amuck, mounts a totalistic assault on any shred of kindness or human regard. For one, Darabont's visual and biblical imagery slowly escalates the malevolent Norton from nasty warden to the arch-demon Satan himself, and his prison becomes a hell of perpetual horrific punishment characterized by unrelenting disdain. So insistent is Darabont in flaunting the titanic evils of Shawshank that it seems to constitute a kind of inverse transcendence, a separate, undiluted sphere of malice wholly discontinuous from the usual mix of evil and good that characterizes the range of human experience.

Oddly, as for personal evil, the first glimpse of that is Andy Dufresne himself as he sits in his car drinking hard with a handgun in his lap as the camera crosscuts to the rough passion of his wife and her lover. That sequence and Andy's trial leave little doubt that Andy, no matter how mild-mannered he looks, did his own crime of passion, though looks might deceive. Even good people fall into a rage and do horrible crimes, and this might readily apply to Dufresne, for he looks civil enough, and all the evidence (as much as Darabont gives this early in the story) points to his guilt. Whether he in fact did murder remains one of the central questions in the film—that is, until a young convict's tale of a prior cellmate's tale of his own perfect crime. For much of the film, though, Darabont usefully defers the question of Dufresne's guilt, a tack that differs from King's relatively early announcement of his protagonist's innocence.

For his own crime, be it murder or otherwise, Andy seems to more than pay, running a foul, even hideous, gauntlet of crimes done to him, as they are to just about everyone else in Shawshank. Many are the handiwork of Warden Norton, who seems the incarnation of every imaginable caricature of all benighted, hypocritical Christians whose belief and piety mask ravenous ego, thirst for power, and sadism. In this instance, invoking God or quoting the Bible cloaks a magnitude of evil well beyond the usual Gothic horrors. So extreme is Norton's conduct that it is never really clear if he actually buys anything religious or simply deploys a religious guise to cover his corruption. Whether sane or mad, from start to finish, he's diabolical, ever relishing the pain he inflicts on his wards. While he does not tolerate blasphemy—"Rule number one: no blaspheming"—he blinks not at all at the constant rank obscenities and endless brutal violence directed at the prisoners by the guards or other prisoners; indeed, *The Shawshank Redemption* stands out for the frequency and extremity of its obscenities, in which pious Norton also indulges: "I believe in two things. Discipline and the Bible. Here, you'll receive both. Put your faith in the Lord. Your ass belongs to me" (13:24). The last statement in particular is significant because *Shawshank* is one of the few films about prison life that is forthright about the realities of rape and sexual domination. And Warden Norton himself is not beyond using them as a threat, as he does to Andy when he promises that if he fails to sustain Norton's schemes of graft Norton will cast him down among the "sodomites" where he'll think he'd been "f— by a freight train" (1:39:36). So extreme is Darabont's portraiture of contradiction in Norton that it often seems implausible and fantastic.

Beyond his reign of unholy terror on the inside, on the outside Norton sells his inmates' labor, making them work for slave wages while he rakes off the cream and undercuts the local labor market. In just about every way, Norton seems the full-blown embodiment of the postmodernist and neo-atheist caricatures of Christianity as a cloak for the hegemonic imperialism that in the name of God has ravaged the indigenous cultures the whole world over.

If Norton seems like evil personified, made the more repulsive by his smug piety, his malignancy is multiplied by the institutional system that gives him the domain and prominence to let the abominable run free. Power intoxicates and disinhibits whatever social, legal, and moral restraints he might still feel. The penal system bestows on Norton complete freedom to damn or bless as is his wont, and what human can resist becoming a rule and god unto himself? For his diabolical ends, Norton enlists a cadre of protean guards who set forth to desecrate any notions of penal reform or human dignity. His chief guard, the enormous and vicious Byron Hadley (Clancy Brown), is brutality unfettered, fulminating obscene execrations when he is not physically beating *and* murdering whomever he (or Norton) pleases. On Andy's first night, Hadley gleefully beats to death a timid "fish," as the inmates call new arrivals, for making too much noise while quietly protesting his fate and crying in his cell. And on it goes—*ad nauseaum infinitum*—in what is in just about every way overkill, meaning that the official violence done far exceeds what is necessary to accomplish whatever ends prison is intended to accomplish, in this case, at best, inmate reform or, at worst, simple compliance. That this sort of systemic horror can flourish with abandon and even glee, even among the supposed "good guys," is more than clear given recent terror scandals in the American military treatment of Iraqi prisoners and international terror suspects. Or, for that matter, consider child sexual abuse by priests and football coaches. Or, last, the too-eager compliance of college students in the celebrated docudrama *The Stanford Prison Experiment* (2015).

And what the guards cannot bring themselves to do, they essentially consign to "the sisters," an inmate gang of sadistic thugs, "bull queers," the film calls them, whose delight is ultraviolent rape in which they seem to derive more pleasure from the violence than from the sex. In his first months in Shawshank, Andy suffers their "attentions" to the point that he seems to deflate psychologically. When Andy is nearly beaten to death and spends a month in the infirmary, Hadley and the guards step in—not because they wish to do right but because Andy has become an important resource in helping them with their tax questions and returns. And then the violence swings the other way: in retaliation Hadley beats the sisters' leader, Bogs (Mark Rolston), so se-

verely that he ends up paralyzed and must for the rest of his life drink all his food through a straw. Late in the film, in response to Dufresne's pleas, Norton threatens to remove the protection of the guards and hand Andy over to the violent whims of the "sodomites" for a new kind of hell. Not even Dante's abundantly inventive hell conjured such tortures.

All this transpires in the dreariest of settings. By happy chance, for the prison, set by King in Maine, the production designers stumbled upon the recently abandoned Ohio State Reformatory in Mansfield, a heavy pile of Gothic stone whose very look is forbidding, if not miasmal, a fortress whose glacial heaviness seems meant to enclose and oppress. The wonderful long aerial shot of the place on Andy's arrival, inmates scurrying in the yard, offers a full enough glimpse of its expanse and formidableness. This pall sinks in further still when the audience recognizes the thickness of its walls. And the interiors are no different, full of hard, clanking surfaces and unremittingly dark spaces of drab, cold colors. Inside and out, the only color variations come within an unremitting gray splotched with rust, a scheme that echoes the prisoners' worn denim uniforms. Moreover, the place is notable for its lack of light and warmth of any kind. It is no wonder, then, that its inhabitants dream of sunlight and the blue of the Pacific.

Roger Deakins's cinematography bleeds the palette of any warmth, conjures ample shadow, and often supplies only enough light to make people and events just barely visible, hauling viewers into the very experience of a darkness where all strain to see light of any kind. Even Andy's nighttime liberation in the creek plays in stark black and white, as if Shawshank has permanently stained the prism of the soul. The same is true for the Shawshank afterlife of Brooks Hatlen (James Whitmore) and Red, so much so that Brooks ends up hanging himself from a rafter in a grim boarding-house room. Even after their release, they seem to carry the drabness of Shawshank with them. No small part of the reason that the very end of the film plays so exultantly is that Darabont finally provides a radiant display of sunlight and deep bright color. For inmates and viewers alike, Shawshank seems some sort of vortex that sucks color and life from everything, just as the place itself exacerbates humankind's deepest longings for deliverance from the pitiless, tragic storm that is for most people around the globe what it means to be alive. From start to finish, story and setting cry out for light of any kind whatever, from the physical to the psycho-emotional or spiritual

(Light), anything that will move the deep self from desolation to hope and, better yet, as the film displays in the story of Andy, to love itself.

Mystery Man

Into this world comes Andy Dufresne, an enigma whose mysteriousness from the very first grabs the curiosity of Ellis Boyd "Red" Redding, a savvy and seasoned lifer, whose tender, ruminative narration animates the whole of *The Shawshank Redemption*. Andy is indeed strange, perhaps the strangest "con" ever to take up residence in Shawshank, and lifer Red is probably the one con in all of Shawshank capable of "getting" the strangeness of whatever makes Dufresne tick. Red is some years older, amply smart, and more than a little philosophical himself. In the hands of Morgan Freeman, one of the medium's great actors, the role is splendidly inflected with a mix of wonder and sobriety.

The history is given retrospectively, and meditatively, from the vantage point of the characters' reunion on the shores of the Pacific (Darabont wanted to end the story with the beginning of Red's journey to Mexico in hopes of finding Andy, which is where King ends his novella, but the studio urged a less ambiguous ending that delivered greater cathartic clout, an approach that Darabont first considered warily and then embraced). That last scene is also necessary narratively in order for Red to access much of the information about what happened to Andy in different stages of his story, especially since Andy is not very talkative, or at least not so in his first days in Shawshank. As such, the story runs on a threefold mystery: the riddle of Andy's peculiar, enduringly hopeful self; an account of what both Andy and Red learn in the course of the story—and they both have much to learn; and finally, a memorial to their own redemption into an unlikely friendship of love and mutual care. Throughout, in part because of Darabont's scripting and Freeman's acting, the story plays out in a peculiar zone comprised of both realism and parable, one that lifts the story from the particular into a kind of universality.

The mystery of Andy starts in the first frames. He is a smart and respectable young banker, an early vice president, who is very reasonably convicted, amid protests of innocence, of killing his wife and her lover during a booze-fueled rage. That seems a likely supposition, given the circumstance; by the prosecutor's litany of facts, Andy looks dead-on guilty. Despite that, the audience does not quite buy it because, one, that conclusion runs counter to narrative formula, and two, in Hollywood film nobody this attractive is ever guilty of anything (the chief exception to this is Michael Corleone in *The Godfather* [1974], but then the well-conditioned audience pretty much refused to see his guilt, thus necessitating a sequel, *Part II*, in which Coppola emphatically condemns his protagonist). Red starts his narrative with Andy's arrival at Shawshank with other "fresh fish," and Red wagers heavily that Andy, a "tall drink of water with a silver spoon up his ass," will be the one to break down in tears on his first night in the pen (12:10), but Andy's inner fortitude costs Red two packs of cigarettes.

It is a month into Andy's two consecutive life terms that he first approaches Red, the "man who can get things," the trader in contraband every prison has, to get for him a rock hammer so he can continue his hobby of collecting and carving rock. While entirely civilized, the two are wary of each other, each sensing that he's run into another who's a match for his own capabilities. After all, if Dufresne is the fancy banker on the outside, Red is the inside banker, the chief engineer and importer of the "inside economy" of Shawshank prison. Still, alike as they are in intelligence and practical wherewithal, Red is fully aware of the strangeness of Andy, his detachment from the "normalcy" of prison humanity in particular. After that first negotiation for a rock hammer, as Andy walks away, Red comments that he understands why others thought him snobbish: "he had a quiet way about him, a walk and a talk that just wasn't normal around here. He strolled, like a man in a park without a care or worry in the world, like he had on an invisible coat that could shield him from this place" (28:34). Such are Andy's inner resources: a deep self-contentment combined with irrepressible hopefulness.

That self-enclosure holds up pretty well until the "sisters" get to him, periodically beating and raping, though he tries to fight them off every time they attack him. This continues for two years, and Red suspects that this routine of violent assault will eventually sap all of Dufresne's mysterious inner strength, bringing him to despair or self-destruction. And perhaps Dufresne senses the approach of the end of his resources.

This early juncture in the story introduces two central thematics in the film. In the first, in an amply surprising pivot, given what the audience has learned thus far of Dufresne, the self-sufficient Andy actually risks reaching out for help, and quite a risk it is. Red angles a special roof-tarring detail for himself and his circle of friends, which by now includes Andy. In the midst of their labor on the roof, head guard Hadley is heard complaining about the taxes due on his wife's inheritance. Andy rather daringly leaves tarring to tell Hadley he knows how he can escape paying any taxes, although his first words to Hadley—"Do you trust your wife?"—seem uncharacteristically clumsy, and their implied insult just about gets Andy thrown off the roof (35:34). For Dufresne, the gesture is an admission of his plight and his need for help. Additionally, while Andy's bravado in posing the question is remarkable enough, even more notable is what he requests from the sadistic Hadley as payment for his services, namely, three beers apiece for each of his "coworkers" (36:52). Again, Dufresne reaches out to connect with others, though he seems more than a bit inept in both gestures. In any case, it seems that Dufresne has taken a first small step toward human connection, a suggestion that his self-contented autonomy cannot survive in Shawshank.

The second feature of the sequence is the nature of the "payment," a gesture that elicits from Red a lyrical tribute to the wondrous strangeness of the event, both that it should happen at all and that it should impart such delight and gratitude. Red's voice-over is made the more hefty by echoes of the phrasing, cadence, and imagery of the King James Bible: "And that's how it came to pass that on the second to last day on the job the convict crew that tarred the plate-factory roof in the spring of forty-nine wound up sitting in a row at ten o'clock in the morning drinking icy-cold Bohemia-style beer courtesy of the hardest screw that ever walked a turn at Shawshank State Prison" (37:22). If that were not enough, Red goes on to elaborate on the experience of the event, waxing sacramental, emphasizing their commonality, the inherent dignity, and the goodness of life itself: "We sat and drank with the sun on our shoulders and felt like free men. Hell, we could have been tarring the roof of one of our own houses. We were the lords of all creation" (37:53).

Remarkable for its presence in a mainstream film, the eloquent prose-poem is helped by Deakins's fluid camera. This eucharist of "suds" takes in one man after another in one long take, the camera dollying, panning, and tilting, ending on Red's face in his priestly role attesting to the miracle of creation. The golden sun transfigures the inmates' grime, and the music gently swells and rolls over the scene, imbuing it with the blessedness of the full sweetness of being alive amid the simple, rich pleasures of ordinary existence, "if only for a short while," as Red notes (38:44). Red is more than clear that it is Andy who has delivered the men to whatever they share on that rooftop, which is about as close to heaven as these men get in Shawshank, though Andy's playing of Mozart will bring them another such glimpse from within the hell they inhabit.

What is puzzling about the scene is Dufresne's posture within it, even though his gesture is a first instance of reaching out. Andy Dufresne is still Andy Dufresne, however. Throughout, Andy sits apart from the others, even refusing a beer for himself, saying that he's given up drinking (probably because of what happened the last time he got drunk). His only sign of pleasure is "a strange little smile on his face, watching us drink his beer" (38:09).

The sequence emphasizes the uniqueness of his insularity. Red speculates on his motives for extracting this "payment" from Hadley. After all, it hardly seemed necessary if Andy simply wished to endear himself to the ghastly Hadley, which he did despite his request for payment. Or maybe, Red speculates, he wished to befriend the other inmates, or, finally, just to feel "normal" again. While there is no doubt truth in all three, this last motive signals the right direction.

After all, Dufresne seems to have a profound grasp of the wonder and sweetness of "normal," the gift of the remarkable richness of being alive, a good part of what used to be called "common grace." Others mostly take life for granted, paying it scant attention amid routine. Andy consciously relishes the pleasure found in the ordinary, ranging most notably, again, from rocks to Mozart. Indeed, notably more than Red, Dufresne seems to grasp and savor the exquisite, full goodness and significance of this rooftop celebration. It is not Mount Sinai, to be sure, but for Dufresne it approaches, as imagery used by Red in the first part of his speech suggests, the full goodness of creation itself, the sweet munificent delight of sun and beer and pals, though Andy holds himself at a remove from it all, more the observer and provider than those who partake. The note struck here is Andy's sense of the way the world should be, which is Edenic, full of beauty and majesty in small things and large, and all for human savor. Indeed, Andy's supreme accomplishment, and his own unique and separate source of strength and his much-vaunted hope, is his supreme relish of the goodness of the created world; it is, however, a largely personal and private enjoyment, though he seems repeatedly to want to share it with others. The same is his flaw, for while he properly venerates the gorgeousness of this world, he remains aloof from others even in his provision of something good to share. Dufresne is indeed a strange bird.

This theme of intense appreciation of the present splendor of life brackets its opposite, which is one pole of the ideological melodrama contested at the center of *The Shawshank Redemption*. These realities play off one another, intensifying the existential stakes of survival in Shawshank—and beyond. Following the incident of the roof comes the extended treatment of the opposite, Brooks's institutionalization, specifically the way in which imprisonment slowly devours the appetite for freedom, the ache of longing for a life that allows for imbibing the fullness of life on the outside. In terms of the perception of the world that Andy brandishes, institutionalization depletes the soul's thirst to embrace the wonder and varied glory of being alive. Instead of savor, there is fear. After fifty years in prison, Brooks finds himself paroled into a lonely, fast, and overwhelmingly alien world that both ignores and terrifies him, and finally, quite simply, it is too much, and he opts for "just leaving," so tired is he "of being afraid," as he says in his fare-well letter to his friends back in Shawshank (1:03:52). The pertinence of the Christian notion that "love casts out fear" seems more than clear (1 John 4:18).

To make his point clear, with the thematic of the beauty of being alive front and center, Darabont follows the story of Brooks's mortal inability to handle freedom by showing the portal to wonder and relish. Fear precludes and opposes relish. This thematic comes in the events surrounding Andy's playing of an aria from Mozart's *Marriage of Figaro* over the prison's loudspeaker system. It is a breathtaking sequence. As if some angelic choir were descending from the heavens, the horde of convicts in the yard stop to look upward and listen as the camera itself mounts upward to survey their expanse, and meanwhile in the infirmary the sick rise from their beds and even the guards go to the window to see what the stir might be. It is not the Rapture, as Red jokes at another point in the film, but the effect is one of revelatory magnitude imparting awe and wonder to the stolid but ravening souls of Shawshank's inmates. Darabont's work here, as in the rooftop sequence, leaves off the pedestrian shot/reverse-shot scheme that necessarily characterizes the film in order to wax lyrical visually. And again, Red's quiet eloquence conveys the effect on the host of cons in the yard, and the speech far surpasses his lovely, albeit brief, description of the pleasures of drinking beer on the plate-factory roof. The whole of it, at least for Red, seems liminal; it exposes a borderland between the mundane and some sort of overwhelming numinous beauty:

> I have no idea to this day what those two Italian ladies were singing about. Truth is that I don't want to know. Some things are best left unsaid. I like to think they were singing about something so beautiful it can't be expressed in words and makes your heart ache because of it. I tell you those voices soared, higher and farther than anybody in a gray place dares to dream. It was like some beautiful bird flapped into our cage and made those walls dissolve away. And for the briefest of moments, every last man in Shawshank felt free. (1:09:15)

In *The Shawshank Redemption*, freedom is the capacity to relish beauty, to be taken up by the beautiful bird into a realm of delight, unto ecstasy and joy. It is this belief and expectation of the goodness of beauty that institutionalization slowly squashes to an obscene fear of life itself, and of this the fate of Brooks is the chief example, though later Red will in a fear-soaked freedom contemplate following Brooks's way out. Freedom is a much-bandied and finally vague concept. It is much to Darabont's credit that he repeatedly specifies what that much-vaunted freedom is for—the adoration of the goodness of being alive within the quotidian glories of ordinary life.

The whole time Andy plays Mozart he sits like a king with his feet propped on Norton's desk with that same strange smile that covered his face on the rooftop, and when the warden comes pounding on the door, Andy responds by turning the music still louder, as if to drown out all that Norton embodies, namely, the crushing, demonic aegis of antilife and antifreedom. For that Andy gets two weeks in the hole, but he emerges with that same smile on his face, a phenomenon that launches a long-running debate between Red and Andy over hope and institutionalization. Hope is what Andy has, in spades, and it is nurtured from the depths of his relish for both the ordinary and the exceptional beauty of living. As he tells his friends, the two weeks in the hole were the easiest time he ever did because the music of Mozart embedded in his head and soul got him through: "That's the beauty of music, they can't get that from ya. Haven't you ever felt that way about music?" (1:11:36). While for Andy the recollection of beauty invariably spills into hope, his inmate friends, save for Red, look at him with incomprehension; this response accentuates both Andy's uniqueness in relation to the other inmates and the extent to which the most meaningful parts of his life are interior and solitary, that ambiguous trait that, we soon learn, got him into trouble in his marriage in the first place.

Red concedes the wonder and glory of music, confessing that on the outside he once played a mean harmonica but it "didn't make much sense in here" (1:11:45). In return, Andy argues with as much passion as he shows in the whole film that "here is where it makes the most sense. You need it so you don't forget . . . that there are places in the world that aren't made out of stone. There's something inside that they can't get to, that they can't touch. It's yours" (1:11:55). This Andy names hope, as nurtured by recollection and relish of things past *and* present. Red is incredulous, calling hope "a dangerous thing. Hope can drive a man insane. It's got no use on the inside. You better get used to that idea" (1:12:30).

Red's argument seems to be that cultivating the exquisite pleasures of being, like playing the harmonica, only increases longing for freedom and all the hopes and dreams that will not be realized "on the inside," and thus it only frustrates and depresses. Longing and relish hurt too much. Better to live, he thinks, on the cheap, sleepwalking through the half-life that is prison, even as institutionalization withers the soul, even though that sacrifices one of the core elements of humanness.

The debate continues when Red is again rejected for parole, and Andy presents him with a harmonica, a gesture of affection from the usually reserved Andy that Red very much appreciates. Nonetheless, Red cannot bring himself to play it, either when he receives it or when, later, he is alone in his cell. For him, the instrument becomes something of a symbol of his own reckoning with the conditions and consequences of his life, stirring the roots of what Red was once upon a time, a long thirty years ago on the outside.

Beyond Hope

Nine years later, life in Shawshank takes a dramatic turn for both Andy and Red. Andy has put his time to good use, working as a tax consultant for the guards, minding Warden Norton's accounts, creating a wealthy fictional entity named Randall Stephens to help the warden launder money, and, of special note, establishing a thriving library for Shawshank through which he occasionally tutors cons seeking high school diplomas. For his labors his life turns privileged; he enjoys protection from assault by either cons or guards and all the contraband he wants, and he has cushy work in the library, the newly named Brooks Hatlen Memorial Library, for which he is able to get Red released from his labors in the woodshop. And so things would have gone for the rest of his life if not for a young convict, Tommy (Gil Bellows), who can testify that a former cellmate of his confessed to murdering Andy's wife and lover. But the warden turns a deaf ear on Andy's pleas; this so frustrates Andy that he first calls the warden "obtuse" and then brings up the matter of his graft. This puts Andy in the lightless hole for a month, and then immediately after that come dire threats of the loss of privilege and still another month in the dark.

It is at this nadir of Andy's experience in Shawshank and life, for Shawshank has by now become his life, that two things happen, one followed by the other, and the relationship between the two seems more than coincidental, as suggested at the beginning of this discussion of the film. The first is that Andy emerges from solitary sober and chastened. This time there's no trace of a smile and not a mention of easy time or Mozart. Rather, there's a diminished and self-doubting Andy, one who has finally been caught, perhaps necessarily, by the walls of Shawshank, just as the cramped setting for this sequence plainly suggests (1:40:35).

It is here that Andy confesses to *in effect* murdering his wife by failing to provide emotional intimacy. He was cool, aloof, detached, remote, and his distance drove her to the golf pro and to her death. With that insight, Shawshank has at last become a genuine penitentiary, a place of penance, in which Andy now recognizes, as Red implies, that he has already done penance aplenty, more than enough to account for being a "bad husband" and for the "storm" of bad luck that has engulfed his life. Having finally come upon the recognition of his own guilt and gaping, even lethal, personal shortfall, and having confessed it to another, Andy is now "free," psychically and spiritually, and more than that, ready to be free physically, spiritually, and morally.

And so, amid thunder and lightning, the very groaning of the created universe in which it is rumored God speaks, as with Moses on Sinai, Andy breaks out and free of Shawshank. This happens by crawling through five hundred yards of sewer pipe—an apt symbol for the heretofore unrecognized transgressions of his own life and for the suffering of nineteen years in Shawshank. At last, amid lightning and downpour, he spills into the creek, at which point he tears off his excrement-soaked clothing and lifts his arms to the light and rain as he is washed clean by the waters of rain and creek (though the water of the creek cannot be very clean, given what empties into it). Here Andy in laughter exults, raising his face and arms to the rain and the heavens, for hope has been made real, consummated, new life washing off the old, a notion that derives from orthodox Christian practices of baptism, and it is as striking an image of the meaning of baptism as film has ever conjured (save perhaps for the end of *The Godfather* where Michael Corleone stands as godfather at his nephew's baptism while his goons massacre the opposition).

Fittingly, the sequence perfectly captures both Andy's exultation in the beauty of the moment and, in his gestures, his gratitude and relish toward the heavens, a fitting end that seems to have begun back in his cell where he sat quietly waiting with his hands folded. As his deliverance befits one now properly penitent, Dufresne goes about setting the skewed world of Shawshank aright. One of the more satisfying sequences in the whole melodrama comes in the post-escape account in which ogre Norton gets his comeuppance, and then some.

First comes Norton's recognition of Dufresne's escape, replete with a host of ironies. Andy has departed Shawshank without the slightest trace, and Norton is in a cosmic stew when he throws one of Andy's polished stones at the poster of Raquel Welch only for it to pass through and tumble and echo down Andy's still undiscovered hand-chiseled passage. Though Norton had just seconds before characterized Dufresne's sudden absence as a miracle, this he and everyone else greet with astonishment, indeed, as a miracle, an ironic sort of miracle of persistent, unflagging hope and, ultimately, redemption bordering on resurrection, a point Darabont emphasizes by placing the camera within the cave-like passage to peer out at Norton looking in, a camera shot that recalls the discovery of Christ's empty tomb as seen from within. The point is not that Dufresne is Christ, but that what has happened here is a like miracle accomplished by another means, and in effect a resurrection. And the joke is on Norton, though he is indisposed, to say the least, to laugh at himself. After all, it is Norton who, in a cell inspection earlier in the film, hands Andy his Bible with the comment that "Salvation lies within," never guessing the literalness of the admonition because, as we soon find out, Andy's copy of the Bible hides his rock hammer, the instrument that allows him to chip his way through the gargantuan walls of the prison. Dufresne rightly guesses that the last thing anyone in Shawshank would open is the Bible.

Further justice, and shock, comes when Warden Norton opens his morning newspaper to find headlines—"Corruption, Murder at Shawshank: D.A. Has Ledger—Indictments Expected"—that show that Andy has spilled the beans about Norton's graft. Then, as Norton hears approaching sirens, his eyes turn to the wall safe where he has kept that ledger, the safe aptly concealed by his wife's framed needlepoint that warns, again ironically, "His Judgment Cometh and That Right Soon . . ." (2:01:55). In fact, the approaching police sirens indicate it is just about to arrive. When Norton opens the safe, he finds not the ledger but Andy's Bible with the inscription that recalls the warden's words: "You were right. Salvation lay within" (2:02:16). The bookmark is at the beginning of Exodus, which is also the spot where the hollowed-out pages accommodate the rock hammer. And appropriately, the warden drops the Bible—not that he ever really embraced it, at least not nearly so much as Andy—for the more immediate recourse of a handgun, with which he much prefers ending his life to getting a dose of the "medicine" he has for so long so self-righteously and sadistically administered to others.

This is indeed, as Frederick Buechner has pointed out, part of the great joke of the coming of a divine justice when the last shall be first and the first last, and the mighty fall and the lowly rise, and all brokenness is made whole.[4] Story and script march in lockstep to pound home the surprise and paradox of the coming grace of judgment, here in the relentless action of the God wherein nothing is as it seems and the impossible happens: after all, as Red recollects, it was Andy "who crawled through a river of shit and came out clean on the other side . . . [and] headed for the Pacific," Darabont's apt emblem for the expansive and encompassing realities of divine beauty and divine love, which in this film go hand in hand, two facets of the one reality (2:04:31).

The film as a whole, narratively and thematically, seems a gloss on central biblical notions that receive endless reiteration in Old and New Testaments. The first comes from the beginning of the New Testament and the second from its last book, and they together serve well enough to delineate the wellspring from which King and Darabont draw their imaginative fire. "The people that lived in darkness saw a great light; / light dawned on the dwellers in the land of death's dark shadow" (Matt. 4:16 NEB). This is as well the land of outlandish hope and promise: "These are the men who have passed through the great ordeal; they have washed their robes and made them white in the blood of the Lamb. . . . They shall never again feel hunger or thirst, the sun shall not beat on them nor any scorching heat, because the Lamb who is at the heart of the throne will be their shepherd and will guide them to the springs of the water of life; and God will wipe all tears from their eyes" (Rev. 7:14–17 NEB). These yearnings and dreams assume mythic weight when they shape tales that depict the centrality of humankind's restless search for personal and social meaning and wholeness.

Redemption?

Of course, in Western culture one can hardly tell any story without reference, witting or otherwise, to some biblical concept or another, so

---

4. Frederick Buechner, *Telling the Truth: The Gospel as Tragedy, Comedy, and Fairy Tale* (San Francisco: Harper, 1977), 58.

imbued is the culture with biblical imagery, historical schema, ontology, and eschatology. The challenge for interpretation is to know how hard to push markers, such as images and possible allusions, in the visual and verbal texts, especially after the supposed death of God and the indeterminacy of signs in general. The interpretive challenge is further complicated by the fact that some of these clear references might be inadvertent, the by-product or residue of what has been a culture soaked in the Jewish and Christian traditions.

Most often religious reference seems the remainder of a bygone ethos that filmmakers grab in order to layer some depth and resonance on the frequently very lame, hackneyed stories they tell. The foremost example of this, regardless of whatever else might be said about the saga, is *The Matrix* films (1999, 2003), where the Wachowski brothers raid the Bible (and Greek culture) for the most gravid names they can haul into their text, and so we have a hero named Neo, a self-sacrificing girl named Trinity, a prophet named Oracle, and a ship named after the Old Testament Babylonian king Nebuchadnezzar. Spielberg and Lucas also borrow shamelessly, and no one more so than the makers of *Superman*, whose story from beginning to end rests heavily on the Christ story, an element that the 2006 remake, *Superman Returns*, emphasizes all over again. In light of this often opportunistic resort to literary free-for-all, the viewer must legitimately wonder how much Darabont's use of the expansive, heavy-duty term "redemption" is meant to cue particular readings, especially religious ones, of the film.

In *Shawshank* Darabont seems dead serious, just as he is in his next film, a torturously slow version of another Stephen King novella, *The Green Mile* (1999), starring no less a luminary than Tom Hanks. Darabont's *Shawshank* screenplay is notable in the way it elaborates and makes central minor notes in King's novella, especially on the matter of redemption. In fact, in *Shawshank* there are three and maybe even four different redemptions, depending on how hard one wishes to push the term. The first of these befalls Andy Dufresne, and this seems the most overtly Christian-seeming of the bunch. This discussion began by arguing that the most important scenes in the film comes after Andy emerges from weeks in the hole confessing to Red his guilt for his wife's death, and it is only after Dufresne's remarkably belated recognition of responsibility that he escapes Shawshank, a revelation of sorts that suggests that full humanity or hope depends on acknowledgment of one's limits and offenses and the posture of humility that proceeds from it. It is Andy's insight into a fundamental error of being: "I loved her. But I guess I couldn't show it enough. . . . I drove her away. That's why she died. Because of me, the way I am" (1:41:22). The implication is that, for nineteen years in prison, Andy has misunderstood his time in Shawshank simply to be the product of "bad luck," and suddenly his understanding changes to embrace the notion that somehow this was all some sort of penance that has long since been paid: "whatever mistakes I made I've paid for and then some." As for now, there is the simple yearning "To look at the stars just after sunset. Touch the sand. Wade in the water. Feel Free." That is Andy's redemption, from blindness to sight, from despair to hope, from isolation to relationship. And now existentially free, he is free, in the film's most famous line, to "Get busy living or get busy dying" (1:45:49). Red, of course, institutionalized man that he now is, and having no knowledge of Andy's tunnel, misinterprets that line to conclude that Andy is about to commit suicide, especially after his friend asks for a five-foot length of rope.

The surprise is that Andy did not earlier recognize his guilt, given the character Darabont has developed, for Dufresne is unique not only in his aloofness and detachment but also in his quiet religiousness. This is a note that Darabont adds to the story, for there is not a trace of it in King's novella. This is revealed in innumerable small and large ways, though audiences tend to slide over even rather prominent clues. For one, oddly, Andy's language is completely chaste. In an institution that personifies obscenity and whose wards endlessly spew the rankest obscenities and blasphemy, nary a bad word—not so much as a "darn"—escapes Andy's mouth. The worst he does is call Norton "obtuse," which sounds more like a compliment, given the monster that Norton is. Some of this might be ascribed to class differences, given Andy's background and profession; he simply wishes not to become institutionalized by miming the foul banter and execration of Shawshank. And too, he is an aesthete, loving music and also, apparently, language, choosing to use it with precision and elegance. He'd no more sully a sentence than hear Mozart ill-played.

The language tack makes more sense in light of Andy's exhaustive knowledge of the Bible. When Norton asks for his favorite Bible verse, Andy gives him, from memory, Mark 13:35, which is impressive enough, but when Norton responds with his own, Andy readily identifies exact chapter and verse (49:39). This occurs after Andy has hollowed out his Bible for his rock hammer, effectively gutting it for any meaningful reading. It seems, then, just as Andy has embossed in his head and soul major portions of Mozart because prison is where one needs them most, he has done the same with the Bible, watering the desert of his lostness with it.

Moreover, it is from the Bible that Dufresne, and Darabont, get their talk of hope as an essential category of being, much as playwright and novelist Thornton Wilder mines the term through the whole length of his Pulitzer Prize–winning 1968 novel, *The Eighth Day*, in which the main character, also wrongly convicted for murder, lives a long exile nursing his daily life on hope. The same elements on which his main character sustains himself through long exile—Saint Paul's great attitudinal virtues: faith, hope, and love—seem to inform the core of the screenplay in a way that differs entirely from King's source material. Again, this Darabont puts at the center of his tale. Talk of hope is there in King's novella, but it appears hardly at all till the very end when Red finds himself released and inspired by finding the rock under which Andy hid the key to his safety deposit box (in the novella, Andy does not give Red any specific instruction to find the rock).

The hope for freedom to relish the fullest loveliness of earth's good pleasures—the focus of Dufresne's rooftop and Mozart gambits—sustains Andy each day, just as Wilder's John Ashley in Chile gains fortitude from the recollection of his family in Illinois. And, like Ashley, Andy must learn love, the goodness and rightness of human care, the thing that got him in trouble in the first place in his marital distance. The fruition of this, the farthest destination of love, is Zihuatanejo, which provides Andy with those pleasures he enumerates but also, with the coming of Red, whose way he had prepared, with the depth of human care and veneration that is love, the thing Saint Paul labels the "greatest" of all postures of being. Andy has at last grasped the fullness of love for the earth, which is love for its living souls. Always kind to people, such as Tommy, Red's commentary makes it entirely clear, in the film as in the novella, that much of Andy's do-gooding was simply to keep his mind off his own plight. It is finally with that physical embrace of Red that Andy finds the fullest embodiment, even incarnation, of freedom and hope, which is love. To this extent, Andy Dufresne's story reiterates the classic trajectory of Christian pilgrims, as in Dante's *Divine Comedy*, into the loving mystery of divine presence.

The second redemption comes to Red. If Andy Dufresne enjoys a surfeit of hope, Red suffers a shortfall, inexorably caving in, it seems, to the crushing momentum of "institutionalization," another theme that Darabont extends beyond King in order to highlight the contrasting powers of hope and relish. Red almost goes the way of Brooks Halten in succumbing to the dizzying, deadening forces of modernity, and would have gone there if not for Andy's ploy to extricate him from the powers of death. Andy takes time from the pressures of escape to leave the money and letter beneath that black rock along the stone fence beneath the tree where he asked his wife to marry him. Implicit in this gesture is a roaring declaration of love, though done in the quietest terms. Andy summons Red to sacred personal ground to issue another invitation to deep and lasting relationship, only this time Andy has a better sense of what this amounts to. He and Red express mutual affection clearly enough, though it is in the muted, oblique terms of midcentury male bondedness. Andy's gesture of love rings out, and the ending of the film, first resisted by Darabont, declares that without any ambiguity whatever. Red is free at last, and now perhaps can return to that symbol of hope he once refused, the harmonica. Indeed, one can well imagine, if Darabont were to undertake a sequel, Red sitting on a veranda in Zihuatanejo quietly playing his once-forsaken instrument.

A third clear display of redemption is the legacy of hope Andy leaves behind. The inmates of Shawshank regale each other with tales of Andy's exploits, relishing them over and over again, whether the beer on the rooftop or the building of a library; his miracle-like liberation from captivity recalls the possibility of their own liberation from despair and futility. Andy's course represents a pathway for their own lives.

Last is the fullness of redemption offered in the film's final sequence. The film was to end with Red's words as he begins his long bus ride from Maine to Mexico, and these words express the hope that he too will see the Pacific and all that it represents imaginatively and symbolically. It is, in the end, a hope realized, and no more so than in the quietly rhapsodic walk of Red down the sunlit blue-Pacific beach to where Andy happily toils away refurbishing an old boat. This pure, ravishingly beautiful setting is the place beyond memory and tears, the gift of hope realized in the fullness of love as evoked in the relationship between Red and Andy, a relationship that has been characterized by a history of gifts, whether musical instruments or posters, all of which constitute hints about the nature of the universe—namely, that it is a gift, the profoundest, essential inescapable one, one that at its core is founded in love. In the end is the glimpse of the fullness of the world, the hope of "shalom" that God infuses deep into the souls and yearnings of empty-hearted, hope-haunted humankind.

Some suggest that Andy Dufresne is a Christ figure of sorts, but that simply doesn't wash, since all along *he* is the one in need of redemption, and what suffering and sacrifice he undertakes seem mostly self-wrought for the self. Furthermore, what hope he has is mostly for the liberation of the self, and no matter how much he relishes the beauty of the earth, he has yet to learn love for people. The same bars him from sainthood. What he is, though, is that most common of all types, the pilgrim, the benighted soul thirsting and stumbling his way with hope toward freedom, relish, and relationship. The great surprise for him, religious and self-assured though he is, is guilt, specifically guilt over the failure to love and venerate the inner realities of other people, the lesson he belatedly absorbs as manifest in his tender, trusting relationship with the most unlikely of people, an ill-educated confessed murderer and black man named Red.

CHAPTER SIX

"IT'S TAKEN ME SO LONG TO FIND YOU"

Search and Rescue in Paul Schrader's *American Gigolo*

The opening minutes of Paul Schrader's *American Gigolo* (1980) show a young man on the make who is enjoying the best minutes he'll have for virtually the whole length of the film. For him, in those few minutes, this is as good as it gets, for all is right with the world: he's the darling of his own hard-won universe, and a glittery future is his for the asking. With his long opening credits montage, writer-director Paul Schrader tidily sketches that realm and self of his protagonist's world. Julian Kaye (Richard Gere) drives the Pacific Coast Highway in his fancy Mercedes convertible, top down and hair tousled in the wind. The camera lavishes attention on the details of the car and the driver and the setting, leaping in rapid cuts from one to another much as a lover tries to take in the whole of the beloved. All the while the rock group Blondie belts out the insistent, even rapturous, "Call Me," an apt anthem for Kaye's line of work, which we know well enough already from the film's title. The verses, as also the chorus, could hardly be more pointed, over and over again: "call me" repeats eight times in five brief lines, and of course, at any time at all.

From the seaside cruise the camera alights on Rodeo Drive in the posh retail heart of Beverly Hills, giving it much the same sort of adoring treatment as the coastal drive. Kaye parks his Benz before meeting a much older, even elderly, and markedly well-heeled woman in mink, presumably a client, who accompanies the impeccably dressed Mr. Kaye for a fitting in a very upscale men's store. The whole long sequence ends with the biggest treat of all; the camera dwells on Kaye as he in his ample prettiness simply walks, gliding with quiet elegance, something between a strut and a stroll, to his car after saying good-bye to his benefactress. Not many actors can gambol on the screen and get away with it; Gere does aplenty, and it greatly serves the film. One glimpse of that walk and viewers pretty much know all they need to know, and that does not differ much from Kaye's own self-understanding, as events soon enough demonstrate.

All this sensuous elegance, from the car to the attire and the walk, and all encompassed by that propulsive music, works masterfully to evoke simple, undiluted intoxication with sheer physicality, and especially a very affluent manifestation of it. It is fair to say, even from the many glimpses that bombard viewers in the first moments, and without any dialogue whatever, that Julian Kaye is a fellow who very much lives not only by but also in his skin, a man of surfaces and externals, fearful of the unwieldy inner terrains of the self. Psycho-emotionally Julian *is* carnal pleasure unalloyed, a creature dedicated to the artful bestowing of sensual pleasure, and by such means he defines his "call," the measure of his success, and a standard for his own fulfillment. And he fully savors the tools of his trade, from his own physique to his drawers full of high-fashion shirts and ties. Jay Gatsby had the same, but only because of esteem and longing for Daisy. In this case, there is little discrepancy between the look and the person, Schrader perhaps punning on the opening lyric and Kaye's own sense of vocation (his calling is "call me"). What you get is what you see, and that is the whole of him, at least until late in the film when Kaye turns murder suspect and fugitive, on the run and incognito and trying very hard to look like just the average anonymous blue-collar working guy.

Until that descent, though, Richard Gere is Kaye, with panache in spades, all pretty boy looks and clothes but still very much heterosexual, though that is not where he began. In his portraiture of Kaye, benefiting from his usual cultural prescience, Schrader repeatedly lavishes visual focus on Julian's stylistic *flambeau*, in his style and manner a precursor of the large cultural shift that has since spread the camera's gaze from women to include men, an expansion fueled in part by the emergence of gay culture and new styles of male celebritology (three years before, in *Saturday Night Fever* [1977], John Travolta shook up usual categories of male attractiveness, and at one time Travolta had agreed to play Julian Kaye, only later to back out of the role).

In any case, skin merchant though he is, Kaye does not consider himself, in one of the film's thematic paradoxes, either tawdry or the least bit suspect. Rather, in good American entrepreneurial fashion, he deems himself a man on the rise, fast ascending the distinct tiers of professional success, as is clear in all the conspicuous markers of professional achievement: car, clothes, elegant apartment, leisure, access to the best country clubs, and so on. In most ways, he is a man who at a young age has accomplished a great deal, especially given the distance he's traveled from the scraggly gutters of the sex trade. Rags to riches; up by the bootstraps; self-made by venerable, quintessential American pluck; the American Adam in la-la land—Kaye could be a latter-day Goodman Brown or even Huck Finn, finding a heaven of opportunity in the limitless West. In the late twentieth-century dreamworld frontier, Kaye prospers in the empty underbelly of LA gentility, at least until he turns uppity and offends the powers that indulge the untidy but discrete (and very private) cravings of its often desolate inhabitants. By the conspicuous material standards by which both the culture and Kaye assess themselves, Kaye has indeed made it, and he seems intent on convincing himself of that reality; after all, he has the American male dream, material boy, and that in spades—more toys and ardent women than he can handle.

To his profound dismay, Kaye will plummet from that pinnacle he deems success into a vortex of woe that strips him of every shred of self-sufficiency, accomplishment, and human connection. An unremittingly hostile, omnivorous world, a domain he foolishly trusted, instead proves to be hell itself, abruptly swallowing him up to spit him out of its lesser end, first on the lam and then into prison. Betrayed by a fantasy of success amid a once-welcoming world, Julian proves, astounded and defeated, bereft of any interior resources—imaginative, moral, intellectual, or emotional—with which to revise his estimate of life's meanings and possibilities. It has all gone smash, and as such, Julian contemplates his impotence and nothingness amid the frailty and error of human constructs of happiness and meaning. Indeed, Kaye will find out that he is, as the Heidelberg Catechism so revered by Schrader's Calvinist forebears puts it, steeped in "sins and misery," another way of saying dust and ashes, nothingness, and no measure of fancy goods or studly performance can paste over the errors wrought by Julian's self-deception and conceit.

Amid this collapse, enshrouded by his own forsakenness, Julian finds rescue from a source and in a measure he did not think possible. And in that *American Gigolo* becomes a perfect visual display of the Calvinist tale of radical grace as first limned cinematically by French writer-director Robert Bresson in *Pickpocket* (1959), a structure and thematic on which Schrader has made no less than three films (*Light Sleeper* [1992] and *The Walker* [2007] complete the trio).

At that point of rock-bottom nothingness, feeling utter defeat and lostness, Kaye is rescued by an unforeseeable, enveloping grace not only from imprisonment but also from his own lethal despair into the precincts of uncontainable love. The intrusion is meant to evoke, and indeed it does, the radical care bestowed on humankind by divine love, a love that is fundamentally unimaginable, unforeseeable, supra-rational, and ungraspable, something that ever so wildly retrieves human lostness. The wonder of both Bresson in *Pickpocket* and Schrader in *American Gigolo* is that their tales perfectly convey the experience of the music, texture, and exhilaration of the recognition of that exultant press of love that retrieves the soul from its confusion and hopelessness. That is a long way to go for material boy.

In *American Gigolo*, Schrader crafts a stark parable of descent from preening self-infatuation to, well, nothingness, a condition soaked in despair and futility. Like Gatsby, Julian has paid a terrible price for living too long with a single dream. Strangely, both end up dead, Gatsby floating in his pool and Julian in utter despair in prison. The difference lies in unexpected, and even preposterous, rescue, free and fortuitous, returning the incredulous (and abjectly grateful) Julian to the land of the living—and at that, life as he never knew it before. A fellow who has known and practiced everything there is to know and do within physical intimacy comes upon, finally, a wild, insensible self-giving love, one that freely sacrifices safety, status, and self in his behalf. And it is a long, tangled journey to arrive at this new realm of love and, well, light, light both shattering and transfixing.

Material Boy

No matter his considerable success at the outset of the story, Julian is by no means content, though he hardly knows it, and this puts him in the distinguished company of both cinematic and literary pilgrims. That appears clearly enough in the very first scene after the opening montage when Julian, or Julie, as his partners call him, visits Anne (Nina van Pallandt), the attractive, well-heeled, jet-set mentor-madam and procurer. Her contemporary beach house is elegantly adorned with expensive art and furniture, and two of her female employees sunbathe topless on the deck. For most of their brief encounter, Anne and Julie haggle about splits and fees for his next assignments, a widow from Charlottesville and, following that, someone from Stockholm for whom he is learning Swedish. When Anne resists Julie's request for a larger share than usual, Julie tells her to get instead one of those "high school dropouts you like so much" (4:25), to which Anne throws back: "Look who's talking," pointedly reminding Julie of his own ignominious past and of the debt he owes her for pulling him out of squalor. He relents, but when Anne invites him to join the idle girls on the deck, he scoffs, and when Anne offers to tutor him in Swedish, a euphemism for sex, he refuses, though Anne, as is apparent by her adoring look throughout the sequence, would relish a friendly romp.

The same dispute over money is soon repeated when another of Julie's procurers calls him to fill in for a quick trick in Palm Springs. Here Julie agrees but protests his cut of a mere ten percent of the five hundred dollar fee. Leon (Bill Duke) responds testily till Julie reminds him that Leon is the one who wants the favor.

And so it goes, Julie clearly always wanting more money to support his elegant life. More importantly, however, it seems that he wants, one, independence, saying he "can't be possessed" (22:25), and, two, ever more refined and prestigious gigs, successes that confirm his distance from a not-so-long-ago world of violent sex and back-alley "fag tricks" and "kink," as Julian names them late in the film (1:44:33). Seemingly, the further he gets from those ugly origins, the better he feels about himself, all those material accouterments providing a palpable reminder of how far he has already come and, as he tells Anne, has yet to go. After all, of all of Anne's "resources," only he is admitted to the ultraposh Los Angeles Country Club, where he can troll for new clients with impunity.

Ironically, this very success will also prove to be Julian's downfall, even though Leon warns that he has gone too far in newfound "scruples" that would have him forsake those who helped him up the ladder in the first place (22:15). Anne's clientele comes from a posh, lucrative world far above what Leon can arrange for Julian, a world where that Swedish gig will pay eight grand. For this Julian is more than eager, though Leon warns him, in graphically vulgar terms, that he risks betrayal by all his wealthy clients and by Anne herself. Alas, Julian's own self-confidence is getting the better of him, though that is a possibility that Julie plainly finds difficult to comprehend. As Leon lays out his pointed warning, all Julian can do is smile in self-content at his glittering future (23:40).

Immediately following this cautionary advice, Schrader deftly elaborates on the nature of Julie's pleasure in his own hard-won comfort. A wordless, and dazzling, two-minute montage simply observes Julie as he slowly, deliberately prepares for his night's work while music plays on his stereo and he dances and sings. The closet holds an array of designer sport jackets, and drawer upon drawer display tidily arranged designer shirts and ties. Like a child testing clothing on a doll, Julie happily spreads out on the bed a host of possibilities for that night's work. Schrader's camera lovingly takes it all in. For Julie this is a ritual of pleasure, as he delights not only in the loveliness of his garments but also clearly in what they represent of his accomplishment.

The significance of his elegantly but casually appointed apartment, another artifact of character that Schrader constantly surveys, comes

clear when an unexpected and unwanted woman visitor shows up. Julie tries to send her away, telling her that "This is my apartment, women don't come here" (27:05). For Julian the apartment, as much as his inner life, or what there is of it, comprises a separate sanctum or retreat walled off from "work" and women and maybe even himself. The apartment has become a shrine of sorts where Julie seemingly exults in the surfaces of self-portraiture.

So also later, when the same woman, whose introduction will come forthwith, asks in postcoital chat where Julian is from, he replies that he is "Not from anywhere. From this bed. Everything worth knowing about me you can learn by letting me make love to you" (39:05). The limits of that self-description appear starkly clear later when the one woman about whom he begins to care complains that when he makes love he goes "to work," sealing himself off, maintaining control and power by refusing to receive pleasure (1:02:30). The truth of this he finally admits, and he fully knows what is at stake: "You're talking about me giving up what I am, what I do" (1:03:00). "It's all I'm good at," says Julie. Indeed, in that same conversation Julie reports his skill at bringing sexual climax to women who have long gone without.

In such statements Julian again echoes Jay Gatsby, also of humble origins, defining himself almost entirely by what he possesses—mansion, clothes, cars, parties, and "gonnections," as gangster Meyer Wolfsheim puts it—and what he wants, the unachievable Daisy. Much like Gatsby, Kaye reveals a remarkable lack of interiority in which the self achieves solidity almost entirely by exterior material standards of what it does and owns. The apartment constitutes a separate, inviolate realm, something akin to Gatsby's famous green light, the closest thing Julian has to a self, externalized and prettified. And, like Gatsby, the goal of achieving identity by palpable goods will prove elusive, probably delusory, and ultimately fatal. There is only the vague expectation that ever more achievement will effect a magical completion of some sort. Midway through the film when Julie argues with Anne about working only for her, he explains that he cannot because "Things are different now. I'm more than what I used to be. I'm getting older, Anne, gotta keep moving, forward, just move," though Julie could not guess where exactly he wants to end up (1:00:32). This restless, ceaseless search for God knows what leaves Julie ill equipped for the storms that follow, storms that show just how flimsy a structure Julian has unwisely built upon sand (Matt. 7:24–27).

Storm

From his charmed pinnacle Julian Kaye is headed into a maelstrom the likes of which he never dreamed, even amid the cautions from Leon and Anne. It is partly his own doing in his thirst for autonomy, but at the same time there seems to be a special devouring malice in the retribution that engulfs him. In part because Julian is out there on his own, having severed the ties of business and sponsorship that assisted him in his rise, he is susceptible to disposal, either to protect others or to be rid of him as an obstreperous nuisance. After all, as his "friend" and occasional employer Leon tells him, Julian is "frameable" (1:44:58). And before long, Julian finds himself a prime suspect in the sex murder of a onetime client, the "violent trick" that Julie took on to do Leon a favor. A couple of days after Julie's peculiar Palm Springs tryst (the watching husband instructs Julie to beat his wife during sex), the woman dies from sexual assault. Though it allows viewers to wonder for a while, the film eventually makes clear that Julian did not commit the crime, though he lacks an alibi for that night. And when he petitions others for that crucial alibi, they all, as Leon predicted, desert him without a twitch of hesitation or remorse. This is the unimaginable hell into which an increasingly desperate Julie descends, through one ring of

146

desertion and terror after another, all seemingly designed to teach him lessons about human connection and about a voraciousness of evil that shreds his outsized sensually charmed existence.

In the tightest plotting of any of the films Schrader has both written and directed, Julie moves from seeing the initial police inquiries as a minor annoyance to the alarming recognition that he is "in a frame," a predicament that leads to desperation and terror as his entire array of professional "friends" deserts him. The descent is not pretty to watch, Schrader masterfully, and slowly, upping the stakes. After the conversations with comical but dead-serious Detective Sunday, wonderfully played by Hector Elizondo, and the searching of his apartment by the police, Julian petitions Anne for help, but she insists that Julian work only for her.

After a lineup, Julian is informed that the search of the apartment turned up handcuffs with the victim's fingerprints, and that Sunday, who has acted like he is Julian's friend, thinks he's guilty as hell itself. Julian then flees to the estate of the wealthy client seen in the film's opening and on occasion thereafter, in whose house he was on the night in question. Amid the twilight, she is upset that he gave her name to the police, impugning her reputation, after which her husband comes to the door to give her an alibi. That night Julie is confronted by would-be Senator Stratton (Brian Davies) at a fancy LA country club, where Stratton threatens Julie with the loss of the "good graces" of LA's wealthy, who allow him entrée into their world of glamour and wealth. To his credit, Julian does not back down, telling Stratton that he and Michelle, Stratton's wife, see each other because they want to.

From that point to virtually its end, *American Gigolo* hugely darkens in plot, setting, lighting, and palette, as Julie moves from his fancy sunlit world to the violent nightmare of LA's sexual underground. Desperate evil is not in the least contained or shrouded in that world; the polite, sunshine world differs little but bothers to mask its predilections behind facades of social nicety and conventionality. Amid his peril, Julian searches for Leon in the underground of LA's gay nightclub scene, places where Julian, with his exalted status, no longer works, in this instance a darkly lit macho S&M bar where Leon is showing off his "new little boy," as one patron puts it (1:21:22). Kaye has even less success with him than with Anne. When Leon barters with Julie—you do my tricks and I'll do your alibi—Julian still rebels, no matter the deep trouble that has beset him, telling Leon that he's "sick of doing your shit," meaning "no more fag stuff, no more kink" (1:23:25). Leon avers that's he's only being fair, for "how do you expect me to help you" if Julian will not help him (1:24:00). It is, alas, a relentless mercantile world of mutual allegiance dictated entirely by self-interest and profit, and that ethos effectively dooms Julie in his pride of accomplishment and autonomy.

As if this were not bad enough, Julie spies Leon's "new boy" lurking about his apartment parking garage. Now engulfed, justifiably, by an ample dose of paranoia and dread, Julian proceeds to rip apart his own cherished refuge in search of planted evidence, specifically the jewels that were supposedly taken during the murder for which he will be charged. Through his search, as a marker of his worsening plight, the apartment is half-lit and striped with the shadows of window blinds, a device Schrader has used before in the film, foreshadowing not only Julian's eventual imprisonment but, more importantly, his own imprisonment in the limits of himself. As Julian searches, crawling the walls of his apartment like an insect, his frustration slowly morphs to full-blown rage, and he begins to throw vases and rip audio equipment from shelves; all those baubles and toys his career has bestowed on him that have become emblems of his achievement and independence now offer no protection. They have become meaningless and hostile, the very attractions that have eventually plunged him into the very pit that seeks to devour him. His search ends when he again crawls, this time ripping apart his sacred Mercedes, destroying yet another symbol of what has invested his life with meaning. Sliding beneath, even though nicely dressed, he finds taped to the undercarriage the jewels from the murder, and Julian now knows for sure that someone is working hard to frame him. Wisely, and symbolically, he goes incognito, donning gray workman's clothes and driving a cheap rental car, leaving behind for good all the prizes of his gig-hood. Fugitive that he now surely is, he rides through the garish fluorescent dark. The golden land has come to look like hell itself.

The last circle of Julian's descent comes in Anne's renunciation of him, especially since Julian in his flight has neglected a client Anne has taken six months to arrange: "I'm through with you, Julian. You'll have to fend for yourself. I don't care what happens to you anymore" (1:37:01).

Then, finding Leon in his gaudy high-rise apartment, Julian grovels, begging for his life back, offering to give Leon his savings of thirty grand and agreeing to "break in new boys for you. I'll work just for you . . . 50-50 split. . . . I'll do anything you want me to do" (1:44:08). To all this Leon has one simple and consistent answer: "It don't make no difference how much, Julie. The other side will always pay more" (1:42:40). As for the reason for Julie's plight, Leon simply states the obvious: "because you were frameable, Julie. You stepped on too many toes. Nobody cared about you. I never liked you much myself. Now get out." Unfortunately, as Leon himself exits to walk onto his balcony to watch below the real murderer, his "new little boy," Julie angrily pushes him and, inadvertently, over the railing he goes. Julie grabs his legs, only to have Leon slide out of his fancy boots to fall to his death many stories below. His fate sealed, Julie returns to the darkened living room, where, appropriately, he sits on Leon's black snakeskin couch, a boot in his hand, waiting for the police to show up. For a full thirty seconds the camera slowly retreats, watching a plain-looking Julian slumped, defeated, resigned. As the camera retreats, Julian in gray, engulfed in the cavernous darkness of Leon's apartment, blackness ten times black, as Melville said of Hawthorne's work, he literally shrinks (the camera retreating), as if imploding as the last ember of self wanes (1:46:30). For Julian, ever naïve and hopeful, this is malice unforeseeable and unimaginable. Hell has come and swallowed him whole.

From there, in jail, Julian simply goes silent and still. This new inertness in a man who has embodied hustle and swagger gives an apt

indication of the obliteration that evil has wrought on him. Julian even refuses to help his lawyers mount a defense, though one wealthy client, Michelle Stratton, has offered to foot the bill for a high-priced celebrity defender.

All would indeed be lost, and Julian would rot away his life in prison, if not for, in the terms of Schrader's Christian parable, the coming of a radical love—unforeseeable, welcoming, and enveloping. Michelle's words in response to Julian's query as to why she cares fathom the Christian mystery of inexorable divine self-emptying and sacrifice, the crux of orthodox notions of the meaning of an incarnation, are simply "I had no choice. I love you" (1:53:22). This Julian gladly receives, and at last discarding his prized autonomy, he gladly relinquishes himself. The film's last words are Julian's words, adapted from the end of Bresson's *Pickpocket*: "My God, Michelle, it has taken me so long to come to you" (1:53:36).

Love Unbidden

That homecoming arrives embodied, in and through another person, therein amply illumining the relational crux at the core of Christianity's metahistory (in this view final reality is neither material nor spiritual but relational and reciprocal, as represented in the incarnation and the eventual sacrifice of Jesus in the crucifixion). And like that ur-story, love comes slowly, welling up through the most unlikely sources and circumstances, as in the biblical incarnation. Indeed, within the rich imaginative possibilities in the many parables of Jesus that give dramatic shape to the nature of God, Julian clearly becomes the one lost sheep for whom the shepherd risks everything (Luke 15:1–7). Also fitting is the story of Jesus's encounter with the adulterous woman at the well (John 4:1–26). Most fitting of all, though, is the account of the woman about to be stoned for adultery but who is instead, while at death's door, made free and new, in spite of her own misbegotten self, by a blinding gesture of rescue and welcome (John 7:53–8:11). This at last is something to which Julian, thirsty gigolo control freak that he is, can wholly, in its self-giving splendor, give himself, unhesitatingly and unreservedly.

That person is, of course, the lovely, and very lonely, wealthy woman who resolutely pursues Julian through the first part of the film, though it is by no means with any intention of saving him from anything. Far from trying to redeem Julian from his life of perdition, Michelle Stratton (played by fashion model Lauren Hutton) wants more and more of him, even to the point of actually wanting him himself, as a person, far more than merely the well-crafted body, fancy attire, faux sophistication, and, most of all, sexual pleasure from a pro. The wife of a Kennedy-esque state senator with his sights set on Washington, Michelle first sees Julian in an ultrachic hotel bar that seems eerily engulfed in a warm, deep pink, an appropriately exotic setting for their first encounter. Both alone, Julian sees a likely client, but when Michelle gets over-bold, willing to pay for "just one f——," Julian backs away, offended by the indelicacy of the proposition (16:05). Unfortunately for her, her approach is exactly the sort of street-dealing crassness that Julian is trying to escape, and he politely rebuffs her.

Not taking no for an answer, Michelle tracks down the secretive Julie, learning exactly who he is and where he lives and showing up at his fancy apartment just as Julie is about to leave for a night's work. Once inside, she in effect begs for his "attentions," dropping her bravado to show desperate need for some measure of human connection. Such is her desolation and thirst: she is caught in a loveless, high-profile marriage to a man-on-the-make narcissist who sees her as an attractive and necessary prop in his own rise. And much against his principles, Julie relents, for his apartment is a place where he keeps his inviolate self and where women never enter. Something in Michelle's undisguised vulnerability and hunger, something well beyond mating games and mere physical desire, strikes some chord deep within Julian, more than likely one he has never before heard or felt within himself.

And against all odds, the relationship becomes just that, a relationship, much to Julian's surprise and the audience's. At least some of Julian's eventual welcome of Michelle lies simply in his desire to prove himself yet again. He is, after all, the sex pro who takes pride in performance and success. There is, though, in Julian a minor note that responds, simply put, to need. This he confesses to Michelle after another encounter in which she has again come in petition. Julian tells of an older woman, long neglected by her husband, for whom he has labored long to bring a measure of sexual satisfaction. As he tells Michelle, "Who else would take the time, cared enough to do it right?" (40:25). And her genuine liking and gratitude for Julian both surprises and ingratiates her.

Julian himself is taken aback because Michelle does seem to care about the actual person Julian, a posture that is very different from what we see of his "work" relationships, which seem comprised of boy-toy sex dalliance, some polite and some bluntly vulgar. Uncharacteristically, at least for Julian's "trade," Michelle seems to want to engage who he is as a person, however clichéd that might sound. He skitters away and gets ironic when she wants to know about his past and where he is from. Julie is not used to these sorts of questions that probe beyond his usual hooey about being from France. Julie is clearly not used to caring *for* himself, and he clearly does not know how to receive that. Given Julian's humble beginnings on the street and the self-loathing that sometimes seems to run just below the surface, this is new territory. Moreover, Michelle pushes Julian toward personal candor and honesty, especially on the relationship between the personal and the vocational, so to speak. While he pushes Michelle toward self-care in her marriage to "take your pleasure when you can," he himself is not good at self-care, except in the most superficial ways (52:22). To her question of "How about you? Where do you come in? How do you get pleasure?" there is no answer, for Schrader cuts to the police station and a shot of the handcuffs used in the murder of Mrs. Rheiman (52:27). That cut serves as a possible answer to Michelle's question, though it is not the one right or complete answer.

How substantial the barrier is for Julian and for Michelle becomes clear when she, late in their relationship, in a pivotal scene, refuses to make love, which is itself a reversal of the dynamic that first attracted her to Julian. She now complains to Julian that "when you make love, you go to work" (1:02:30). In the middle of the frame, spread out on the bed, as if the shot is to recall Julian's statement that he is from this bed, Julian plays dumb, deflecting the charge, as he typically does when pushed, but then, finally, in a rare moment of honesty, he admits the truth of her charge. The point here is not the revelation that Julie has difficulty dropping his professional detachment, but that Michelle cares enough to push him to deal up front with the guises and limits of his own person. As an exemplar of prototypical American man-on-the-make individualism, Julian has a difficult time moving beyond the instrumental to genuine intimacy. And this he knows: "You're talking about me giving up what I am, what I do." And having come that far in candor, Julian admits that "I care about you, I really do . . . [but] it's all I'm good at" (1:03:10). Michelle is not happy, though, with the expression of care for her; she wants more, the actual real Julian, though he contends he cannot leave his world because "the people I know care about each other" and take care of each other, and he now needs their protection.

Such blatant concern for Julian and the relationship dents the barriers of Julian's well-fortressed self, as does the countermovement, namely, the increasing danger of a murder charge. Much of the remainder of the film chronicles Julian's mounting recognition of the startling reality that these supposedly caring sponsors and suppliers are either orchestrating the frame-up or acquiescing to it. It is no wonder, then, with all his assumptions about the world turned upside-down, that Julian ends up betrayed, defenseless, and defeated, an ordinary human engulfed by devouring enmity. That is, save for Michelle, who will not let him alone no matter what he tells her.

What he does tell her in a last, wholly accidental meeting before his arrest is: "Just stay away from me. . . . I'll ruin your life, your husband's. It's all over" (1:38:20). However, Michelle will not be deterred, in what amounts to a foreshadowing of the end of the film. Julian grabs her roughly to demand that she tell him she knows he's innocent. Her unhesitating reply is a simple "Yes," a simple word that seems to knock Julian over, for he's never ever before run across this kind of affirmation and trust, a plain, simple belief in his value (1:38:38). Indeed, he's at a loss for words, half angry at her for believing in him more than he does himself, telling her as he hurriedly leaves, "Forget me. I never loved you" (1:38:48). And that is exactly what she will not do.

For the climactic scenes of the film, all set in the jailhouse, Schrader both slows and quiets the film, inserting long tracking shots and stills, three-second fades between scenes, and long pauses in conversation. Moreover, the setting itself seems the fruition of Schrader's visual motif of bars, enclosure, and imprisonment; Julian here, though, has become everyman, acknowledging the reality of everyone's existential reality, isolated and cast out, imprisoned, inert, and futureless. The slow pacing generates a sense of momentousness, especially in contrast to the increasingly fast-paced suspense of the last half of the film. In the first scene of the closing sequence, when Michelle unexpectedly comes to visit the imprisoned Julian, she informs him that she has decided not to go abroad, as she had promised her husband; the breaking of her solemn spousal pledge is another gesture of her concern for Julian. While Julian tells her not to come back, when the guard comes to indicate the end of visiting hours, he spontaneously, desperately blurts out, "Don't go, Michelle," a rare expression of actual need on his part. Clearly conflicted between his own despair and the hope and comfort Michelle represents, he emphatically tells the fancy lawyer hired by Michelle not to bother, and tells Michelle, through the lawyer, to forget him.

All that resignation goes smash when Michelle quite literally gives up her life of comfort and status to provide Julian with an alibi that will free him. In the stunningly eloquent last scene, a humbled Julian asks Michelle, separated still by the jailhouse glass, why she did it. Her response is simple, direct, and laden with parabolic theological meaning: "I had no choice; I love you," gigolo and accused murderer though he is (1:53:22). Such radical self-giving seems to be the nature of genuine love, and of the sort that only a radically kenotic God can muster; it is diametrically opposite to the paltry sort of loving Julian has dispensed. Authentic love, different also from the self-interested business interdependence of Julian's world and, for that matter, Michelle's husband's world, plainly and fully sacrifices all for the other, and this is what Michelle has done, as her name well indicates. In Hebrew, Michael is the angel "who is like God." It is more than appropriate when Michelle shows up at Julian's door in the middle of the night that her first words are "I'm Michelle," which proves to be the case within this searing parable (26:24).

The words "I love you," much like Michelle's belief in his innocence, seem to lash Julian across the face, for he reels slightly, closes his eyes, and shakes his head as if at once both denying and savoring. And Schrader, in the film's last line, makes the God reference still more overt, as Julian says to Michelle, though he has put down the phone, while slightly shaking his head as if in incredulity: "My God, Michelle, it has taken me so long to come to you" (1:53:36). After that, in the film's most telling gesture, Julian smiles slightly and then slowly lowers his head to rest it on the glass where Michelle's hand rests, allowing himself finally to bask and revel in its embrace and its meaning, though the glass separates them still (and the glass is clear, no longer dark, obviating St. Paul's caution that in this life we invariably see through a dark glass [1 Cor. 13:12 KJV]).

Julian has at last found something that infinitely surpasses and alters any previous notion of what love might be, though he has had to lose everything in order to find and exult in this unforeseeable gift. Schrader underlines this finale with the synthesized organ music that

has resonated through the film, here finally welling upward in volume and morphing into a strangely hymn-like melody and fullness. That solemnity continues as the screen fades to black and the credits begin to roll.

Fini

Coming to Julian to save his skin and soul is that very thing that "All my life I've been looking for," though Julian has had no idea of "what it is" (1:26:32). And to his restless, thirsty soul the deliverance comes in Christic form, plainly announcing that "I'd rather die" than forsake him (or humankind), and in fact, while Michelle, who is like God, does not quite die, she does give up just about everything—privilege, status, respect, wealth, power, glamour, *ad infinitum*—to embrace ignominy as the mad woman who throws it all away for a murdering gigolo who has only recently crept up from the sewers. It is the intrinsic, inexorable character of God, Schrader suggests with this scenario, to simply care, irretrievably, no matter what, for whomever, against all measures of common sense. Michelle substitutes her loss for Julian's crimes, legal and otherwise. Apparently, it takes this much to reach the likes of Julian, who has imploded after a dream gone smash. The society dame's self-sacrifice is the completely gratuitous gesture that addresses Julian's profound sense of worthlessness in himself and existence as a whole. For him, captive and bound as he is, the deed is finally, simply there, dead center in front of him, inescapable, unimaginable, and ungraspable, and it does welcome and redeem, as seen in Julian's glad, smiling acceptance of the soul's pleasure in the fullness of Michelle's love for him. There is more to him, finally, than his skin and sexual prowess, though he has terrible difficulty in believing that very different kind of proposition. Those last words—"It has taken me so long to come to you"—recall Augustine's famous dictum that the heart is restless till it finds its rest in God. In this, though, he can rest and repose, knowing there is love even for the likes of him, rejected and woebegone though he be. Such is the gist of Schrader's remarkable parable of love gone right.

CHAPTER SEVEN

"HOW HIGH CAN I FLY?"

Murder and Sacramental Ascent in Tom Tykwer's *Heaven*

Right at the start, at the close of its opening scene, *Heaven* (2002) poses the question directly—nothing roundabout, or fancy, but right there, up front, uttered by one of the story's two central characters. It is a logical sort of question in a simple scene that seems innocuous, a throwaway unlikely to have much consequence for anything that follows. In fact, the viewer is even likely to forget the question and even the scene (it was added after the film was shot to clarify its ending). That sort of forgetfulness, however, especially when entering the cinematic world of screenwriters Krzysztof Piesiewicz and the late Krzysztof Kieslowski, can make for a usually fatal error, for their fictive world is dense with meanings of all sorts—meanings hidden, strange, unforeseeable, and, ultimately, deeply sacramental—and nowhere more so than in *Heaven*, a film shot after Kieslowski's tragic early death in 1996 by well-known German director Tom Tykwer (*Run Lola Run* and *Cloud Atlas*).

As brief production credits eke by on a black screen, the faint sound of helicopter rotor blades loudens, and the screen turns to the greenish landscape of a flight simulator in which a trainee tries to fly his craft over a computer-generated landscape of ever-higher hills. When the student pilot flies too high, the faux machine crashes, the simulator screen going black, prompting what will prove to be the film's central question: "How high can I fly?" (2:42). So ends the prologue, the black screen again briefly overlaid by credits and then the sound of a ticking clock.

A dissolve moves from darkness to the blonde hair of the film's protagonist, Philippa Paccard (Cate Blanchett), a very frustrated but deliberate elementary school teacher who is preparing a homemade bomb. The bomb is intended, we soon discover, for the high-rise office of a businessman named Vendice. Only later do we learn that this fellow's commercial respectability has cloaked his success as a drug-trade kingpin in the northern Italian city of Turin.

This descent into mayhem and murder seems a long way from heaven, or any soaring high, and so begins, cryptically, the story that will offer a wild and improbable metaphysical journey to answer that very mundane, ordinary-sounding question about altitude and personal survival: Given the troubles of this tear-sodden earth, how does anyone fly? And by what means, if any, do we fly—really, really fly, as suggested by the film's peculiar title? All the way to heaven? Very strange indeed.

Only much, much later—actually, only in the story's very last frames—does all circle back to the beginning to raise again the question of how high one can fly, although by the end the notion of flight has assumed a wholly different meaning. Only then, at long last, does the pertinence of that question come fully clear, and then stunningly, unimaginably so. And so it is, as Stephen Holden of the *New York Times* concludes, that *Heaven*'s account of "romantic and spiritual transcendence" leaves one "breathless."[1]

As far as endings go, *Heaven*'s denouement astonishes in its boldness (only *Places in the Heart* [1984] rivals it). An ending that no one could possibly foresee illumines—and goes so far as to wholly re-envision—the significance of everything that has happened before. That conclusion asserts a kind of retroactive refractive power, transposing and even transfiguring the meaning and significance of everything that has preceded it. In a "certain slant of light," in Emily Dickinson's memorable phrase, ordinary, unremarkable events assume wholly different meanings. What seems ordinary, and even incidental, abruptly goes fraught. Here the light shed is metacognitive and transfiguring, the world suddenly assuming a wholly different, and radiant, guise. In *Heaven*, what seemed throughout like plot contrivances transmute to

---

1. Stephen Holden, "Film Review; When Fate Intrudes, Death on Screen as Well as Off," *New York Times*, October 4, 2002, http://www.nytimes.com/movie/review?res=9B07E2DF1F38F937A35753C1A9649C8B63.

necessary passages in a lambent sacramental ascent. In *Heaven*'s last few seconds—surprise—*Heaven* answers its own question, to which— surprise—heaven is the answer. That's how high one can fly, and the route there and what makes heaven heaven constitutes the great wonder of the film, both as story and as cinematic achievement. In this case, remarkably, it has nothing to do with an otherworldly realm of bliss and forgetfulness, and everything to do with the despair and elations of the human self. Nor does heaven have anything to do with a metaphysical locale or postmortem existence, and everything to do with a particular ferocity of love in being alive. Stranger still, the route there is ascent by means of sacrament, specifically by means of Christendom's oldest passages on the route toward fullness of being and Light, meaning the realization of Love itself, and a wild, unimaginable journey it is.

Traditionally, the term "heaven" has denoted an otherworldly spiritual realm of blissful reward above and beyond earth and mortal life to which the faithful journey after death. In *Heaven*'s central surprise, writers Piesiewicz and Kieslowski, and director Tom Tykwer, flip that over, yanking the essential character of heaven down to earth, seeking to dramatize and thus clarify the psycho-moral necessity of a very this-worldly, fully embodied posture of radical love and belovedness. Here love is brought down and enacted, effecting heaven, a full experiential realization of a redemptive sacramental journey, and heaven as another extraworldly destination comes to look anticlimactic.

All of that happens in the here and now, and the great accomplishment of the film is that this arduous journey is made palpable, plausible, and very fleshly, ending in relational physical consummation and then ascent. Indeed, it presents a wild rupture with the mundane ordinariness of living insofar as one arrives finally at personal and relational newness and wholeness—an inmost condition of conciliation and relational wholeness accesses the very inmost nature of divine reality. Here the arduous path to that destination is marked by Christian sacraments of confirmation (Eastern Orthodoxy fittingly calls it chrismation), contrition, forgiveness, reconciliation, Eucharist, and union, all necessary passages to achieve holiness (wholeness), a beatific rupture with enmity and despair. It is divine Love that, in the profoundest, agapic sense of the word, re-forms the individual self to love others, even the outcast and criminal in a very broken world. One critic has aptly labeled *Heaven* a "philosophical parable," one that here assumes a distinctly Catholic Christian itinerary and flavor.[2] The screenwriters embed their characters firmly within a sac-ramental journey that finally brings them to an exultant blessedness (for lack of a better word) that imbibes and manifests divine love and delight. Again, very strange.

That sort of "spiritual" destination is a stretch, needless to say, for any art form, though particularly so for film, a very modern medium whose success from the first has by and large depended on its capacity to convey this mundane, quotidian material world. Infusing film stories with some element that is essentially nonvisual, invisible, or transcendent has been a risky enterprise, yielding many sanctimonious clunkers. The accomplish-ment of *Heaven* lies in sliding viewers, virtually unbeknownst to them, into the glowing core of the Jewish-Christian understandings of divine care for a lovingly created but now sorely broken world. The film argues that, yes, God is love; indeed, virtually *everything* in the film works to foster a warm, radiant translucence that in some measure inducts view-ers into a liminal zone of apprehension of a numinous reality. Against all odds, with remarkable cinematic ingenuity, *Heaven* configures divine presence, especially pictorially and musically, as lovingly, intimately en-meshed in individual destiny and events so to bring souls to comprehend the wonder of being and the call of Love. With Tom Tykwer's ingenious di-rection, *Heaven* slowly but very surely, and with fetching cogency, morphs from what seems for a long while like a mostly conventional, albeit grip-ping, crime-and-escape romance into an exultant, pluriform meditation on the mystery of love, particularly the ever-strange admixture of human and divine love. For this, Tykwer deploys a wonderful array of cinematic strategies that slowly mount and gather to achieve by the climax a clam-orous, numinous heft. All leads to that radiant closing ascent in which viewers sense what the redemption of the world might look like, even for the likes of the murderous Philippa Paccard.

Crime and Punishment, Sort Of

Before ascent, however, there is descent from which the protagonist must rise, and in that journey we witness the encroachment of a mea-

---

2. Jonathan Rosenbaum, *Chicago Reader*, October 18, 2002. Quite the opposite view was set forth by Owen Gleiberman of *Entertainment Weekly*, who deemed *Heaven* "softheaded metaphysical claptrap." October 25, 2002, http://www.ew.com/article/2002/10/25/heaven.

sure of hell in multiple relentless, devouring fractures of this world. And, frankly, from that vantage point notions of love or heaven have neither bite nor credibility. So it is in any serious rendition of darkness. While the opening sequence tries to fly too high, to escape this world, the story itself pivots abruptly, and scarily, to the very earthbound assembly of a bomb, the bomb maker attaching a timer to a small block of plastic explosive. As the credits eke out, we track the maker, the fierce, very resolute Philippa, played by the dauntless, peerless Cate Blanchett in a startling display of her quicksilver emotional intelligence. We follow her from apartment to bus to a fancy high-rise office building where she deposits her bomb in the inner-office wastebasket of the respectable-looking businessman she apparently wishes to kill. All would end well, at least from her perspective, if it were not for the pure happenstance of a janitress soon after emptying the wastebasket into her trash cart before boarding an elevator already occupied by a father and his two daughters visiting the building for the pleasure of riding its glass-enclosed exterior elevator. The lengthy sequence zips along with the suspense of an action-adventure film, all the more suspenseful for its comparative wordlessness and its female villain (we have no idea why Paccard is planting the bomb).

What words the script does provide only complicate audience estimates of the blonde woman bomber: immediately following the planting of the bomb in the skyscraper, she stops at a phone booth in the plaza below to make two quick phone calls that show viewers that this person, for a bomber at least, is apparently a tenderhearted sort. First, she rings the receptionist-secretary whose desk adjoins the inner office where the bomb rests to tell her that her car alarm has gone off in the underground garage and that she must attend to it immediately. That done, Paccard calls the police to warn them of the bomb *and* to give them her name and her reasons for planting it. Immediately afterward, the audience learns what Paccard does not know—that the bomb has gone hideously astray and killed the four in that elevator. Tracking down the villain is easy enough, given that she has delivered her name to the *carabinieri*, and in the middle of the night a SWAT team raids her apartment and puts her in custody. And so begins the film, and a tough fix it is for villain and viewers alike, especially as all try to understand what drives this comely but crazed evildoer.

In what seems a head-on affront after this opening dose of destruction and death in murder gone awry—of hell itself, in short—Tykwer, having gotten to this dismal turn, slows the film by abruptly cutting to the film's title, *Heaven*, starkly displayed over a stunning, and regularly recurring, down-looking vertical shot that slowly floats over the tiled, red-roofed housing blocks of Turin.

For nearly a half minute, as the first liquid piano notes of Arvo Pärt's

Für Alina drip out, the camera slowly, even meditatively, moves over the city below.[3] With this abrupt shift in perspective, both visual and dramatic, Tykwer takes his first of many incremental steps that induct the viewer into one of the film's most prominent stylistic signatures, namely, an insistent verticality. Cumulatively, this motif suggests far more than travelogue or simple aesthetic indulgence. Rather, as one critic succinctly put it, the film's many down-looking shots suggest a kind of divine observance of the human world below. To be sure, this perspectival motif initiates a distinctive manner of seeing the world—specifically, the suggestion of the presence of a transcendent divine witness that in some manner or degree watches and takes account of

3. Arvo Pärt, *Für Alina*. Much of the music in *Heaven* comes from two pieces by Pärt, a celebrated contemporary Estonian composer. The source for both *Für Alina* and *Spiegel im Spiegel* is the 2000 release by ECM Records of *Arvo Pärt: Alina*.

manifold human horrors such as viewers have just witnessed. That this might be benign or caring is suggested by the delicate, aching tenderness of *Für Alina*. If it were not for this artful melding of arresting visual beauty and exquisitely tender music, viewers might conclude that this striking visual motif was meant to be ironic, given what we've seen thus far. By the end of the credits, however, no matter how enticing this slow visual dance, we land very much back in this mess of human affairs as the vertical down-looking shot dissolves to a horizontal still of Philippa Paccard sitting alone on a bed in a bare cell. In any case, the juxtaposition unsettles and vexes the usual expectations of how a movie should move from scene to scene, especially one that for all the world looks to be a crime thriller.

It is in the course of her first police interrogation that Paccard learns of the horrifying failure of her attempted homicide. When the charge is read by the police superintendent—the murder not of a drug lord but of four people—she simply cannot grasp the fact that her plot, going hideously awry, killed innocents. Numbing incomprehension soon turns to tears. Here Blanchett wordlessly limns the self-repulsion of conscience and soul. She tries to explain to the police that she intended to kill the man who runs the "drug scene" and on whose wares her husband overdosed and her pupils also now die. Incomprehension fast turns to dread, "grief upon unbearable grief," as Roger Ebert put it,[4] and she soon faints dead away, the camera again looking straight down, though now it is not at rooftops but at her body splayed on the floor.

Assisting the staff physician as she lies unconscious is a young policeman (Giovanni Ribisi), who serves as an interpreter during the interrogation (though an elementary school teacher in Turin schools and fluent in Italian, Paccard has insisted on interrogation in her native tongue, English, and the young police stenographer volunteers to translate). While the doctor prepares an injection of some sort, for she has not revived by other means, the fresh-faced young fellow kneels by the young woman's side, holding her hand as the physician rolls back her sleeve.

Already, strangely, the young policeman is far from disinterested. Throughout the interrogation, the camera has regularly watched him watching her, and while his face has remained largely impassive, there

4. Roger Ebert, *Chicago Daily News*, October 18, 2002, available at RogerEbert.com, http://www.rogerebert.com/reviews/heaven-2002.

plays on it in a minor key a wondering curiosity, especially at her depth of sorrow and remorse at the news that her plot killed bystanders. That remorse shows a measure of sensitivity not usually evident in mass murderers. As she stirs toward consciousness, the camera assumes the kneeling policeman's point of view to look yet again, tellingly, straight down, and it focuses, as it will in critical moments throughout the story, on their intertwined hands. As she slowly regains consciousness, he explains who he is and where she is. In that first interchange between the two, the plot begins to turn, and quickly so, from a simple who-done-it to romance, and then, after escape, to what-next. For now, though, it is hard to imagine a more ill-fated time for the heart to tumble. After all, how often does a fresh-faced, idealistic young cop fall for a guilty-as-hell quadruple-murdering damsel, especially amid the kind of legal and moral finalities at which she has arrived?

Soon after the day's interrogation, we see, in another vertical shot, the young man on his side in bed, wide awake in near darkness as midnight approaches. He stares at his hand, and as piano notes drip out, the camera slowly descends till only the hand fills the dead center of the frame. In its emphasis on connectedness and consequence, that image says with due eloquence all we need to know. Some sort of connection, however mysterious or bizarre, has been made.

If there be any doubt about the depth of the young man's reaction to this criminal damsel in distress, the mildly comic events of the next

morning elaborate and at the same time keep the film's tone light amid the story's enormous potential for tragic funk. From an exterior dawn shot of the lovely home in which he lives, the camera cuts to the young man's hands washing sheets in a bathroom sink (so much for never washing that hand, as the smitten often proclaim). A knock on the door and a call to "Filippo," for that is his name, brings in his father (Remo Girone) to ask what he is doing. "Washing," replies Filippo, for he has "wet the bed," something he hasn't done for ten years, says his father (24:15). Able to tell that his son is upset by something, the kindly father asks what disturbs him, to which Filippo replies that he "fell in love," though the father at this point has no inkling of which lucky girl has won his son's affections (24:40). And forthwith Filippo plots to free this murderous young woman, and by elaborate and ingenious means he pulls it off.

Such is this young man, a bit mad perhaps, but also pure and single-hearted, falling for the least likely romantic prospect. He is one of those mysterious humans that Kieslowski and Piesiewicz regularly insert into their tales (the most famous is the reappearing silent man in *The Decalogue*). From the start, Filippo does not look quite, well, "normal," but more like a cherub, full-grown fellow though he is. He is smartly uniformed (with enough filigree to make an angel jealous), pale, possessed of strikingly red lips but without the least touch of effeminacy (a bit of makeup helps), and always with a remarkably attentive and patient look of silent concern. Throughout the escape plot, he remains focused and calm, almost preternaturally so, especially as it becomes clear that the stakes are very high, with his own life at risk as well as his family's honor (his father is the retired chief of police in Turin).

What strikes Filippo about the accused is the same singular moral posture that strikes the viewer. Despite her crime, Ms. Paccard is possessed of a rare moral clarity and courage; these emerge in her contempt for the drug lord, her profound sorrow for those who suffer from the relentless evil of others, and also, it seems, from herself. For a still-young person, she has increasingly dwelt in the shadows of suffering and death. After all, her attempt at homicide emerged entirely from grief and indignation at the immense toll of potent illegal drugs, and moreover, she has willingly sacrificed her freedom and life to put an end to it by killing its mastermind. And all the while she knows, and invites, the full moral and legal consequence of the law and is more than willing, and even eager, to endure the likely consequence of a life in prison. That is remarkable moral seriousness and sensitivity. So it is that the news that the bomb went astray devastates her not only emotionally and morally but also, as viewers learn late in the film, spiritually. It is no surprise, then, that Philippa strikes the young cherubic police stenographer, who himself possesses the sensitivity of an angel, as a creature of great inner beauty and capacity for self-sacrifice.

Throughout repeated interrogations, Philippa vainly strives to convince her questioners of her attempts to inform the police of the crimes of her intended victim. Alas, all her complaints by phone and post have been intercepted and destroyed by the corrupt Major Pini (Mattia Sbragia). The question, then, expands beyond rescuing Paccard to exposing high police corruption. Indeed, Pini regularly colludes with the nasty drug lord, and they both know they'll only be safe when Paccard is dead. This much Filippo has surmised, and he duly alters his escape plans at the last minute to outwit the conspirators, who will use her escape attempt to silence her permanently. That dire outcome seems likely because Pini has bugged Philippa's jail cell and hears Filippo's tape-recorded instructions. Happily, at the very last minute, Filippo, one very smart fellow, directs Philippa not to the train station but to an unused attic in the stately old palazzo-style police building. And so suspense mounts, and the escape goes chugging along, for the pair will indeed elude the bloodthirsty *carabinieri*.

Presence

Escape, however, soon begins to seem secondary, for Tykwer has already begun to transpose the story to a different, wholly mysterious metaphysical frame. The viewer can sense its approach though its nature will take time to clarify, a reality that characterizes a lot of elements in living. Put another way, the film increasingly emphasizes that there are higher stakes than concerns about personal freedom and safety such as Philippa confronts. For one, the insistent verticality and evocative shots of hands have only increased until, finally, when the fugitive couple escapes to the countryside, the metaphysical swallows the literal. All this is signaled and prepared by the gradual intensification of visual and musical motifs and events, and ultimately these accrue more narrative significance than the assorted exciting plot twists that pave the way for their flight, a journey that is simultaneously harrowingly this-worldly and surprisingly, radically and very mysteriously, sacramental and redemptive. These visual and dramatic movements gradually intertwine and become more pronounced, to foreshadow another threshold of experience and meaning of which neither audience nor characters themselves are yet aware. Stephen Holden has suggested "dreamlike" for the peculiar aura the film slowly amps up, and that is as fitting a word as any to depict the journey into a strange, parabolic domain.

From the start this verticality converges with motifs of setting and character to gradually elicit from viewers the increasing sense that this cinematic world might just be at the very least observed, if not exactly superintended, by some sort of supernatural power, a mystery both Kieslowski and Tykwer have separately repeatedly explored. This sense amplifies exponentially once the fugitive couple escape into the countryside and the visual world seems to pass through a transfigurative prism, for which verticality and hands imagery seem but a foreshadowing. There they find themselves, it seems, in a liminal world very palpably suffused with a numinous power full of light and surpassing beauty.

The first glimpse of this trajectory takes place midway through Philippa's interrogation. In a long wordless sequence that does not further the plot in any way, the camera looks straight down upon Philippa as she lies on her cell bed; as the camera slowly rises, the image dissolves to repeat the slow aerial tracking shot of Turin's blocks and blocks of red-roofed apartment buildings, which then dissolves into a repeat of Filippo, that wondering trance on his face again, sitting on a bench in the empty plaza before the police building that confines Philippa (viewers saw this sort of sequence when the stretcher carried Philippa after her faint). For most of it, Arvo Pärt's minimalist music plays, this time *Spiegel im Spiegel*, piano and then violin, achingly delicate, soaking the film with, at the very least, a good dose of meditative "tenderness," as music critic Richard Lehnert has labeled the clarion core of Pärt's piece.[5]

Just as the effect of the music is somehow poignant and gentle, though often indeterminate in mood, so the precise meaning of the sequence remains uncertain, though it has begun to intimate the pres-

---

5. Rarely do music critics make themselves quite so vulnerable as Richard Lehnert in his estimate of Pärt's *Alina*: "One comes away from *Alina* with a heart as comforted as it is troubled. I didn't know a human endeavor could be so subtle. I don't know why we can't treat each other with as much tenderness. Which is why we make art. Here is some of the best of it." *Stereophile*, February 2011, 82.

ence of some sort of transcendent reality, looking down, perhaps first bathing the bereft woman and then the wounded city with an enveloping compassion, an impression that wells up from both the music and connotations associated with this sort of transcendent perspective in historic Christian ideals of transcendent divine knowing, presence, and, especially, immanent compassion for the human plight. For now, though, this seems only speculative, a "perhaps" that bears in mind that Kieslowski's habit, going back to *The Decalogue*, was to keep his signs and symbols imprecise, thereby allowing viewers to wonder and startle at their seductive, albeit cryptic, compellingness and freshness. This take on transcendent compassion and presence acquires added cogency, however, when the sequence ends with Filippo on the bench, wondering and transfixed. After all, he will become the primary conduit for whatever transcendent compassion might aid Philippa amid her dire straits. The sequence clearly links the two, the brief aerial transit of the city offering an explanatory glimpse of the how and why of their linkage. Nor does it end there, for Tykwer begins the very next sequence with a vertical perspective on the interrogation room, all the principals scattered about, suggesting an ongoing observing presence even in this arena of murder and guilt. Whatever oversees this world, and perhaps also attends to these people, does so even in this woman's Golgotha.

The same continues after the escape. The morning after, and following their murder of Vendice, after they have taken refuge in the cavernous attic of the aging building, the camera approaches slowly from the piazza outside, dissolving first into a down-looking shot of the enormous clock in its tower, and then to the interior, where in the morning light the pair sleep beside one another on the floor until, once again, the camera looks directly down upon them in medium close-up. In this slow approach, taking well over a minute, Tykwer works hard to slow the pace in order to situate their homicide within another context. It would have been rather too easy after the murder of Vendice to hurtle the story along, cutting directly to the close calls of their escape from the building to the train station. Their murder of Vendice takes place in the dark, and throughout, the camera is always straight-on horizontal. In stark contrast, the next morning the camera descends on Philippa as she awakens in full morning light and comments to Filippo, in surprised tones, as if anyone after her dire crimes would wish to, "You were sleeping beside me" (57:20). To the viewer, though, this hardly comes as surprise, for Filippo had early on informed his father that he had fallen in love, and everything he has done since shows the depths of his care for Philippa.

He has now, like some guardian angel, risked all to free this person, even though he does not know if she cares a whit about him. Throughout most of their time in the attic, they are bathed in the light that pours in through large, circular, church-like windows; indeed, with its vaulted ceilings and circular windows, the setting feels more than a little solemn and churchly, more like a cathedral than a jail. In one instance, just after they arrive in the attic after the escape, Philippa stands directly in front of the window quite literally surrounded, almost taken up, backlit, by the light that pours in from behind. It is here, though, with her face turned away from light, thunder sounding in the distance, that she informs Filippo that the only reason she agreed to escape is to correct her botched murder of Vendice. The visual imagery here deployed in setting, lighting, and composition, all overladen with Pärt's music, conjures the numinous borderland these characters travel, something that becomes all the clearer after their deliverance to the countryside.

Getting away with the crime is easy enough, and apparently escape is too. Wisely, recalling his father's advice about catching criminals,

Filippo changes the escape plan at the last minute and foils Major Pini's eavesdropping on Philippa's cell. Instead of fleeing out the back door of the police station, where Pini's police would have promptly gunned down Philippa, Filippo has sent her to the attic and his little brother, a decoy dressed in hooded sweatshirt and blonde wig, out the front of the building (it is, though, implausible that he would have put his brother at such risk).

A far more arduous escape, however, is from the profoundly difficult moral and, as we later discover, religious fix in which Philippa finds herself (for a police officer, no matter how young, and a son of a police chief, Filippo seems completely untroubled by his role in effecting Philippa's escape, though the murder of Vendice is another matter). As is obvious from the start, Filippa is a clear-eyed moral realist about the significance and personal consequence of what she undertakes; there is about her no softheaded mush about anarchic freedom or social progress; she believes in law and social compacts, no matter how limited or corrupt these may be, and she places herself firmly within them. In this regard, she stands in stark contrast to the intellectual rationalization of murder from such as Dostoevsky's Raskolnikov in *Crime and Punishment*. She will apply this to the murder of drug lord Vendice. She knows that at best this is morally dubious as well as completely legally forbidden, but ultimately she sees her deed as morally necessary—as simultaneous justice for his crimes and compassion for future victims—and she expects to pay the price for her criminality with eons in prison. Indeed, as suggested earlier, this stalwart moral ferocity explains at least part of Filippo's admiration.

So she murders Vendice, knowing full well the inevitability of punishment for her deed, and even wanting the punishment. She has, after all, not only warned the police but also given them her name, bringing sure punishment upon herself for what is perhaps a morally defensible, if not legally defensible, act. She has undertaken vigilante justice, pure and simple, but only after a long campaign to get the police to act against the murderous (and profitable) reign that killed her husband and several of her pupils. If she willingly suffers for that act, we can only imagine that guilt amplified many times over when the plot goes askew and four innocents die. She expects and wants to pay for that, as she tells Filippo upon taking refuge in the attic (48:34), and later she will tell him that with her measure of guilt, something she feels acutely, she can't go on long and wants her life to end soon

(1:10:31). In such collisions of crime and self-punishment, the plot searches the complex, often conflicting, interplay between moral and legal economies. As she will tell Filippo, the fate of those around her has left her to despair about the goodness of life, about hope for its improvement, and, in the age-old theodicy, about the possibility of divine care in so wounded a world. After all, her own best efforts—such as trying to inform the police and, as a last resort, murdering Vendice—have not only come to naught but also run tragically awry, bringing needless death and destruction without accomplishing anything of their intended goal. Nor was she, as she later confesses, able to love her husband off drugs or rescue her schoolchildren from their allure. This globe is indeed a grim, fractured place, and Philippa's efforts to alleviate the sorrow seem only to flail as desperate and angry lament.

Strangely, though, *Heaven* soon leaps beyond moral matters without in the least ignoring the daunting ambiguity of right and wrong, mercy and justice. It is exactly these sorts of concerns, after all, that lie at the heart of *The Decalogue* (1988; also called *Dekalog*), Piesiewicz and Kieslowski's ten-part cinematic masterpiece on the Ten Commandments. The last portion of *Heaven* initiates a profound shift from the complexities of human action to a divine calculus that ever mysteriously trumps humankind's inveterate fumblings at trying to assess right, wrong, and comparative costs. To these tangled moral questions, it seems, there may be no answers, at least no easily definable, tidy ones. For this the screenwriters proffer a very different understanding of how and for what the world might work. It is not, to be sure, for the sort of perfunctory rutting that the escaped pair witness while hiding in the back of a milk truck, their transport away from police headquarters and to the train station. The scene of the couple in the front seat is both graphic and comic for the purpose of contrasting starkly with the complete lack of physicality between Philippa and Filippo; though they are often seen in close proximity, as one might expect, the relationship between the fugitives remains for the longest time entirely practical and chaste, save perhaps Philippa's surprise when she awakens in the attic next to Filippo. Exactly what her words mean at that point is not altogether clear other than suggesting her extreme degree of alienation from others and how alone she has been.

Ascent

As soon as the pair escapes the city by train, a new metaphysical calculus of understanding flares into being in the first of a remarkable
series of visually stunning sequences within a film full of ingenious
and arresting cinematography. In a nearly empty train car the two fugitives lounge side by side, looking silently out the window. Suddenly the
screen goes black save for a dot of light in its middle, the distant exit
from the darkened tunnel the train has now entered; a pinhole of light
shining in the darkness shows their exit not only from the tunnel but
also from life's tangles. In that dark, both literal and figurative, Philippa
asks where they are going (to her hometown is Filippo's answer), and
amid silence, save for the wrenchingly beautiful violin and piano from
Pärt's *Spiegel im Spiegel*, the train exits into a blanched sepia-toned
Tuscan countryside burnished with widely scattered trees. The sepia
landscape looks artificial, very much as if it has been generated by a
computer, like the terrain in the flight simulator that opens the film.

While not exactly passing through the looking glass, like the hapless Alice, the pair seems to enter an altogether different realm, palpable and clear but nonetheless mysteriously changed, transfigured,
both magical and transfixing in its visual power. No one imagines such
countryside, and it is a jolt to see it, as is seeing any such place for
the first time. And again the camera looks down on the moving train
and the blanched landscape, for the fugitives have moved to a unique
realm of experience and understanding. Though they themselves have
not yet understood it, something akin to revelation will soon envelop
both as they walk toward the climax, what the DVD chapter list names
"Ascension." What happens between here and the ending carries them
sacramental step by sacramental step individually and relationally to
the stunning conclusion.

In the first of these steps, as the airborne camera watches the train
pass through the countryside, Philippa for the first time asks Filippo
his name, a remarkable oversight given all they have been through
(1:06:09). The surprising proximity of his name to hers prompts the
question of when he was born. That date, May 23, 1978, prompts her to
ask his time of birth, for not only do they share the same birthday, but,
more than that, on the particular morning of his birth she was under-
going a birth of her own, at least sacramentally. It was her first Holy
Communion, the ritual feast confirming her entry into the Christian

church, that mysterious entity that is meant to birth and embody the sacrificial love that allows for the reconciliation and renewal of all that is, and for this there is the eucharistic feast (1:06:55). On this formal occasion marking belief and entrance, she partakes in, receives, and enters the body of Christ. Moreover, Philippa recalls that her mother attired young Philippa in a bride's gown and then, strangely, burst into tears, as if some deep foreboding sensed something terrible awaiting her pure-hearted daughter. Here the gist of sacrament and providential fate entwine. At the cost of her own life, Philippa's fate will both undertake justice and set free captives to addiction.

Through the whole length of this revelatory conversation, the camera stays external to the train and high above. We simply watch the train move through the countryside. This distant perspective gives the voices an ethereal quality and the camera transcendence, as befits the substance of their talk, for they have moved beyond legal and moral economies to the metaphysical and religious, though these too, obviously, intertwine. At last the train stops, and we watch the pair from above as they walk a dirt road from the crossing, the music providing a solemn but lilting cadence. Both wear jeans and white T-shirts, their faces uplifted and rapt, looking almost like clones of one another, or two halves of one self, made for each other's soul, as indeed their strange, enmeshed histories seem to suggest.

Only after watching the look-alike couple for a long while does the

camera reverse again, and we see what elicits their rapt attention. High on a hill above and before them is their destination, the lovely hill town of Montepulciano, Tuscany, the place where Philippa grew up. From within the visual and thematic prism of the film, the place seems far less a small Italian village on a hilltop than a timeless golden city upon a hill, a new Jerusalem where all things will heal and restore; indeed, it will soon prove the setting for just that. The hilltop destination seems a fair rendition of what Stephen Holden labels an "Italian Eden." Fittingly, Philippa herself, seeing her native place again, in stunned whisper asserts that "It's as if nothing ever happened" (1:07:49). In truth, nothing has happened, and everything has happened, and a sort of timeless divine nimbus absorbs them both as they make their way back to beginnings, a journey into a sort of liminal state that culminates in the film's last scenes.

In short, the fugitives have ventured into a quietly resplendent world, one that for them and for viewers alike seems radically different and wondrous. Clearly, the look of this landscape through which they travel, so well meshed with music, argues that the two criminals have accomplished far more than a train ride but have completed some sort of transit, for nothing in the film has thus far looked and felt so singular and beguiling. The sudden strangeness of this lushly surreal landscape contrasts sharply with the starkly urban visual realism of the story thus far. It is altogether a stunning sequence in its melding of music, visual delight, event, and script. The music and the screen so well display the substance of the words that the script at times seems superfluous. Whatever wonder the language conveys at the strange providences of life is amplified by the elegant, highly affective mating of image and sound, the two seemingly in concert in a measured, elegant dance. Even though earlier elements, particularly the use of light and all those vertical shots, anticipate this radically enchanting realm, this sepia-like treatment is so wholly distinctive and other that it comes with some shock, as have the strange coincidences of birth dates and Holy Communion.

What exactly those coincidences mean never becomes entirely clear, but they surely suggest that the screenwriters see woven into human affairs specific climes and destinies of mysterious and unforeseeable meeting and import. Reviewer Holden, historically an astute commentator on Kieslowski's films, is helpful, calling these oddities "synchronicity." The same has been a preoccupation in Tykwer's work, film after film, "unshackling . . . characters from the constraints and responses that govern everyday life and letting them roam through a universe where fate, coincidence, and chance dominate."[6]

In a more religious time, people deferred freely to a shadowy divine providence that arranged such meetings and turnings. In this case, in more than the similarity of names, important clue though it be, Filippo and Philippa seem strangely linked, he birthing at the moment of her new birth or born-again-ness. And now it seems that as the two arrive in her hometown, the place she was first confirmed, the same will be repeated, for they arrive amid crisis and despair to rebirth Philippa into a new embrace of hope, faith, and love, of which the greatest is love (1 Cor. 13:13). As soon becomes clear, their unique intimacy only flourishes, something Tykwer emphasizes by their increasing visual similarity.

If there were any doubt about this scheme, the very next sequence dispels it, as the two enact the second of the story's four distinctly Roman Catholic sacraments that provide the film's shape and meaning. Upon entering the town piazza, they immediately, strangely, head straight for the church, the same presumably in which Philippa was christened and confirmed into God's body (every town in Italy seems to have a piazza, and on it a church, and here the square and building visually echo Turin and the police station, though a metaphysical world away from them). Perhaps because of the knowledge exchanged on the train, the church seems an urgent destination, Philippa leading the way. Her voice overlay begins before they even enter the door—a long confession in which Filippo, fittingly, given his time of birth, serves as confessor and priest, a role that only expands as the film develops. Again, the visual and musical tenderness of the sequence adds enormously to the power of the words. "I've done a lot of damage, and stupid, stupid things," begins Philippa (1:08:20). Cate Blanchett's bluntness and transparent sorrow in her recitation suggest that these are matters that deeply pain Philippa and to which she has given much thought. As her voice continues, the camera slowly approaches the chancel, glimpsing the confessional on the far side of the sanctuary, then cutting briefly to the backs of the pair sitting side by side in a pew near the front. In the next shot, however, now opposite Philippa,

6. Jamie Russell, "Heaven (2002)," BBC online, updated August 7, 2002, http://www.bbc .co.uk/films/2002/07/24/heaven_2002_review.shtml.

Filippo sits on the back of the pew in front of her, his head turned to one side, mimicking the typical posture of the priest in the confessional with his ear to the screen. Bit by bit, with concise, deliberate enumeration, her face looking down and forward, Philippa recounts her evil, moving from lesser to greater: "I've lied to my mother and my sister, many, many times. I was unfaithful to my husband once, and I didn't do everything I could to save him. Anyway, maybe it's not possible to do everything. Four people died because of me, and I can't live with that. I'll never be able to. I shot a defenseless person, which you know" (1:08:35). As she talks, the violin plays and the camera slowly circles; they themselves, seemingly, are the only source of light in the darkened church.

And then things get serious. In matters as profound as guilt, Philippa volunteers, now looking for the first time straight into Filippo's face, "What you don't know is that I've ceased to believe" (1:09:25). "Ceased to believe in what?" he asks. "In sense, in justice, in life" is the reply, meaning belief in anything that might make life worth living, including God, presumably. To all this self-incrimination, Filippo responds, now for the first time looking straight into Philippa's face, with words of absolution, words that not only absolve but also contain the entirety of one rationale for forgiveness, both Filippo's and, presumably, God's. With intensity but with little emotion, Filippo carefully pronounces, "I love you," a gift Philippa readily acknowledges with a simple "I know," though she finds the timing of this love terrible, for "It's just, it's just that I want the end to come soon" (1:10:15). No matter, though, for Filippo leans forward, gently putting his arm around her, and whispers in her ear, though we do not hear what he says. The words of absolution from the sacrament of confession seem a likely candidate, though he has in effect already pronounced them in his declaration of love.

In acknowledging the reality of Filippo's enormous care, risking all to free her, she at the least admits the possibility of outlandish love despite human failings, a notion that is at the center of the character of the Christian God. To that end, the scene perfectly distills the core of historic Christian theology: no matter the transgressions, mild or major, the reflexive action of God, God being who God is, is a love so extreme that it cherishes and forgives. Suffice it to say that in this sequence, all those visual and musical elements that Tykwer has evocatively sprinkled through the story coalesce to flourish full bloom.

The strangeness of what we've seen only escalates in stark, visual terms when the next shot abruptly cuts to the top of Philippa's head in the process of being shorn right down to the scalp, the whole head, a treatment Filippo has already undergone. Now the two jeaned and T-shirted figures look even more alike, mirror reflections of one another, almost one and the same, two halves of one soul, as they squat, as if again children, along a wall in the piazza eating ice-cream cones (1:11:10).

The striking visual similarity suggests that something more has transpired. That is confirmed when Filippo reappears after making a phone call to find Philippa running to greet him, essentially leaping into his arms, and the pair desperately cling to one another, an emotional and physical gesture that is new to the relationship and prepares the way for a third sacrament. Filippo has called his little brother at school to arrange a meeting with Filippo's father, the retired police chief of Turin, at a nearby tourist destination, St. Biagio Church, which, fittingly, sits atop a hill in the Italian countryside. It is a stunning site, and for what follows, the camera, typically by now, approaches from above, circling and soaring. When the father spies the pair crouched along a wall, he quickly shepherds them down an exterior alcove, stone benches on either side, that looks in shape and scale very much like the interior of a church, especially as they retreat to its depth and the camera stays exterior.

From that moment on, the father acts far less like a parent than like another kind of father, namely, a priest, telling them to sit down while he stands over them. Without offering rebuke or asking questions, he hands Filippo an envelope containing a big wad of cash, at which Filippo smiles in pleasure in the knowledge that that is exactly what his father would do—no censure, no judgment, no threats, just help. The father is stressed, though, as indicated by the fact that, to his son's surprise, he has taken to smoking cigarettes. The father's concern is to get them to freedom; he volunteers to smuggle them through roadblocks, himself risking a lengthy prison sentence and even further public humiliation. There is no longer any doubt about from whom Filippo gets his capacity for self-giving.

A long silence follows, in which both young people look at him with surprise for his complete self-sacrifice. Finally, Philippa informs father and son that she will not go with him in his effort to smuggle them to safety but wishes that Filippo would. In his wisdom the old man then asks if, given the fact that his son loves her, she loves him. After a long while, clearly ruminating on her answer, truth-teller that she is, she answers that she does, prompting Filippo to say that neither will he go with his father. "I know. I do know you a little," says the father. The refusal is, in effect, a marriage vow, a pledge to stay with one another no matter what, which in this case is likely death. The father wonders complainingly, full of sorrow and impotence at the sacrifice of his son, "Why can we never do anything at the most important moments?" Tykwer throughout slows the scene to a crawl, watching faces and allowing the splendid actors to do their nonverbal best to show an intensity of emotion that words simply cannot reach. The father-priest then tenderly offers his benediction, kissing Philippa good-bye and then grasping Filippo, who tells him to give little brother Ariel "a hug for me" (1:23:23). No tears, but the father hurries away, lest he lose his last vestiges of composure. After all, he has given up his loving son to die for a murderess. So we have marriage, and then the giving up of a son for another, an excruciating act, to say the least. Some of this, needless to say, echoes New Testament formulations of God the Father self-sacrificing Jesus the Son for the well-being of humankind.

By this stage in the film, it has become clear that the filmmakers have configured this loving, intimate family of three males as a Holy Trinity of sorts. This is done in a decidedly lighthearted, even playful, manner, as befits the nature of their commonality. Indeed, they seem inextricable, and partake of the same deep well of care and kindness. The loving, utterly selfless father, no less than a retired police chief, of all things (the law keeper, if not exactly the lawgiver), fits well as an emblem of transcendent goodness and compassion, whose understanding of the law is more than a little complex and certainly not black and white (perhaps he has moved from law keeper to love giver?). And, yes, though it seems a stretch, that makes Filippo a Jesus figure, giving all for another, not only seeing in a murderess remarkable spiritual beauty but also expressing his own willingness to forgive all. More than an angelic protector, Piesiewicz and Kieslowski seem to exalt him ever higher as the story goes on, even to the point of delivering Philippa from this vale to some sort of transcendent existence. As for little brother, fittingly named Ariel, well, he works pretty well as an elfin Holy Spirit, conveying information and intervening, as when he was disguised to divert police, to effect the escape of the fugitives (the name has many references, one of which is to the prankish spirit of the air in Shakespeare's *The Tempest*, who is required to use his magic to help Prospero).

The intent here is not to argue for any sort of literal manifestation but to suggest by a parable of sorts the plausibility of a tri-unity that collaborates to mediate the extremity of divine care for this world, no matter what malefaction humankind has done. Indeed, the three might have remained insular and intact if not for the wild, improvident love of Filippo for his strangely paradoxical damsel in distress. Given what he is in his deepest self, this Jesus figure cannot help himself in lavishing all upon the lost. And the same characterizes his family. The relational *caritas* and wholeness within define as well its irrepressible surfeit of love and relish for the created world. It is this drama of the mystery of divine love and *kenosis* (self-emptying) that the sacramental structure of the church intends to display. Remarkably, the filmmakers imbue the film with the texture of this affectional mystery without going didactic or maudlin. Audiences wonder at its substance without necessarily recognizing its origin.

And then on to the final sacrament, the ultimate one, which, like the second and third, takes place on a hilltop. Philippa had earlier seen her best girlhood friend in a wedding celebration on the town piazza; the two manage to talk quietly in an out-of-the-way alcove. The friend first strikes Philippa for what she has done, having read of it in the press, and then embraces her. Philippa asks if she and Filippo can spend the night at her farm outside of town, and it is there that they go after leaving Filippo's father at St. Biagio. Amid birdsong, they walk that same blanched countryside they had traveled in their ascent to Philippa's hometown. Again, the high places, whether attics or hilltops, function as sacramental liminal zones, borderlands where the mundane and holy entwine and exalt.

Once at the farm, the friend greets the couple with full welcome, telling them she feared they would not come and showing them to accommodations in the barn. Later, Philippa and Filippo sit at a small table inside the barn, bathed in the golden light of early evening, sharing a meal to consecrate their coming together, an effectual union, sacramental bread and wine prominently displayed on the table. For a long while, half of their faces showing on opposite sides of the frame, they stare at one another, until Philippa nods ever so slightly, and off they go, fleeing the barn to go to still another hilltop. The camera slowly rises as it watches the pair run atop the long ridge beside the drive that leads to the farmhouse and barn, small figures fleeing through the immense countryside of steep hills, immense sky, and distant mountains.

Their destination is a starkly green hilltop a quarter mile away, on

which stands alone some kind of enormous pine, under which they stand, five feet apart, simply staring at one another as the camera, as in the confessional sequence, circles, this time filming from the air. It is a breathtaking shot: the tableau in time-lapse photography fades to sunset, the sky now a glowing deep orange, the distant camera circling still, the pair yet standing apart, now only in silhouette, the couple and the tree black against the brilliant sky with only the sound of the blowing wind. At last they disrobe and approach one another, shyly, embracing just as the screen fades to black. In one another made whole, their oneness consummated, bound in love, they will achieve sacramental completion, reconciliation in soul as policeman and murderess, and in fullness of being relational physical intimacy and oneness. That is a fitting preparation for the film's finale, a turn of events that measures still more wondrous, narratively and cinematically, in which the mundane transfigures.

Then comes the morning after, one that ends one fulfillment and begins another. The approach of a caravan of black SWAT SUVs shatters the morning silence. The police roust the sleeping farm family from its beds. From under their hilltop tree, Philippa and Filippo awaken to the noise, staring quietly into each other's face. Then, after the police helicopter carrying the desperate Major Pini lands, the pair, remarkably, run *to* the farm. The helicopter is left idling as Pini and the pilot exit to watch the operation, and the fugitives watch as they crouch by a fence on the edge of the farmyard. The camera watches them from behind and then above, focusing on their hands atop a railing, Filippo placing his hand on hers, repeating the gesture of their first contact amid Philippa's faint during the police interrogation. A long way they have come, indeed. He simply asks, "Now?" to which she after a few seconds replies with her own assent, "Now," and they run for the empty helicopter to begin their flight upward and their likely deaths.

Tykwer suddenly cuts the sound level by 80 percent, suggesting that they, the couple, and we too, have entered still another, very different liminal territory, one that is even more surreal than any so far. As the camera looks down from the bubble cockpit of the ascending machine, the police become aware of the suddenly airborne machine and begin to fire away, though no shots at all hit the large bubble canopy (perhaps they're lousy shots). A reverse shot watches the helicopter ascend higher and higher and higher as the story circles back to pose again the film's by-now-long-forgotten initial question of "How high can you fly?" For the story's last fifty seconds, the now silent machine rises and rises ever higher till we hear it no more and then see it no more as it disappears into the blue sky above (the last chapter in the original DVD release, number 14, is simply titled "To Heaven"; the 2011 release replaces that with "Ascension"). The screen goes black for a few seconds, a piano sounds, and the film title again appears, unambiguously answering that question about altitude, though here the reference is not to technological capacity but to humanity's aspiration and completion. Less fugitives than pilgrims, the pair have found renewal and completion marked and fostered by sacrament.

Fini

The radical import of *Heaven* becomes all the more emphatic when placed beside another Kieslowski-Piesiewicz screenplay that was intended to be part of the same metaphysical trilogy as *Heaven*. A tale of utter familial destruction born of shared malice between the parents, *Hell* (*L'Enfer*, 2005) could hardly be more different. It would be difficult to imagine any greater enmity than that harbored by that film's *materfamilias*, who has long hated her husband for a crime that she eventually learns he did not commit; even then, she cannot relinquish her quest for vengeance upon the world. She lives, it seems, simply for raising hell above ground, as she labors to induct her three daughters into the same misery of enmity. Remarkably, all this takes place among parents and siblings in one family—among those who should, in short, most readily understand and care. Destruction wins. In just about every way, then, *Heaven* plays the antipode, celebrating the sway of a radical love between complete strangers as they together journey upon a wounded, tear-soaked earth.

Heaven features the movement from despair to love, a transit of renewal that is at once profoundly moral, relational, and religious. Amid Philippa Paccard's sense of futility, she finds just what she never expected, an unconditional love that instigates her return to the possibility of loving and even belief in some sort of a loving divine something or another. That return hinges on signs, deliverances, and sacrament, all tokens of divine care and presence, all of which are made clear and conjured in music, cinematography, and extraordinary direction. The sacraments, in particular, in the screenwriters' vision of the world, constitute necessary passages in the journey to renewal. Indeed, for them, the sort of kenotic sacrifice of entire self-giving in Filippo's rescue of Philippa instigates the renewal of the self and, by extension, the renewal of the world. Indeed, by this means, as Stephen Holden suggested, *Heaven* in effect reverses the Fall story; in this case, fugitives Adam and Eve return to Eden by means of redemptive love. To miss this is to deem *Heaven* "softheaded metaphysical claptrap," as does Owen Gleiberman in *Entertainment Weekly*,[7] or "smug piety," as does Ann Hornaday in her *Washington Post* review,[8] and to miss both the film and the radical hopefulness at the soul of the Judeo-Christian tradition. Indeed, a center of that tradition has focused on the promise of renewal, the fullness of redemption—personal, social, and cultural, the whole of the globe reconciled and healed. It is in this "exquisitely profound film of rare beauty" that the filmmakers construe a glimpse of the inmost character of heaven itself, the world as it was meant to be in the first place, and last.[9]

7. Owen Gleiberman, "Heaven," *Entertainment Weekly*, October 25, 2002, http://www.ew.com/article/2002/10/25/heaven.

8. Ann Hornaday, "A 'Heaven' More Like Purgatory," *Washington Post*, October 25, 2002, http://www.washingtonpost.com/wp-dyn/content/article/2002/10/25/AR2005033116482.html.

9. Antonio D. Sison, Film Review, *Journal of Religion and Film* 78 (April 2003). https://www.unomaha.edu/jrf/Vol7No1/heavenrev.htm.

CHAPTER EIGHT

"IT CAN HAPPEN"

Frogs, Deliverance, and
Reconciliation in P. T. Anderson's *Magnolia*

Surely one of the brashest, strangest, wildest, giddiest, darkest, and altogether dazzling films ever made is Paul Thomas Anderson's *Magnolia* (1999), written and directed by a twenty-nine-year-old boy wonder (*Magnolia* was his third feature).

More surprising still is that the accolades *Magnolia* has received describe a film whose story is, for the most part, very much a downer, and for darkness of this psycho-relational sort, contemporary audiences, at least American ones, do not have much appreciation. Nonetheless, prodigy Anderson pulls it off, his cinematic pizzazz deftly hauling (even enthralling) wary audiences through the full length of an arduous three-hour trek through misfortune and misery, brokenness and desolation, death and—surprise—*frogs*.

Since its appearance, the film has gained a sizable cult following, in part because not all is doom, gloom, and perdition. In the last minutes, finally, viewers arrive at a very peculiar, and patently incredible, *deus ex machina* deliverance that stuns, puzzles, and then, given all its many reversals of calamity, ultimately elates. Along the way, though, the only thing, and a very big feat it is, that sustains viewers through a whirling, propulsive descent into pervasive brokenness is the jaunty stylistic panache of Anderson's filmmaking. The same tale, told conventionally, would very likely have driven audiences to the nearest drinking establishment. Never has anyone treated woe with such élan. In *Magnolia*, to a greater extent than any of his other films, Anderson's prodigious talent goes just about everywhere—editing, camera, music—and, whether you like *Magnolia* or not, it is unforgettable. It is, for sure, something to behold, and no less so than in the wildness of the implausible dramatic turn that stuns the viewer two hours into the film.

Indeed, the effect was such that it pushed fancy, and usually very articulate, critics to scramble for words to convey *Magnolia*'s allure. Even the venerable Kenneth Turan of the *Los Angeles Times*, though thinking *Magnolia* "frantic [and] flawed," relished the fact that it was "drunk and disorderly on the pure joy of making movies."[1] So also with Roger Ebert, who viewed just about everything at least twice. For him, *Magnolia* inhabited an improbable terrain all its own, mixing diverse elements into an intoxicating brew: "operatic in its ambition, a great, joyous leap into melodrama and coincidence, with ragged emotions, crimes and punishments, deathbed scenes, manic dreams, generational turmoil and celestial intervention, all scored to insistent music."[2] Some reviewers, overwhelmed by so much naked emotion and cinematic verve jammed within one film, simply labeled the film epic. Epic, though, is here a curious term, for the story surveys but one day in one Los Angeles neighborhood (maybe like Joyce's *Ulysses*). And there were naysayers, though not in great numbers. Even the skeptics appreciated *Magnolia*'s daring, though they deemed it pompous and gassy, emotionally exhibitionist, and generally a preposterous, sprawling mess. Not temperate in style or substance, neither were the judgments of *Magnolia*; good thing it's only a movie. In any case, *Magnolia*, in its "operatic ecstasy" (Ebert), most certainly is not tame, and it is not easy to explain just how and why it met with such extremes of devotion and condemnation.

Unfortunately, all the hoopla over the film's methods and melodrama tended to obscure the fact that Anderson's inventiveness and panache were there to show a very human story of people *in extremis*. Story matters, needless to say, and here the story—or stories (there are nine of them, depending on how one counts)—cycles through the descents of multiple dark nights of the soul, paroxysms of raw emotional anguish, that culminate finally in what the DVD edition simply, and fittingly, names "Meltdowns" (chapter 8). For much of the film, the news, comically distilled in the film's periodic weather reports, is not

1. Kenneth Turan, "Random Lives, Bound by Chance," *Los Angeles Times*, December 17, 1999, http://articles.latimes.com/1999/dec/17/entertainment/ca-44701.
2. Roger Ebert, "Magnolia," Rogerebert.com, January 7, 2000.

very good, or at least it gets very bad before it gets any better. The film's small host of wildly assorted, contorted characters, from sad-sack cop to deranged trophy wife, simply "lose it" when running smack into intractable matters of death, truth, loss, fear, ineptitude, self-deception, enmity, predation, isolation, or whatever—all the usual stuff, if truth be told, of being alive in a human skin. Abundant meltdowns do happen—relentless, plaintive, and loud—until Anderson flips his narrative to insert, however unforeseeably, a climax that features a bracing dose of hope for the healing of the many broken and heavy-laden among his woebegone crew of miscreants and losers-in-general. A fulsome happy ending of bells and pixie dust it is not, but hopeful and glad it surely is, and given all the deep woe and pain that have been, it seems very near miraculous.

To the survivors—for not all survive—comes a new, wonder-filled way of seeing the world and themselves in it, one that Anderson clearly urges upon his viewers. In some ways, this pivot in the story exceeds even the wonder of the sky raining frogs. The impossible can happen, and that impossible whatever that "just happens" points the way to a surprising, unforeseen realm of care and amity. It will take a miracle to jostle the afflicted into the light, so sunken are these disparate folks, but so it is. As for explanation, Anderson's peculiar narrator suggests that "these things just don't happen." But that's just it: they do happen, or so Magnolia seems to contend. In fact, Anderson goes so far as to suggest that, improbable as frogs raining from above, a wild, redemptive compassion does indeed happen, and seems to go—especially so perhaps—to the greatest of human messes, and as with the magnolia blossom, petal by petal, a great flowering ensues. Though steeping it in academic jargon and limiting the scope of Anderson's notion of redemption, Anderson scholar Christina Lane comes to a similar conclusion: "the characters circulate within a moral and philosophical universe that privileges redemption and transformation."[3] Remarkably, things can get better, even for these sorry folks. Wonder, delight, and concord, against all odds, they just might have the final say—or the unforeseeable smile that proceeds from care and hope. For now, though, just hang on. Tight.

3. Christina Lane, Magnolia (Chichester, UK: Wiley-Blackwell, 2011), 6.

First, and Last, Strange Things Happen, Don't They?

First comes that peculiar beginning that is perhaps the oddest start ever to any mainstream American movie. A lengthy, comic prologue on the subject of chance and providence sets the mood for the film as a whole and up front poses the question that shapes the narrative, pointing especially to the strange deliverances that close the story. Setting those in motion, that slightly loony narrative voice simply disappears until the very end, when it resurfaces to recall and drive home the point that might have gotten lost amid the swirl of an eventful, very populated film. The outlandish claim is that there is no such thing as coincidence, and on that proposition the narrator fastens his attention, as does Anderson throughout his film. As Christina Lane put the question in her short book on the film, *Magnolia* "ultimately revolves around a question of faith—a refusal to believe only in chance."[4] Apparently, life has meaning, and more than that, it is somehow mysteriously plotted. Going further than Lane, Anderson questions not simply if there is something such as fate or providence that shapes this messy, sometimes pain-ridden circus, but whether that force cares a whit about human well-being. By the end, there's not much doubt that Whatever It Is does indeed care, and radically so, as seen in the event and aftermath of a wild, improbable incursion—or call it miracle—that emphasizes how little humans know about anything important, and especially an outlandish sort of Love that on occasion breaks outlandishly into this dire world.

A good deal of the pleasure of the film comes in the manner in which Anderson repeatedly sneaks up on whatever unforeseeable something he wishes to show. At no place does that happen more than at the very beginning. That chirpy, disappearing narrator (pop raconteur of the paranormal, Ricky Jay) recounts preposterous events that conceal very serious questions about the mysteries of coincidence and fate (or is it providence?). These riddles, as old as Sophocles and Job, loom over the film as a whole: How could all of this happen in the first place, or how could it persist in the film's remarkable turn toward hope, reconciliation, and healing?

To pose that eternally knotty problem, the prologue jauntily lays out three very peculiar events. In attempting to summarize their signifi-

4. Lane, *Magnolia*, 15.

cance, the narrator soon runs out of words, a predicament that seems especially inevitable in the present era of semantic reductionism. If Western culture ever did have ready at hand a vocabulary to describe the strange occurrences of the prologue, modernity's determinism has long since drained plausibility from propositions about coincidence, meaning, and the possibility of some sort of mysterious transcendent intelligence intimately present in the seeming randomness of daily human affairs. So here, channeling modern skepticism, Anderson allows his narrator to struggle, and well he should, for these are unresolvable (at least to scientism), age-old quandaries about meaning, evil, presence, fate, death, and, strangely, even redemption.

In the first and simplest of the narrator's three curious events, three criminals named Green, Berry, and Hill die for a robbery-murder they commit in 1911 in the Greenberry Hill section of London. The narrator concludes that he "would like to think this [coincidence] was only a matter of chance" (1:10). That sort of dismissive conclusion becomes more difficult in the second incident. In 1983, as reported in the *Reno Gazette*, in the aftermath of a forest fire, firefighters find dead in a treetop miles from any source of water a fully equipped scuba diver named Delmar Darion. That in itself would not be so strange, for his arrival in the treetop is quite explainable: while diving, Delmar was scooped from Lake Tahoe by an airplane water tanker swooping down to fill its tanks to drop water on a nearby forest fire. However, then comes the really strange part: the pilot of the plane, Craig Hansen, "an estranged father of four [with] a poor tendency to drink," had two evenings earlier drunkenly assaulted a casino blackjack dealer, namely, Delmar Darion, for dealing him a bad hand (2:06). Racked by guilt, pilot Hansen proceeds to kill himself, and this time the narrator struggles to understand: "And I am trying to think this was all only a matter of chance" (2:44). Questions and more questions.

The last remarkable incident, pushing the limits of credulity still further, is the death in Los Angeles in 1958 of seventeen-year-old Sydney Barringer, who attempted suicide by plunging from the roof of the nine-story apartment building in which he lived with his parents. Die he does, but his mother is arrested for murder since her shotgun blast, aimed toward her husband, exits a window to strike and kill son Sydney as he plummets past his family's apartment. It is judged to be murder because a window washer's safety net below would have saved Sydney's life if he had not first died from the shotgun wound inflicted amid his descent. Furthermore, in irony upon irony, it was Sydney who loaded the shotgun, the typically unloaded weapon his bitterly argumentative parents regularly brandished at each other amid their quarrels. His hope was that one parent would finally point the gun at the other and fire it, thereby killing one parent, sending the other to jail, and finally freeing Sydney from a life of incessant parental combat. All of this Anderson's narrator explains in detail, including diagrams, ending with the odd fact that while Sydney's mother was charged with killing her son, Sydney himself, the victim, was noted as an accomplice in his own murder. By now, the previously cautious narrator seemingly has no choice but to declare that "in the humble opinion of this narrator . . . this is not just 'something that happened.' This cannot be 'one of those things. . . .' This, please, cannot be that. And for what I would like to say, I can't. This was not just a matter of chance." Moving from the tentativeness of his comment on the Green-Berry-Hill episode, the narrator now seems quite convinced of the fact that, to quote the last sentence of his comment, "These strange things happen all the time" (5:44).

It is by this means—protracted contemplation on the strangeness and mysteriousness of events—that Anderson extends the questions about chance and coincidence to ponder what role these oddities that "happen all the time" might play in the ordinary lives of pretty much ordinary run-of-the-mill people (5:56). What makes these events so very strange, and who sponsors such implausibility, and for what purposes? Indeed, such questions begin and shape the whole film. As Lane comments, the "roaming, questioning quality of this opening serves as preparation for the remaining three hours," pushing viewers toward a posture of wonder and curiosity as *Magnolia* cycles again and again through an array of sorely bruised lives, only, finally, to have their psycho-emotional slides miraculously disrupted—to good effect, to say the least. Apparently, the greatly implausible does happen, and for very good reasons.

Just One, the Loneliest Number

With the prologue's mounting vexation about the meaning of events firmly in mind, Anderson leaps into a brief but telling serial catalogue of the flock of characters in whose lives he will, in effect, test out the speculations set forth by the narrator. To this end, amid a black screen following a very brief title credit of a wildly unfolding magnolia blossom, Anderson begins the first of an array of Aimee Mann's songs (this one written by Harry Nilsson; the others are by her), the urgently sorrowful "One," the song that defines the preeminent reality, isolation and loneliness, of all those lives that swirl by for the next three hours under Anderson's wrenching scrutiny. With the song loudly reiterating over and over again—"One is the loneliest number / That you'll ever do"—Anderson launches a lengthy montage survey of just which lonely people he has in mind for testing out his thesis about the role of chance, and they are indeed a mournful, disconnected bunch.

We glimpse all the principals, and a long list it is: the odious Frank T. J. Mackey (Tom Cruise) in an infomercial pitching his loathsome *Seduce and Destroy*, a video series that pitches sex as a counter to relationship; Claudia Wilson Gator (Melora Walters) hooking up, snorting, and then paying for the snort, part-time hooker that she is; her father, long-running quiz show host and "family man" Jimmy Gator (Philip Baker Hall), rudely copulating with his secretary before he heads to his doctor's office to receive a terminal cancer diagnosis; a contestant on Gator's *What Do Kids Know?* quiz show, the angelic-looking Stanley Spector (Jeremy Blackman), whose brilliance is a meal ticket for his bullying, narcissistic would-be actor father (Michael Bowen); bumbling and needy quiz-kid veteran Donnie Smith (William H. Macy), whose 1968 $100,000 quiz-show jackpot was pilfered by his parents; the embittered, self-loathing *paterfamilias* of all these people, the soon-to-die television magnate Earl Partridge (the brilliant Jason Robards Jr., himself during shooting suffering from terminal cancer); his nurse (and confessor) Phil Parma (Philip Seymour Hoffman), whose tender care for Partridge sears the film; Partridge's guilt- and grief-stricken, and presently hysterical, mink-clad youngish wife, Linda (Julianne Moore); and finally, straight arrow but inept LA cop Jim Kurring (John C. Reilly), whose plaintive *Cops*-style self-dramatizing monologues wrench the soul. Viewers glimpse the long catalogue of misery great and small that mostly derives from an excess of guilt and self-loathing. It is not a pretty sight, and it goes on and on, one character after another, isolated and lost, succumbing to the threshing machine that life can be. Everyone, after all, in Aimee Mann's opening hymn, is just "one," and one is the "loneliest number."

And so it goes among the disconnected, whose mutual loneliness is about the only thing that links them together. At once clarifying and balancing the downward arc of tragedy is Anderson's pervasive use of the work of Aimee Mann, whose propulsive music and witty, incisive lyrics simply dominate—omniscient, wise, cajoling, hounding, consoling, and always haunting, on and on. Most of all, it connects those disconnected many, and as such, as a dimension of style, forecasts an eventuality of which the characters themselves have no inkling. After all, Mann's music and singing provide still another narrative voice, a prism, both affective and cognitive, that counsels audiences on what to make of the people and the lives they witness; it is a crucial help throughout, a complex host that inhabits the film.

While Mann's lyrics enliven, link, and illumine themes, the music itself sustains and carries the narrative, even setting the rhythm for scenes and editing. In its heavy reliance on score as a narrative prism, *Magnolia* extends movie music beyond its usual atmospherics to become, in its own right—so pervasive and smart is its constant presence—another major character, in this case a brooding lyrical interpreter of the action of the film. In short, the music itself becomes a nondiegetic presence, external to the story, a narrator more important than the official one who appears first and last, for this voice clarifies, deepens, and links the pained and vexing experience of those random folks the camera visits. Moreover, to confirm the centrality of Mann's music, Anderson confesses that the whole of the film grew out of one line from friend Aimee Mann's yet unreleased new album, subsequently entitled with the release of the film *Magnolia: Music from the Motion Picture* (1999). More than that, Anderson says he listened to the album constantly through the writing of the film.[5]

And it works, the music's liveliness, jive, and smarts carrying viewers through virtually every stricken character's dire emotional paroxysms. Moreover, songs often supply and coalesce narrative pivots toward the notion that all this sorrow and madness do not wholly define the world, and its own interpretive voice throughout supplies, especially in songs "Wise Up" and "Save Me," a kind of supranarrative referential frame for sustaining action and supplying hope. After all, the singer's presence throughout, commenting and interpreting, suggests that these characters are not finally lost and alone, for another someone broods and sings over their plight even if it is only to proffer some hard reality from which they typically flee.

5. Lane, *Magnolia*, 8, and chap. 4 on the role of Mann's music in the film.

This role reaches a crescendo of sorts in one of the most effective and implausible sequences in the whole film, as the assorted host of characters, each followed by another, join in singing "Wise Up," something that almost all of them desperately need to do. Indeed, "It's not going to stop till you wise up." That sequential chorus even includes, one, the dying and comatose Earl Partridge and, two, wife Linda, also comatose and at that point dying from a suicidal overdose.

While the device shows the thematic proximity of the lyric to the substance of the narrative, the songs simultaneously, and perhaps oddly, with their hip commentary work to distance viewers, imparting the sense that the story is after all an artificial construct and not life itself. And they also sustain one gist of the prologue, namely that there is an intelligent presence external and superior to the characters that not only sees but also comments on, empathizes with, and admonishes them, and, at long last, intervenes on their behalf amid their plight. Indeed, the omnipresence of Mann's music suggests that some non-diegetic something (or Something), external and beyond the story, is aware of their dire straits and counsels and sings thereof in a way that seems virtually psalmic. In short, that very present Presence reassures viewers that at the very least some knowing, savvy intelligence of some kind attends and, late in the film, intervenes in their troubled lives. At the very least, the music provides for viewers an interpretive life raft as they witness the assorted characters themselves thrash about in their individual seas of personal apocalypse.

And always over all of this, often smothering the characters' words, is Mann's "One Is the Loneliest Number," which becomes both lament and dirge for the woefulness of everyone's relational and psychic condition. The lyric says it all: "One is the loneliest number you'll ever know."[6] And in case the listener does not get the point about the mournfulness of rejection and isolation, the second verse repeats the word "loneliest" seven times. One thing that *Magnolia* is not is subtle.

If this constant woe of these many lives were not enough, the forecast is not so good either. After the initial survey of the heapings of desolation in the lives of Anderson's separate characters, Mann's music ceases, and Anderson throws up on the screen the first of his many weather forecasts. Though clearly meant to be whimsical, the forecasts do foreshadow what comes next—in this case, more bad news, "Partly

6. Aimee Mann, "One Is the Loneliest Number," Azlyrics.com, accessed January 14, 2016.

Cloudy, 82% Chance of Rain," in which the chance of rain echoes the constant reference, some fifty times in *Magnolia*, to Exodus's rain of frogs (12:57).

If that forecast were not enough, Anderson now gives a protracted up-close look at the unhappy lives of his protagonists. Policeman Jim Kurring, on a disturbance call, encounters the belligerent Marcie (Cleo King), an African American woman, who delivers for three and a half minutes a profane, obscene, and darkly comic rant to divert Kurring from finding what looks to be a dead white male in the closet (the first of several DWMs). Throughout Kurring is polite and also, seemingly inevitably for him, officious, oh-so-aware of his role as a helpful cop and "doing good," as his *Cops*-like exposition of his philosophy has recounted (12:41). Anderson then cuts to more death, as the beautiful, minked-up Linda Partridge, now shrouded in both literal and figurative darkness, rants to Earl's doctor that "he's dying, . . . dying as we're sitting here. . . . How can you tell me to calm down?" (16:46). For Earl's mounting pain and, by extension, Linda's hysteria at Earl's pain, the physician prescribes a heavy dose of liquid morphine that will ease his suffering but also smother all traces of the distinguishable Earl, a prospect with which Linda has more than a little trouble, as becomes apparent as the camera slowly dollies toward her anxious, twitching face. For Linda, as the loss of Earl approaches, things will only get worse, as is also true for her fast-dying, self-recriminating husband, to whom Anderson quite logically next attends.

In contrast, and far from a man who's losing his mind to pain, the very-soon-to-die Earl Partridge seems to have a better grasp of himself than ever before. Apparently, in this instance, the approach of death provides a clarifying tonic for the soul, though his is bitterly rancorous, particularly toward himself and his life, and it is to matters of self and guilt to which Earl incessantly returns whenever he regains consciousness. Unlike employee Jimmy Gator, whose many crimes are lost in a lifelong swill of booze, dying Earl remembers all too well. For this Anderson again summons the foulest possible language of moral loathing as the mode of Partridge's screed, so much so that the immensely reassuring Phil Parma first teases him and then asks him why all this self-hatred. What sets off the vitriol this time, it seems, is the thought of his son, who lives nearby but with whom he has not had contact for five or ten years (he complains about his inability to keep in his head a "time line").

Here, as in his later discourse on the "love of his life," Partridge turns all into a kind of aria of self-condemnation, to which Anderson's lighting plays as descant, first deeply shadowing Earl in assorted close-ups and concluding the scene with a medium-distance shot of the living room, in which seemingly beatific light pours down on Earl, having finally confessed his crimes, as he lies on the king-sized hospital bed that sits in front of the fireplace (an echo perhaps of the fireplace, or entrance to hell, before which Charles Foster Kane, another media magnate, stood in his enormous but empty mansion).

In this last contemplative shot, the measure of light far exceeds any plausible light source or explanation, unless there are blindingly bright spots in the ceiling, which would be a cruel thing to do to a fading cancer victim. Some measure of light seems to have at last come to old, forlorn, and, by his own reckoning, corrupt Earl Partridge. As Phil walks about wondering how to accomplish Earl's request to find his son, the opening strains of Strauss's *Thus Sprach Zarathustra*, oddly, begin to play and continue even as Anderson cuts to a black screen that stays black for ten seconds as music and cheers mount. It is a flamboyant leap to the world of Earl's estranged son, Frank T. J. Mackey, to whom Tom Cruise contributes his best-ever acting.

The peculiar lighting of Earl Partridge's deathbed carries nicely into Mackey's vilely misogynistic fantasy, a bizarre, Gothic half-world of psycho-ethical death for himself and his deluded acolytes. The music that seems ill fitting for closing the sickbed scene of the father of Jack, as Earl called him, is used to stoke the adulation of a horde of benighted males attending Mackey's weekend Seduce and Destroy seminar. Remarkably, the actual-factual reality of Frank/Jack and his gospel of female destruction proves even more repugnant than the glimpse provided in the infomercial running on a television in the film's opening character survey. As the music mounts in the darkness of a hotel meeting room, high key spotlights slowly brighten to outline Mackey doing some sort of balletic body birth ritual that is meant to display his hard-body virility—or whatever—especially as he ends his pantomime with a pose that suggests he is displaying an enormous male member. It is amply repulsive and, in its narcissism, misogyny, and obscene verbal violence, only barely watchable—and that is the point. There is such a thing as obscene, not because of what it depicts sexually but because of its radical narcissism and vicious reduction of women in the extreme vulgarisms of mere "bush" or "cherry pie" that Mackey typically uses to describe them. Like a bad Holiness televangelist turned Nietszchean sexual *Übermensch*, or Satan himself, Mackey preens, struts, shouts, thumps, gyrates, and grinds, even to the point of simulating sex as his minions cheer and chant along. He opens with his mantra, "Respect the cock, and tame the cunt," and then riffs graphically on the notion that biology justifies all, no matter the cruelty to other people. And on it goes: "It is animal. We—are—men" (26:55).

It is a remarkable notion, to say the least, and it is a remarkable performance, in which a long-haired (greasy), leather-vested (black) Mackey lays out in blunt terms a coercive, if not tyrannous sexual ideology (or is it rationalization?) of instrumentalizing women that runs just below the surface of American male culture. This is moralist-satirist Anderson at work, and surely by the time we learn the name of Mackey's personal assistant, Captain Muffy, even the most enamored must understand that Mackey's comic-book fantasy is a land of infantile wish and fantastical compensation. The really sad thing, as we soon find out, is that self-created Mackey learned it all from the father of Jack, a man Mackey thoroughly and plainly hates. While Mackey has rejected father Earl Partridge to the point of taking a different name than the one his father gave him, he nonetheless *is* every bit, as we find out, his father's son, only writ large. A good deal of what fuels his self-help positive power-thinking is plain revenge, though he has misdirected it toward women, doing as Daddy did with Lily, the mother of Jack, whom Earl abandoned to their pubescent son Jack as she slowly died of breast cancer. Psychologically, while hating his father, he has taken the one route, the abuse of women, that subconsciously he believes will make his father proud of him. As the film's oft-repeated mantra has it, "You may be done with the past, but that past is not done with you." To be sure, as Anderson proclaims at one point in the film, the sins of the fathers are visited upon the children to the third and fourth generations, for the fathers bequeath their wrongs to their children, and perhaps their sons in particular.

Throughout Anderson pushes this exacting maxim with relentless, driving energy, and it is prominent in the connection between scenes and between all the characters. Just as Frank Mackey is advising his gang of faltering males to resort to deception and trickery as routes to seduction, even advising faking a personal tragedy to win female sympathy, the scene cuts to one unabated thoroughgoing tragedy, a case in point, namely, the plight of Claudia Gator, who's sleeping off her night of quick sex and drugs when her father Jimmy comes calling, wanting to "talk" because, as he informs her, he's fatally ill and will die soon of cancer. For him, though, there is from Claudia only screaming rejection, a violent, deeply visceral repulsion at which audiences wonder, not yet knowing, as they discover near the end of the film, that Gator sexually abused Claudia as a teenager. So much for Mackey's gospel of unfettered male sexual access to whomever. For now, Anderson simply lets the wreckage and antipathy that is Claudia flare across the screen, providing still another instance of profound father-child hostility.

Then, in quick succession, follow three more instances of parent-child wreckage: inept, deluded parent exploitee Donnie Smith losing his sales job at an appliance store, even though he needs money to pay for braces on his already perfect teeth (his Arab American employer, Solomon Solomon [Alfred Molina], is incredulous at Donnie's plan); police investigating the murder of the dead man found in Marcie's closet, the husband she has murdered to protect her son and grandson from abuse (this is another, and rather complicated, story line that Anderson, happily, deleted from the final cut; read the shooting script or view the extras on the DVD); and finally, sweet Stanley Spector hustled along, literally and figuratively, by his always indignant father so Stanley can continue to support his narcissistic parent by winning even more on the Partridge-produced and Gator-hosted *What Do Kids Know?* All in all, fathers don't look so good.

Light Showers

From "One" and the worlds of individual characters, *Magnolia's* psycho-social realism not only gathers steam but further clarifies and deepens the streams of woe that explain the many inner troubles of the be-leaguered characters. Things do not for anyone get better, in the near term at least. Rain it does, steadily, as the lives of the separate charac-ters deteriorate further, although all this misfortune hardly amounts to a sprinkle given what will soon fall from the sky. Stanley is late to the broadcast of *What Do Kids Know?*, Claudia snorts more coke, Jim responds to an apartment-house complaint about screaming and loud music, Linda needs more head meds, and Frank sits for a lengthy inter-view with television newswoman Gwenovier (April Grace). In general, for all these principal characters, all goes from very bad to much, much worse. The predominant tone throughout, though mixed with ample humor, as the camera and music whirl and cycle in relentless momen-tum, is a kind of gleeful lament, best understood perhaps as of exultant relish for the film's brutal honesty about the woe-filled lives of just about everyone. Indeed, the tone here echoes the sort of high-spirited dark humor of Jonathan Swift's *Gulliver's Travels*.

The most sensational of the glimpses in this cycle of visitation of his central characters, following upon Linda's tirade, is talk-show inter-viewer Gwenovier's encounter with Linda's stepson Frank T. J. Mackey, who cavorts around, trousers around his ankles, in white jockey briefs, in the afterglow of his Seduce and Destroy "lecture," absolutely stone-cold stark manic and embarrassingly talkative, bragging fantastically of his sexual prowess and triumphs. Clearly, he celebrates his personal mythos, one that is infantile in its narcissism and wounded in its pro-fane self-captivation: "I swear to . . . God, I am Batman," he crows, and that's just a bit of his self-congratulatory drivel. After all, as he tells Gwenovier, "I am what I believe. I do as I say. I live by these rules as religiously as I preach them. . . . I will take what is mine"—and that is every female he might possibly want (50:45). If it were not for Tom Cruise playing the role, who has played nothing but good guys, we'd right off think this fellow is a nutcase sexual predator, as in fact he is, even though he advises trickery to get what he wants, no doubt to keep the law off his back. Finally, Mackey strikes one as a case of the arrested development of the small boy who plays by himself in the backyard dreaming of hitting home runs. Indeed, there is no indication whatever that Mackey has even a twinge of the slightest self-doubt or that the audience is to take him for anything but what they see, for he does finally, incredibly, take himself and all that monumental hokum as ultimate truth.

With this portraiture of Mackey, one that is only extended by the actual interview in which Gwenovier exposes his concocted personal history, we witness another instance of the American capacity of self-invention, the penchant for self-creation that is an art form in Hollywood (and so it will be again with Anderson's *The Master* [2012], an eviscerating take on L. Ron Hubbard's and Hollywood's Scientology cult). In fact, Mackey has fabricated his education and reverses the fate of his parents: his father lives and his mother died and is not around to bless his "go get 'em [women], honey" obsession (1:11:02). Throughout Mackey claims, as he argues in his Seduce and Destroy manual, "the most useless thing in the world is that which is behind me" (1:29:16), a view the film pointedly disputes ("you may be done with the past but the past is not done with you"). For Mackey, grinning his best leer, there are "more important things to put myself into" than the past (1:28:59).

For Mackey, the past is irrelevant and an encumbrance to his compensatory fantasy. He has no truck with the film's coda that the past shapes the present and "is not done with you." Indeed, the past does haunt, as Anderson repeatedly avers, even unto the third and fourth generations. Again, Anderson seems to suggest that to evade that reality there is no idiocy or offense or fantasy that a good part of the culture, and the male part in particular, will not embrace. Gwenovier's question, the one that turns hyped-up Mackey silent for the rest of the interview, applies not only to his life history but also to his philosophy as a whole: "Why would you lie, Frank?" (1:31:30).

And so it goes, as the film reiterates over and over. The desperate sadness of it all overwhelms. A stunningly beautiful woman, and running errands in a full-length mink, Linda is seemingly without any inner resources whatsoever, especially now that she has at last come to love a dying husband she married for money and on whom she has habitually cheated. Linda rants and screams to the suspicious druggists who think beautiful women only party and never dread and grieve. She waxes Kierkegaardian: "I'm sickness," indeed sickness unto death, who has "sickness all around me" (1:13:20), a telling personal confession that amply fits the whole of the culture in which she partakes. So acute is her sense of guilt that she begs to change Earl's will in order to *exclude* her from getting any money. Another redhead, Donnie Smith encounters a rival (Henry Gibson) for the affections of a muscular bartender, a fellow who himself sports orthodontics. Smith promptly gets roundly drunk, blubbering to his rival that he "used to be smart" but then was twice struck by lightning, perhaps meaning his parents, and is "now . . . just stupid" (1:27:50). The whole bar then hears about Donnie having "love to give" before he finally ends up in the bathroom with his head in the toilet vomiting and mumbling about the sins of the fathers and reciting the film's mantra on the inescapability of the past (1:56:00).

In what is perhaps the film's most poignant misadventure, officious and very lonely Jim Kurring instantly falls for Claudia Gator Wilson, even though it is blatantly obvious that the woman is either unhinged or has an enormous drug problem. Here the bathos of two lost lives spills into comedy as Kurring lectures her on the dangers of loud music and hearing loss, which is the least of her storehouse of problems, proclaiming that "I'm here to help you," though surprisingly that claim will prove true enough. The full measure of Kurring's ineptitude soon appears when during the pursuit on foot of a suspect in a rainstorm he commits the greatest of all cop offenses and loses his gun. He sobs, distraught, "Lord, what is happening to me? I'm lost out here. . . . Please God, help me find the gun" (2:01:53). His desperate prayer is answered much later and after much agony, and by quite miraculous means.

Or, for that matter, God—or some supernatural something, for that is what it will take given the magnitude of the ills—help everyone in general find the way, for these assorted benighted pilgrims are lost and desperate, feverishly grabbing at whatever wild anything that promises to give them some semblance of a life or happiness. And that task seems harder than ever, given the massive distortions of meaning and goodness their culture promulgates.

In that regard, Claudia's father is in no better shape, another contorted grown-up, collapsing in the middle of an installment of *What Do Kids Know?*, "America's longest-running quiz show," on which the kids, meaning entirely Stanley Spector, have in eight weeks amassed a half-million dollars (1:05:40). Apparently reckoning comes eventually to everyone, even the aptly named Jimmy Gator, sexual predator that he is, for he recites the film's mantra, though he is the one least capable of recognizing his torrent of evildoing: "The Book says we may be through with the past, but the past ain't through with us" (1:05:15). The past, it seems, does come to get us, and the reckoning is not easy—or easy to watch.

Confession

All these collapses, rendered with a raw emotional realism that makes them both wrenching and mournful, are what Anderson labels "Meltdowns" (title for DVD chapter 8), and in virtually every instance these meltdowns constitute a necessary prelude to what follows. For that, the only term that fits is "confession," one statement after another by the array of characters that one's life is indeed calamity, whether as a result of their own meanness or self-destruction or the malignancy of others, though the former seems to emerge from the latter.

Some culprits have devoured the lives of others, such as the cancerous old men in the film, Jimmy Gator and Earl Partridge, who have blighted the lives of spouses and their profoundly damaged children. For them, Claudia and Jack/Frank, as for the film's other victims of abuse and neglect, Donnie Smith and Stanley Spector, life has amounted to a fevered effort to stanch wounds that have only resulted in further disasters: hard-core drug addiction; fantastic self-mythologizing sexual aggression; naked, plaintive neediness; and, in the only seemingly healthy response to abuse, intellectual curiosity and mystical openness, though Stanley has more than enough time to lose that before he hits voting age. Within the course of the film, all these assorted characters, transgressors and victims alike, are in effect stripped naked, made to recognize, like King Lear, the pitiless storm of evil that has ferociously enveloped them. This is the dire bad news of how voracious life can be, as novelist Frederick Buechner has put it.[7]

In *Magnolia*, the storm has reached a critical intensity that prompts recognition and, upon that, different sorts of confessions, remarkable displays of moral culpability that prove every bit as wrenching as the meltdowns. And confession itself prepares the way for recognizing the necessity of changed perception and behavior. Aimee Mann's "Wise Up" swirls up and over, like a whirlwind gathering the disparate lives, as explanation, judgment, and counsel: indeed, things will not stop or

---

7. Frederick Buechner, *Telling the Truth: The Gospel as Tragedy, Comedy, and Fairy Tale* (San Francisco: Harper, 1977), 71.

improve until you "wise up."[8] Recognizing errors and wrongs seems a necessary prelude to gaining any wisdom at all. First, though, the storm intensifies, dense with remorse and futility.

The wising up is the hard part, but this they do, and it displays thoroughly mortifying self-recognition, uttered not to a priest or a god of some sort but to the deepest, well-buried mainsprings of selfhood—to psyche, conscience, soul, whatever. After the anguish of saying goodbye to her unconscious husband, Linda Partridge turns to apologize to nurse Phil Parma, a man of immense empathy and compassion. She full well knows what a fool and scoundrel she is, having confessed to her lawyer and also to Phil her serial abuses of her marriage. That has gone so far, as mentioned earlier, to try to get herself *removed* from Earl's will, a bequest that would very likely make her a very rich woman. For her, in short, no penance could possibly prove sufficient to lessen her avalanche of guilt, all of which seems quite well deserved. So she apologizes to Phil, amid her tears tenderly stroking his face, for she had earlier furiously berated and slapped Parma for trying to contact Frank. Clearly, Phil here serves as a proxy for the unconscious Earl. It is a blanket, full-hearted confession, blunt and vulgar though it be: "I do things, and I f— up. I f— up. Can you forgive me?" (2:04:35).

And then, emerging into full awareness one last time before death, comes Earl, who has his own mountain of guilt and self-condemnation. The guilt hounds him through his very last breaths of self-awareness. Earl's confession is a stunning ten-minute monologue pulled off effortlessly by the late, very great Jason Robards. Though Linda has come to love him, however belatedly, Earl's only concern is his multitudinous crimes against his first wife, Lily, whom he here labels the love of his life (he thinks Linda "nuts" and "daffy," albeit a nice girl, as he says early in the film [20:48]). A quiet aria of self-recrimination, the speech is self-lacerating vitriol: "And I cheated on her [Lily] over and over and over again. Because I wanted to be a man, and didn't want her to be a woman . . . a smart, free person who *was* something. My . . . mind then . . . so stupid that . . . mind . . . stupid. . . . What would I think, did I think for what I'd done? She was my wife. For twenty-three years I went behind her over and over, . . . a— that I am" (2:11:00).

Moreover, when breast cancer began to ravage her to ugly death, he abandoned her, leaving his fourteen-year-old son, Jack, to nurse her.

8. Aimee Mann, "Wise Up," Azlyrics.com, January 14, 2016.

Old Earl failed even to call her before she died, something for which the son cannot forgive the father, as we soon find out. Guilt over the enormity of his offense now shreds his very soul: "I loved her so. She knew what I did. She knew all the . . . stupid things that I'd done, but the love was stronger than anything you can think of. G— regret, the g— regret" (2:14:45). As the narrator says, "so it goes," people chewed and devoured by their own stupidity and self-concern—so much so that as Earl nears the end of his speech, the lives of other characters silently play beneath his words, suggesting the desperate moral and existential proximity of their lives to his. So great is, in the words of the bygone radio series *The Shadow*, "the evil [that] lurks in the hearts of men," that it spurns even the flagrant, unconditional love of Earl's Lily or Jimmy's Rose (Melinda Dillon), both named after flowers, as is the film.

As Earl talks, muttering observations like "Mistakes like this you don't make," his words become voice-over commentary as the film again surveys the errors of others. With Earl's self-excoriating words echoing, viewers watch other characters in different stages of either undertaking or regretting similar "mistakes." Or sometimes both, as in the case of Donnie Smith, who breaks into the Solomon brothers' store to rob the safe to pay for his braces, only to afterward confront sudden regret that will bring him to try to put the money back. That will be made especially difficult because, as the bumbling Donnie finds out, he has broken off his key in the lock to the backdoor of the store.

As for Jim Kurring's story, the police search for Kurring's suspect and Kurring's gun, and Kurring himself will admit to Claudia on their date that he's a bad cop and a laughingstock, a far distance from the bromides of "doing good" with which he has tried to cover over his self-doubt and quite real inadequacies (he rides alone, no other police wishing to partner with him). Claudia snorts coke in the bathroom to try to get through her date with Jim but then bolts, even though she knows it's possible to have with him an actual relationship: "now that I've met you, is it all right if we never see each other again?," the line from Mann that proved the seed for the creation of *Magnolia* (2:41:03). With her it is perhaps not so much insecurity as just plain fear of betrayal, a liability inflicted on her by her predator father, a gator if there ever was one. After the betrayals of father and "family man" Jimmy, Claudia simply cannot risk that sort of pain with another man named Jim. Then, alone in her Mercedes convertible in an empty, rain-soaked parking lot, an apt representation of her real predicament in life, Linda swallows a lethal dose of Earl's narcotics. All mire in the fractures of the betrayal of relationship, a cyclone that devours all. Throughout this long catalogue, Anderson pounds home, as insistently as the music's rhythms, the absolute preeminence of relationship in human well-being. Indeed, as all his many remarkable films since *Magnolia* show, this seems for Anderson the central pivot of metaphysical reality.

Meanwhile, back at Linda's house (which is also Frank's father's house), nurse Phil Parma having at last reached him, Jack/Frank parks in front, mustering the courage to go in to face the man he loathes— and his own tangled self. Frank, or Jack, as his father calls him, is not in a happy state, for Gwenovier has thoroughly "exposed" the "facts" of his bogus life story, and why, as she calmly and persistently asks him about his imposture. In fact, Frank/Jack's whole adult life, especially as Frank T. J. Mackey, has proven a sham, a flimsy, if boisterous, compensatory protective covering for his own double whammy of suffering in the profound losses of his mother's death and his father's desertion of both his mother and himself. Frank had begun the interview strutting about the room in his white briefs, his pants about his ankles, boasting to his female interviewer of his prowess with every woman and seemingly on the verge of exposing himself entirely (he will be exposed, though not in the way he intended). In this, oddly, in ways it is clear that Jack does not begin to understand, he simply repeats his loathed father's desire "to be a man," which is as much a rationale as his father gives for his own loathsome behavior. By the end of the interview, however, Frank has encountered quite another and altogether terrifying kind of nakedness he had not expected or desired, and the full measure of that will come clear when he again meets his father, a test indeed for his constant stream of misogynist playacting. The stark, undeniable fact, the truth that cannot be spun by fantasy, is that there is no answer to the question of Jack's "why" or Earl's "why," except for compensatory avoidance, which the scared and silent Frank can no longer pull off.

But for poor Jack/Frank, his day goes from very bad to much worse. No sooner does he gets smacked with the lies of his fabricated self than he receives a call summoning him to his father's deathbed. And that is a bridge the macho man cannot cross, or so it seems as he sits in that car singing about "wising up," waiting and waiting to confront the beasts, specifically his father *and* himself. Finally, in he

does go, at least into the entryway, after first making sure that Phil has cleared away the dogs. There, at that way station, he again has to gather his strength. And when he finally travels all the way across the kitchen to his father's bed, all of fifty feet, he lets loose with a vile stream of epithets attached to the furious wish that the old man die forthwith. And on it goes, and on it goes, for a full two minutes, as Frank seethes, a condemnation that rather matches his father's earlier self-indictment; there has been nothing else like it ever on screen, which can also be said for the other parallel meltdowns afoot, from Stanley to Jimmy to Donnie and Claudia. And then, after a quick survey of the other misfortunes, Anderson returns to Frank, writhing in emotional pain and beginning to cry. And then, and then, something really strange happens. Frank slowly becomes Jack, the deserted boy he once was.

Over the next painful minute, the rage turns to tears as Jack begins to beg his father *not* to die, bawling into the bedclothes, "Don't go away, you . . . a——" (2:42:00). His loathing turns to loving. Strange. Scared and silent at the truths of his life, Jack cries, and Phil cries, confessor and mediator that he is.

And on air, Stanley Spector, another spurned son, also has moisture problems, wetting himself and then chastising producers and audience for regarding him as "cute" or a freak, a message that seems to be heard by Jimmy Gator. As for Gator, he soon after admits to wife Rose that he might indeed have molested daughter Claudia but that he—the unstated likely culprit is booze—cannot really remember, after which Rose flees to her daughter, telling Jimmy that for such crimes he deserves to die alone, and sure enough, what follows insures that he does, and by fire no less.

Save Me?

And what follows, outrageously, incredibly, quite beyond anyone's expectation, and utterly unforeseeable, to enormous salutary effect, is frogs, an abundant downpour of big, plump amphibians plummeting from the sky to smush and splat and goo the streets, turning LA's roads to vehicular skating rinks. To repeat, two hours into a film whose trajectory has been nothing but descent, full of graphic meltdowns and pure despair, amply testing the patience of viewers thirsting for some glimmer of hope for anyone, comes what? A storm of frogs, a crazy, antic frog-fall amid the heretofore unrelentingly dire psycho-relational realism of the film. Indeed, if unto this point viewers doubt the plausibility of quite so many human creatures facing utter bleakness in the very human menagerie Anderson churns up, well, they have not seen anything yet.

Throughout this extraordinary supernatural storm, Anderson's camera has enormous inventive fun observing from every possible perspective, watching upward from the point of view of Donnie Smith as frogs plummet downward, or watching downward as a frog plunges to break through Jimmy Gator's skylight to strike the gun whose discharge will start the fire that will consume Jimmy, sort of the fires of hell coming aboveground.

The big question, then and still, is what to make of this downpour? At first the frog-fall seems a stunt, a preposterous gimmick to disrupt and lighten that increasingly grim descent into swamps of despair. Still, we had been warned by that peculiar prologue—Greenberry Hill and the murder-suicide of Sydney Barringer—about strange occurrences that seemed to have behind them a measure of intentionality by, well, Something or Another. A more conspicuous reference for the coming of the frogs, and one that is far more cogent and thematically pertinent, is the Exodus account of the assorted plagues, frogs being one of them, that fell upon ancient Egypt as a part of Moses's "negotiation" to free the enslaved Israelites. Each time the rulers backed away from a pledge to let the enslaved Israelites depart, Yahweh zapped them with another storm of woe. That this is a primary referent is emphasized by

Anderson's decision to sprinkle throughout the film some fifty times the numbers that cite a specific chapter and verse in Exodus (8:2): "And if thou refuse to let them go, behold, I will smite all thy borders with frogs" (KJV). There, like the other plagues, the invasion of frogs works simultaneously as a judgment upon the stone-heartedness of the Egyptians *and* as a means of deliverance for the captive Israelites into freedom, autonomy, and, eventually at least, the Promised Land, a place of harmony and milk and honey, though they would first wander for forty years.

What is crucial about this preposterous event is not so much that it happens but what role it plays in effecting a diametrical shift of direction for the story. Specifically, the frog storm initiates a series of profound reorientations—deliverances, if you will—for a broad array of characters, save for one case of unequivocal, and well-deserved, judgment. In this instance deliverance is a first step toward an expansive sort of redemption that leads to forgiveness and, more than that, new empathy, care, and mutuality.

That judgment comes to one of the thoroughgoing scoundrels in the film, Jimmy Gator, whose name reflects his predatory moral history, especially toward women and children. He has habitually, if not compulsively, cheated on his wife, who has bathed her sorrows in alcohol, and he also sexually abused his daughter, though the film is skimpy on the extent of the abuse, something Jimmy himself is not sure of given his own long swim in a flood of booze. What is clear, however, given Claudia's unbridled rage toward her father, is that the profound betrayal of trust has destroyed the woman, now a serious cokehead and part-time hooker. Upon Jimmy's reluctant admission of his "maybe" crime to Rose, she promptly leaves him "to die alone," because in her eyes that is what he deserves, though that is only the half of it in Anderson's moral vision. Cowardly narcissist that he is, Jimmy, after Rose leaves, heads straight to a kitchen drawer to retrieve a handgun that he intends to use to blow his head off, only to have a frog fall through a skylight to knock the gun askew and cause it to fire, the bullet hitting an electrical appliance that causes a short that starts the fire that will consume Jimmy. In short, morally speaking, Jimmy deservedly dies in a fiery hell of his own making. Of course, it is the frog that initiates this just and timely fate, depriving Jimmy of the quick, painless exit he planned from his cancer and his life, though the two can hardly be pulled apart. After all, both he and Earl Partridge *were* cancer upon others. Jimmy's end provides fitting judgment on his moral stature and the wreckage of his deeds.

Mostly, though, for all the principals in *Magnolia*, the frog storm initiates another sort of dramatic turn, and a decisive break from their isolation, namely, a deliverance that promises to heal their ample woundedness through a balm of hope, renewal, and a renewed capacity for bonds with others. That surely includes what remains of the Gator family. When Rose departs from Jimmy, she heads straight to Claudia's apartment, having now finally understood the cause of Claudia's self-destruction. En route she is beset by the frog-fall, and Claudia herself, at the spectacle of frogs dropping past her window, falls into pure, screaming terror. After crashing her Jaguar into another car, Rose somehow makes her way through the falling frogs to Claudia's apartment, to find her huddled on the floor. The two clasp each other, the mother embracing her daughter for the first time amid new knowledge of the source of the heretofore mysterious ravages her daughter has suffered. Indeed, the hope in the title of Paul Simon's song "The Mother and Child Reunion" has finally occurred, which for Claudia is the beginning of a new beginning. To emphasize his point about deliverance, Anderson cuts briefly to a print that hangs above the television in Claudia's apartment. In the corner of that print, someone has pasted words from a newspaper headline, "It Can Happen," and indeed, against all odds, it surely has. As preposterous as raining frogs might be, still more unlikely is that the enmity and woe of lives can begin to ebb amid understanding, empathy, and embrace. Those are odds that not even the film's skeptical narrator could possibly calculate.

The same transpires with Jack at the side of his father's deathbed. The impostor Frank has moved from a quaking, vitriolic tirade at his father and his crimes to the sobs of a son, himself once again the amply vulnerable adolescent, the abandoned Jack, imploring his father *not* to die, to "not go away." In the frog storm's last scene, a now calm Jack, over his own storm of rage and sorrow, sits quietly at the comatose man's bedside, listening to the racket of frogs falling on the roof and into the pool outside. From the oblivion into which the opiates have thrust him, Earl awakens to see his son's face just a couple of feet from his own, and he tries desperately to talk, to say something to Jack. Jack listens intently, himself mouthing inaudible words to his father. And then and there, in his effort to speak to his son, Earl Partridge dies. Here, albeit wordlessly, in the intense look into each other's eyes, something like reckoning, forgiveness, and reconciliation seems to have transpired.

The other notable reversal ignited by the frog storm is the peculiar, fortuitous meeting of Jim Kurring and Donnie Smith, perhaps the two loneliest people in the entire film. Jim drives home in his old clunker of a car in a deep funk from his disastrous date with Claudia, who chickened out, snorted, and ran simply because the date had gone *well*. For poor Kurring the futility of trying to connect with anyone seems painfully apparent. Driving down a deserted street, he sees in the corner of his eye Donnie Smith trying to climb the downspout of the Solomon brothers' store where he had earlier robbed the safe. Driving home, the hapless Donnie had come to a moment of self-realization and turned around to return to the store safe the money he'd copped. When he discovered that he broke off his key in the lock when leaving the store, he attempted to get to the roof to enter through a skylight. And then came the frogs. When Donnie looked up, a plummeting frog smacked him in the face, knocking him from the downspout to the ground, where he lay unconscious, his glasses broken, bleeding, and missing some teeth (recall that he had stolen the money to pay for braces to "fix" his already perfect teeth).

The good-hearted Jim runs through the falling frogs to pull the limp Donnie to shelter under the canopy of an adjoining gas station. Miraculously, as much so as the phenomenon of falling frogs, the hyper-legalistic Jim decides to help Donnie return the money to the safe, now caring more for the fate of this ill-fated clown he has come across than for the niceties of the law and being a "good cop." Indeed, he even refers Donnie to a clinic that will fix his now seriously damaged teeth. More than that, after saying good-bye to Donnie, Jim sits in his car reckoning with the need to forgive, something his sanctimony has kept him from seeing. As for Donnie, he sees himself as a fool and seems now, finally, to have some sort of purchase on who he really is—and a new and genuine friend in Jim.

Everyone who witnesses the frog storm initially reacts in incredulity and terror, save for one, who greets it with wonder and delight. Young Stanley Spector, the sensation of Jimmy Gator's exploitive quiz show that pits adults against children (leave it to Hollywood, specifically Earl Partridge Productions, to make money on generational conflict). As the frogs fall, Anderson's camera locates Stanley alone at a table surrounded by open books in the dimly lit, deserted school library in which Stanley has sought refuge after his TV meltdown. The camera at first sees him from middle distance but then slowly dollies in for a close-up, a strategy that infuses the sequence with more than a little gravity. Bright light flickers on his face as he looks aside and upward with a wide smile of pleasure upon his face. He whispers that "this happens," the very sort of assertion that we find in the prologue and on the print on Claudia's wall. Indeed, we have earlier seen in Stanley's perpetual pile of books a best-seller on the paranormal and extraordinary by Ricky Jay, which provides something of an inside joke because Jay, as the credits indicate, is the voice of the film's unseen narrator (2:50:57).

For Stanley, the event offers confirmation of a whole different realm and understanding of human experience, one that differs markedly from the hopeless and loveless constraint in which he finds himself, as merely a "product," whether for Earl Partridge or his father. The logic seems to be that if something so extraordinary as frogs falling from the sky can happen, it is also possible that the conditions of his life might improve. And such seems to be the case. We see Stanley but one more time in the film, to witness the fruit of this confirmation of hope for a different kind of world. "What do kids know?" asks the title of the quiz show, and Anderson answers that with the suggestion that they know a lot more than the ordinary adult, for no one else in the film understands and imagines so clearly and fully as Stanley.

"It Can Happen"

"And So It Goes"

That is the question, after all. Not the usual weather report to begin the climax of this sprawling saga of lost souls beset by preposterous wrongs and even more preposterous frogs. Instead, the last intercut promises to address the perplexity, if not incredulity, of viewers and give some sense of what this all finally amounts to. Anderson first returns to the commentary of the narrator, who promptly recalls the beginning of the film and his assertions that the extraordinary events of the film do not "just happen." Much to his credit, Anderson moves well beyond the mere assertion that such things as frog storms happen to explain their consequences in the way his surviving characters thereafter experience and navigate their painfully troubled lives. It is indeed one thing to claim the reality of some metaphysical intrusion into the course of human affairs. Such claims merely attest to the reality of some sort of mysterious supernatural power, and the display of frogs could well be no more than an arbitrary display of that power for the sake of showing off, power for the sake of power. It is quite another thing, however, and more meaningful by far, to suggest that miraculous events arrive to effect human well-being. Are they something more than mere metaphysical fireworks or self-display, more than a cosmic calling-card? Their meaning manifests itself not merely in the fact that they happen, which is where most of the discussion of *Magnolia* has settled, but in what sort of consequence they signal. In short, they happen for reasons quite beyond themselves, and on this Anderson recalls that rubric of judgment and liberation from the exodus story. As the narrator suggests as the body of Earl Partridge is removed from his home, "It is in the humble opinion of this narrator, that strange things happen all the time, and so it goes and so it goes, and the book says, we may be through with the past, but the past ain't through with us." Indeed, at last the assorted characters have recognized the constricting, if not blinding, weight of their pasts, and from that insight have begun to move beyond. After that comment, Anderson will by and large let events do the explaining.

Fittingly, as those last words play, the camera cuts to Jack Partridge sleeping on his father's couch. His father's death would suggest that a chapter in his life is now closed, but he is awakened by Phil Parma with a call from the hospital on the condition of the dreaded Linda, who has emerged from her overdose and ambulance accident (the speeding vehicle flipped on the frog-slick streets to crash in front of the emergency-room entrance). Significantly, Jack has been awakened from his sleep (symbolic perhaps of his long nightmare as Frank Mackey) to deal with the one actual human relationship left over from his father's life. As the narrator suggests at the start of *Magnolia*'s conclusion, the past is not done with us, and what the past demands in the present is a posture of care for others, even those we abhor. As if to add to the point, while Jack speaks on the phone, the camera, providing a model of this very thing, watches Phil clear the linens from Earl's deathbed, weeping as he does so. Phil, through all and after all, is the embodiment of pure *caritas*, a posture of being that is fundamentally alien and opposed to the exploitation that seems to pervade the media empire of Earl Partridge. Next we see Jack walking—not strutting, for once—down a hospital corridor to visit Linda, who is awakening from her multiple brushes with death to a doctor's reassurance that she will get through it all. Jack, it seems—and not Frank—will help her do that, as she will no doubt help him, for they seem, indeed, to have been delivered. In particular, they have been delivered to the possibility of sympathetic human connection.

The cut goes to a close-up of another sleeping figure, Stanley's father, Rick, who is awakened by his son. Stanley enters the room to insist to his callous father that "You've got to be nicer to me, Dad," who in response tells him to go to bed, to which Stanley repeats his demand, the father replying the same (2:54:49). The scene in effect repeats the previous one, with the human demand for kindness firmly in the center. The point here is that Stanley has finally gotten the courage to stand up to his tyrannical father, for whom Stanley has been nothing more than a burdensome source of cash. The suggestion seems to be that the display of frogs, a wondrous event for Stanley, has confirmed his hunch that the impossible can happen, and in Stanley's immediate life, the impossible thing is that his father could possibly be nicer to him. Whether that will happen is beside the point; instead, the consequence of the miracle of the frogs has delivered Stanley to a new condition of hopefulness; his flagging soul has been renewed, at least for a time, in the frog storm's confirmation of his vision that this world is an extraordinary place where anything can and, indeed, does happen, even family members treating one another with simple kindness. And here Stanley's hopefulness stands in stark contrast to Donnie Smith's life of despair and isolation.

Perhaps the clearest indication of the intention behind the frog storm comes in the major changes that transpire in the forlorn, halting Jim Kurring. First, we see Kurring lose his legalism and judgmentalism, which have been two sides of the side coin. That appears in his measure of compassion for hapless Donnie. He first rescues him from the storm and then listens to the bloodied Donnie's plaintive tale of misadventure, bad judgment, and raw yearning for connection: "I really do have love to give; I just don't know where to put it," something Jim himself feels deeply (2:55:38). Anderson cuts to Jim to witness his look not of judgment but of aching compassion for Donnie's messiness, a condition well represented by his appearance; Donnie is now missing front teeth and covered in blood and tears, amid the frogs lying all about. So extraordinary is Kurring's reaction that Anderson endorses it by returning to Jim his missing gun, dropping it from the sky on the pavement before the pair. In short, Kurring has stumbled on the complex and often ambiguous demands of real-world moral choice. And he goes further still. The previously moralistic Kurring helps Donnie return the stolen loot to the store safe.

Kurring's voice-over commentary as this takes place recognizes that a greater good lies in forgiveness. Anderson gives Kurring a remarkable, protracted meditation, one that comes out haltingly, bit by bit, as Kurring himself tries to think his way toward a new posture of seeing and being in the world. And it could well serve as a coda for the film as a whole, spoken to himself as he sits in his car after his encounter with Donnie: "Sometimes people need a little help; sometimes people need to be forgiven, and sometimes they need to go to jail. And that is a very tricky thing on my part, making that call. The law is the law, and heck if I'm gonna break it, but if you can forgive someone, well, that's the tough part. What can we forgive? Tough part of the job, tough part of walking down the street" (2:57:02). It is the last time we see Jim's face in the film, and Anderson spends a long time just looking in close-up at the silent Jim; between long silences, Jim speaks aloud to himself, *Cops*-style, his series of personal insights, each time extending the realm wherein forgiveness is necessary and inescapable.

The first fruit of his insight is the case of Donnie. Kurring has in his mercy already proven a profound help, even providing a lead on fixing Donnie's badly damaged mouth. One has the sense that this collision between the two could begin a meaningful friendship. For Kurring, who can hardly forgive "bad" language, this constitutes another enormous moral leap, and this time he actually is helping someone at some cost to his own heretofore rigid moral code. The shooting script makes his progress even more emphatic than the final cut of the film. The film has Jim brooding and talking to himself in his car for a long while and then driving off. The shooting script extends the shot to watch Jim drive until he "starts to cry a little bit to himself."[9] Indeed, so profound and central has been Jim's epiphany that he moves from the posture of a censorious moralism to one of forgiveness and compassion. It is more than appropriate, then, that the first chords of Aimee Mann's "Save Me" rise to supply a bridge to the film's last scene, wherein Jim continues his new perception of the world and the people in it, very specifically the afflicted Claudia.

A distressed, tearful, red-eyed Claudia sits alone in bed against the wall in her pajamas as the lyrics play over her. Someone else is there attending her, no doubt her mother, but the camera simply looks at Claudia as the lyrics to "Save Me" again begin to play, and its trenchant lines could not be more fitting: "Can you save me? Come on and save me."[10]

It seems a summons that Kurring has heard. As we watch the solitary Claudia, another voice is heard, though barely audible, beneath Mann's piercing, poignant vocal. Kurring has arrived to visit Claudia, and he speaks to Claudia at length, though the audience can hear only, and then but barely, a few scattered phrases of what he says, and viewers never see more than part of his back. For the entire length of the closing scene, done in one take, the camera remains fixed on Claudia, and viewers can only speculate on Jim's words by watching the reaction on her face. We do hear him recall their dinner conversation about honesty, but after that his words are sketchy, and *The Shooting Script* supplies nothing of Kurring's monologue. His monologue once appeared on the website for the film on the Internet Movie Database, and that account seems plausible: "I can't let this go. I can't let you go. Now, you . . . you listen to me now. You're a good person. You're a good and beautiful person, and I won't let you walk out on me. And I won't let you say those things—those things about how stupid you are and this and that. I won't stand for that. You want to be with me . . . then you be with me. You see?"

9. Paul Thomas Anderson, *Magnolia: The Shooting Script* (New York: Newmarket, 2000), 194.

10. Aimee Mann, "Save Me," Azlyrics.com, accessed January 14, 2016.

Kurring moves from judgment to affirmation, again evidence of a radical turnabout, dispensing with his moralistic self-enclosure to agapic love. For Kurring has again forgiven, this time Claudia for walking out and for drugging and God knows what else, and in the snippets we hear of the conversation he promises to make a habit of forgiving. For Claudia this seems more than enough. The gist of Kurring's words is to ask Claudia if she is up to being loved—for her sake and his own. Suddenly, breaking out fully on Claudia's face, comes something not seen before, and that is a fulsome smile of delight. Such is the work of a love of the sort of which Frank Mackey's destructive credo had no clue. Love and delight are possible in the land of forgiveness and reconciliation, and that is cause for deep and lasting wonder and gratitude.

Fini

In effect, Anderson has slowly inducted viewers into the increasingly mysterious territory toward which he hauls everyone, characters and viewers alike. That destination consists of a very strange, liminal horizon, one of the "thin places" where a mysterious providence works, unbeknownst to most everybody in the middle of it (quiz-kid Stanley Spector may be the one knowing exception), to console, admonish, and finally redeem most in *Magnolia*'s array of the lost, lost to themselves and to others. So it is, then, that in their serial meltdowns the afflicted, all "weary and heavy-laden," move to a desperate sort of self-knowledge that yields confession and/or despair and then, finally, for most, remorse (what the dying Earl Partridge aptly calls "g—— regret"), mutual forgiveness, reconciliation, and hope, much of which is instigated by that incredible, miraculous downpour of frogs. And here Anderson displays an exultant portrait of a redemption personal and relational that ever-mysteriously brings about new being.

The spectacle of raining frogs dropped into the group implosion of psyches provides a sensational marker of a divine presence that is inescapable in its reality and power; in the plagues on Egypt in Exodus, the destruction God rains on Egypt effects condemnation in order to set free the captive Israelite slaves into the fullness of life. The frog-pour certifies that, contrary to modernity's commonsense presumptions, life is indeed played out on an amply mysterious metaphysical stage whose essence is at once profoundly and inextricably moral and religious. This news comes as a shock to just about everyone, save perhaps Stanley and Jim Kurring, who seems to be a rather devout Catholic, kneeling to pray before the crucifix that hangs above his bed before he heads off to work. The outcome for all these aggrieved children, as for the children of Israel, is liberation from solitary enslavement within their assorted psycho-emotional captivities, much of which results from soul-withering abuse by narcissistic parents, especially fathers. In the close, the paternal ogres are by various means dead, and all the children, previously alone and desperate, have moved toward the hope that lies in miracles of reconciliation and healing, the very sort of re-lational wholeness for which the Judeo-Christian God of love strives.

To this the utterly surprising frog-fall furnishes a wild, even prepos-terous display of the ultimacy of love, a radical *caritas*, in the very fabric of the universe. To his credit, Anderson would rather show than tell, and he, in a posture of admirable moral precision, entirely eschews labeling any of these mysteries. Better still, throughout the entire course of this very long film, Anderson lays out all the attributes and significations of love without ever giving in to Hollywood's penchant for trivial, very goopy renderings of it. In what happens, the events themselves weigh, as this analysis has tried to show, far more than the words with which the film might label its driving forces. Throughout, *Magnolia* struggles to make words, events, and images stretch sufficiently to capture the flavor of the unforeseeable, unimaginable turnings that pervade the film, of which frog storms are *not*, in a way, the most spectacular. Here Anderson follows Emily Dickinson's dictum that one should "tell the truth," but necessarily, given the blinding character of truth, "tell it slant." Indeed, how to describe in words the bloom of the magnolia?

CHAPTER NINE

"THE GLORY SMILING THROUGH"

Wonder and Beauty in *The Thin Red Line*

The Thin Red Line is a war film only insofar as that greatest of American novels, Herman Melville's *Moby-Dick* (1851), is a fish story. Comparing Terrence Malick and Melville, though, sheds light on Malick's intentions and means in *The Thin Red Line*, for Malick and his film seem to have absorbed and transposed a good deal of Melville's ambivalent vision of the world.[1] In *Moby-Dick*, a naïve narrator (much like the would-be reader) sails as an ordinary seaman to hunt whales aboard Nantucket whaler *Pequod*. Only when far out to sea does Ishmael learn that the ship's commander, the one-legged Captain Ahab, seeks to hunt down the very white whale that chomped off his leg. Ahab thinks that he will not only avenge his maiming but also, more importantly, resolve his metaphysical quandaries by striking a blow against the deity he holds responsible for the aggression of a mere "dumb brute," as First Mate Starbuck categorizes the whale.[2] What seems most to bother Ahab is the very inscrutability of the white whale, its metaphysical ambiguity

---

1. A small number of the many interpreters of Malick have made reference to Melville's novel. See, in particular, Ron Mottram's essay "All Things Shining: The Struggle for Wholeness, Redemption and Transcendence in the Films of Terrence Malick," in *The Cinema of Terrence Malick: Poetic Vision of America*, ed. Hannah Patterson, 2nd ed. (London: Wallflower, 2007), 14–26.

2. Herman Melville, *Moby-Dick*, ed. Harrison Hayford and Hershel Parker, Norton Critical Edition, 2nd ed. (New York: Norton, 2002), 139.

and ultimately its opacity.[3] What starts as an adventure tale soon transits to a metaphysical dispute. In their respective tales, Melville and Malick push genre conventions to carry rather unusual freight—specifically, a host of perennially vexing philosophical and religious questions about the possibility and character of a divine something both behind and within this world. Genre here becomes the stage on which to contest dilemmas heady, heartfelt, and profoundly metaphysical.

Film scholar Lloyd Michaels has sensibly described Malick's project as posing "eternal, unanswerable questions through a new, especially nonverbal, and often mysterious cinematic language."[4] Michaels's description could apply as well to Melville's novel, a venture that pushed the limits of fiction by stretching both genre and language as a means of metaphysical exploration. Like Melville, Malick stretches genre constructs and cinematic language to stage a demanding, and finally revelatory, journey to a similarly complex reckoning with nature as either unceasingly predatory or, alternatively, even simultaneously, dense with "glory."

The former is easy enough to understand, the latter dauntingly problematic. The whole of the film suggests that Malick means by "glory" the very palpable, transfixing press of a "shining" numinous Presence manifest in the resplendence of the whole of the natural world, something that First Sergeant Edward Welsh (Sean Penn) in particular has a difficult time recognizing. In the depiction of the second alternative, this world as profusely and luminously sacred, lies the origin of Malick's desire to move cinema to embody and freshen thought and even perception itself. Insofar as this is the case, he strives to lift the blinders from modernity's disenchantment, so to speak. In modernity, the first option is a truism, the inexorability of nature's and humankind's incessant carnage, a notion amply conceptualized in Darwin's survival of the fittest. In his turn to the second, however, Malick sets forth a complex, and compelling, counter to Darwin's notion of how the world works. Much of this he ventures to render with a suitably fresh use of cinema's rich storehouse of means of address—visual, aural, musical, and verbal. It is no small task to bring viewers to see the world as luminous and transfixing—to see it, in short, as Malick sees it and, just perhaps, in the furthest extreme of his proposition, as God perhaps

---

3. Melville, *Moby-Dick*, 140.

4. Lloyd Michaels, *Terrence Malick* (Urbana: University of Illinois Press, 2009), 75.

sees it. In Malick's remarkable film, perhaps all things, to adapt the film's closing line, do shine, metaphysically, to be sure, and, without doubt, cinematically.

Melville's masterpiece began with his reading of a survivor account of the sinking in 1820 in the South Pacific of the Nantucket whaler *Essex* by an enormous whale that twice rammed the ship, a story recently twice retold, first in Nathaniel Philbrick's 2000 historical account, *In the Heart of the Sea*, and again in Ron Howard's 2015 film adaptation of that account. From this event Melville eventually wrote the story of mad Captain Ahab seeking vengeance on the white whale (or God) who removed his leg. Maddened by the horrors of this world, the magisterial Ahab moves from grief and perplexity to defiance and damnation.

As Melville did with his historical source material, so Malick expands, complicates, and deepens James Jones's fictionalized account of the costly World War II battle for the South Pacific island of Guadalcanal. From Jones, Malick draws a title, characters (roughly), and the outlines of a plot, but those ingredients only provide narrative rudiments, for Malick's film works insistently and ingeniously, much like Melville's novel does, to haul viewers into the same surprising sorts of metaphysical questions about divine absence and presence. To be sure, both insist upon the inescapability of the terror part—"the horrible vulturism of the earth,"[5] Melville called it—whether it lie in the terrors of furious, very canny whales or the omnivorous caprice of battle. In *Moby-Dick*, the reader cannot but help feel that nature wins, humankind proving fodder for the steady consumption of life in all its forms; in *The Thin Red Line*, however, Malick labors to take exception by providing a significant and fetching counterweight to Melville's mostly bleak estimate of the way things are.[6]

5. Melville, *Moby-Dick*, 248.

6. At the very end of *Moby-Dick*, Melville seems to consider alternative endings to his novel, especially one that allows Ahab to quite literally recover his senses, at least momentarily. For a few moments, he leaves behind his always "smoking brow" to feel again, as Ahab himself puts it, "a mild, mild wind, and a mild looking sky." Or, as Melville comments, "the lovely aromas in that enchanted air did at last seem to dispel for a moment the cankerous thing in his soul. That glad, happy air, that winsome sky, did at last stroke and caress him, the step-mother world, so long cruel—forbidding—now threw affectionate arms around his stubborn neck, and did seem to joyously sob over him." Amid this sway of beauty, Ahab himself wonders at his own dismissal of "all natural lovings and longings." The spell of regret and longing is broken, tragically, when Moby-Dick again shows up to challenge his pursuer (405–6).

And a big dissent it is, and this constitutes the chief distinction between Melville and Malick. Through the considerable length of *The Thin Red Line*, Malick steadily tacks away from the grim finality of that vulturism. In fact, Malick's central character, an ordinary GI named Witt (James Caviezel), moves by a tangled route from contemplating the cold finality of death to embracing a meditative, notably religious recognition of a signal, exultant meaning-fullness within the very fabric of reality. Abandoning an initial posture of denial of any meaning whatsoever, Witt slowly moves, pilgrim-like, to revere an effulgent, variegated beauty that suggests this world was framed in and for love by a transcendent Love—and, amazingly, that recognition comes amid the toughest of all crucibles of doubt, the horrific slaughter of modern warfare wherein humankind ravages itself.[7] Over a decade later in *The Tree of Life* (2011), overtly fashioning a theodicy of sorts, Malick re-enacts and extends this wrestle, but there his setting and interpretive lens become very distinctly Christian in the film's overt exaltation of divine love as manifest in life's pervasive beauty and in humankind's profound thirst, amid loss and enmity, for Light, restoration, and reconciliation, all facets of the same entity. A good word for that path, especially in *The Thin Red Line*, is "meditative," and that, main character Witt surely is. The term "mystical" also fits, though it ventures into more problematic turf, for it clashes with the reductionism of philosophical modernism.

This clash between darkness and light Malick works out dialogically, as if the two reckonings with the way the world works were in conversation. This transpires amid multiple other voices within the film, creating a dense network of perception and experience that provides a wide range of human response to war and combat. This exchange Malick stages with a meticulous "polyphonic" orchestration of multiple elements in the cinematic toolkit—events and words, sound design and music, and preeminently, as is the case with movies especially,

---

7. The word "effulgent" is not used often, and even when it is appropriate, it seems rather arcane and pretentious. Here, though, it works as few words do to capture the character of the mysterious beauty that Malick strives to evoke in script, image, and sound. His sense of beauty as divine expression seems to echo the great American theologian Jonathan Edwards's meditation on the means and texture of beauty and divine care. See William Danaher Jr., "Beauty, Benevolence, and Virtue in Jonathan Edwards' *The Nature of True Virtue*," *Journal of Religion* 87 (2007): 396.

images.[8] These address the different registers of human access to the physical world. The practice throughout juxtaposes one philosophical and experiential pole with another, often prompting viewers to experience what Carl Plantinga calls "affective incongruity," a strategy that sustains throughout a posture of "wonder and rumination" not only for the film's characters but also for viewers.[9] For example, Malick constructs delicate but insistent motifs of vision and light to dramatize riddles of perception, evil, inwardness, and beauty, to name but a few of the prominent contests the film enacts. In fact, the film's dialogic wrestle proceeds as much (or more so) by multiple visual and aural means as by action or the verbal exposition set in characters' mouths, though the verbal text of the final screenplay regularly echoes and underlines Malick's many nonverbal strategies.

In *The Thin Red Line*, then, Malick strives to render affecting and cogent the path by which central character Witt, and viewers with him, journey through war's hell to finally apprehend some measure of a numinous loving presence, or "shining," as Witt puts it portmortem, within the unfathomable beauty of people, the natural world, and also, finally, the prospect of immortality, the last a question that every day looms large for soldiers facing violence, suffering, and death. In bringing Witt to these junctures, Malick depicts a human self of greater amplitude and depth than that allowed by the reductionism of Enlightenment rationalism. That posture of being, so to speak, features a variety of embodied perception wherein the sensorium gradually encounters a complex, multivariate richness that culminates by multiple means and routes in a radical doxological embrace of an effulgent, loving reality.[10] Malick's tale happens slowly, as befits Witt's own slow but clear movement through recognition and doubt to acceptance and exultation. Fit-

---

8. The term "polyphony" is also used by Christina Lane in her book on P. T. Anderson's *Magnolia* (Chichester, UK: Wiley-Blackwell, 2011), 85–90. She seems to limit it, however, to describe the assorted points of view of Anderson's host of characters. She does helpfully suggest that the camera can also provide still another point of view, especially an omniscient or transcendent one. The extent to which Malick's complex use of the camera assumes a transcendent point of view merits careful consideration.

9. Carl Plantinga, "Affective Incongruity and *The Thin Red Line*," *Projections* 4 (2010): 92.

10. The notion of embodiment comes largely from academic philosophy, deriving in particular from the work of phenomenology. The best brief introduction to the topic and its role in *The Thin Red Line* is David Davies's "Vision, Touch, and Embodiment in *The Thin Red Line*," in *The Thin Red Line*, ed. David Davies (London: Routledge, 2009), 45–64.

tingly, and in a bold departure from Hollywood conventions, Malick insists on displaying in image and sound Witt's nonrational and mostly ineffable transit to a posture of being where "glory" shines all about, even amid the darkness of war. That is, to put it mildly, a daunting task to situate within any film, one that merits a patient unpacking of an unconventional, complex, and engrossing film.

"This War in Nature": The Problem and the Means

In posing the deeply vexing puzzle at the heart of the film, Malick wastes no time. More than that, the dialogic exchanges in the first minutes form the primary structural and thematic core of the film as a whole, and as such, the first minutes merit close examination. The very first frames abruptly plunge viewers deep into the thick of the sort of discomforting questions Malick poses throughout. In a deft, startling prologue, Malick seeks first to elicit the fear and confusion of most everyone who confronts a natural world that thrives on predation and death, therewith initiating one portion of the dialogic collision that cycles throughout. The title credits, simple white letters on a black screen, and overlaid by birdsong, portend something pleasant, but instead the film's first image, dominating the screen, emphasizes a very different reality.

The camera watches a large crocodile slowly submerge in a jungle pond, and the camera then approaches, moving from medium distance

to a spooky, uncomfortable close-up, as the creature slides below the surface of the green, algae-covered pool. The take goes on for a very long while, almost a half minute, an eternity of screen time, making sure the viewer gets the point, letting the predator's ominous physicality seep in. Both the approach of the camera and the shot's duration seek to discomfort the viewer, as well they should. The denotative gist of the shot, especially when lasting so long, seems inescapable: pure predation, huge, dreadful, and devouring, sliding below the surface in an otherwise tranquil jungle glade. Indeed, the submersion offers an apt summative image for how evil usually works, stealthily and below the surface, and especially so, as *The Thin Red Line* will argue, when it comes to the military and war where it roars up where and when one least expects it. In any case, something approaching dread seems the goal, and at best nature in the guise of this closely inspected crocodile does not look in the least inviting.

If that were not enough, and to dispel any ambiguity about the nature of the crocodile, the shot's visual clout is greatly amplified by another potent cognitive register that figures decisively in the experience and meaning of the film. The long take on the croc is initiated and throughout overlaid, in surround sound no less, by one low, intense, and increasingly loud organ peal that by its end becomes in intensity and volume so thunderous that it borders on aural assault, veritably drubbing the reader with the impulse to flee (DVD editions of the film begin with advice to play the film louder than "normal"). Here volume, tone, and mood exponentially inflate the character of that forbidding creature on the screen. In short, if the image does not spook viewers, the shattering visceral roar of the organ well indicates the nature and stature of what they see. As foreshadowing, the sequence does not bode at all well for the story that follows. Why this, now, here, already in the first minute, so very lethal and imposing, so emphatic in setting and sound, and for so long? It is amply forceful, the first of Malick's many disarming meditations, both fearsome and exultant, on people, landscape, objects, all packed with a sort of quizzical, metaphoric richness of possibility. This first look at nature is a long way from the inviting jungle birdsong of the title credit.

Then, having duly jolted his audience with a dose of dread, Malick does an about-face, abruptly initiating what seems an altogether different sort of presence within the natural world. The scene moves by dissolve from the crocodile and organ to a tranquil jungle glade, shafts

of sunlight bathing the trunk of an enormous tree, the camera soon tilting to look straight upward at the thick canopy through which the shafts of light cascade.[11] In this juxtaposition, the typical invisibility of light is made palpable, weighty, arresting, and, to borrow an apt word from Marilynne Robinson's prize-winning novel *Gilead* (2004), "irrefragable."[12] This too is startling, as inviting as the first shot is forbidding, especially as the organ very slowly fades to a complete silence that is in seconds followed by a slow, delicate, and confidently exultant choral overlay. Here Malick deploys the "Im Paradisum" from Gabriel Fauré's *Requiem* (1887–1890), the segment of the funeral Mass designated for the exit of the casketed deceased from the sanctuary for burial, a movement that symbolizes the transit of the soul to paradise. Paradise, indeed, and again image and sound infuse and inform one another, all without words (unless one understands Latin), pushing hard toward a mood of rapt, quietly exultant enchantment.

Through this second display of image and sound, Malick suggests that what viewers encounter in this lyrical adoration of the natural world counts for something every bit as important in its cognitive heft as the specter of the crocodile and all the predatory horror it conjures. Two ever-

11. In an informative and entertaining glimpse of Malick's directorial habits, Nick Nolte recounts the peculiarities of Malick's filming, notably including Malick's habit of stopping the day's shoot to have the camera crew film random scenes of light falling and birds. *Charlie Rose*, December 21, 1998. The interview is readily accessible on YouTube.

12. Marilynne Robinson, *Gilead* (New York: Farrar, Straus and Giroux, 2004), 11.

present realities, fierce destruction and supernal beauty, have run smack into each other. With this dialogic juxtaposition of the crocodile and sun-lit glade, Malick fully achieves Plantinga's "affective incongruity," meaning a healthy state of cognitive and affective dissonance, if not confusion and contradiction, that prods the viewer affectively and intellectually to ponder anew the nature of this world. Moreover, Malick seems to suggest that as much epistemic credit should be given to aesthetic delight as to terror, thus running counter to modernist notions of a forbidding, totalizing sublime. The sequence suggests that perhaps, philosophically, a predatory "Nature [blood] red in tooth and claw" (Tennyson's rendition of Darwinian natural selection) does not have the final say on the way things in general finally are, however much modernity contends that it does. Indeed, this second sequence is ever so lovely, in image and music, quietly rapturous, and is wholly opposite from that enormous, fierce predator sliding below the surface to hide its omnivorous presence. This delicate counterpoint—wonder at the splendor of the physical world, even if only episodic and fleeting—betokens another experiential, if not metaphysical, possibility. Already, with his amplitude of cinematic means, Malick prods the viewer to begin to consider the aesthetic and possibly religious significance of, in philosopher Simon Critchley's words, the "immense natural beauty" of the setting in which the story transpires.[13]

Whatever perplexity the viewer might have about the relationship of these two potent, starkly juxtaposed sequences, predatory horror and visual splendor, Malick then intensifies in a third layer of meaning, a voice-over commentary—initially mysterious, as in who's speaking?—that aptly summarizes the conflict already wrought in images, sound, and music. Indeed, this bold, perplexing contrast is the point, and it reiterates the recurring dialogic structure wherein Malick's characters interrogate and ponder life's enveloping mysteries. In this third foray into his subject, and only after image and music have had their "go" at it, some unseen someone, in a soft but earnest Southern drawl, itself as smooth and melodic as Fauré's music, speaks the riddle: "What's this war in the heart of nature? Why does nature vie with itself, the land contend with the sea? Is there an avenging power in nature, not one power, but two?" (1:45). The speaker seems to assume the benign char-

13. Simon Critchley, "Calm—on Terrence Malick's *The Thin Red Line*," in Davies, *The Thin Red Line*, 25.

acter of nature but marvels at the ferocity of the "war" within nature because of a destructive "avenging power" therein.[14]

The opening minutes make overt by multiple means the central puzzle of the film as a whole, that persistent, deep metaphysical clash between fearsome predation (terror and death) and exultant beauty (relish and delight)—vying, contending, wrestling, warring. On the one hand, this is the world after Darwin, the fellow who made fully clear the hard reality of natural selection, meaning the brutally omnivorous nature of nature. On the other, there is "glory" smiling through all that is, as the speaker of these opening words, meditative character Witt, will later describe. While others in the film, like the despair-laden Sergeant Welsh, see only evil and ugliness, Witt recognizes an effulgent, arresting beauty in people and nature that for him will prove revelatory, though exactly of what constitutes the largest part of a fierce interpretive debate among philosophers and film scholars. Here interpretations range from seeing *The Thin Red Line* as starkly naturalistic and materialistic to deeming it pantheistic and mystical, a domain of numinous disclosure amid a fearsome world.

This essay contends that Malick, to the surprise of many, pushes toward the latter, specifically embedding the journey of his central character within a long tradition of Christian relish of the natural world, one that begins with Augustine and continues through Jonathan Edwards, Emily Dickinson, and Henry David Thoreau to such remarkable

---

14. The view here stands in contrast to that of Michael Chion in his book *The Thin Red Line* (trans. Trista Selous [London: BFI, 2004], 12–13), where he claims that for Malick "nothing in nature ever gives any signs to human beings." Chion compares Malick's film to composer Charles Ives's *The Unanswered Question* (1906), in which Ives notes the juxtaposition of beauty and terror "without ever seeking to answer the question." This essay contends the opposite, and locates in the backdrop of Malick's film and thought a traditional American Protestant idea about divine revelation. American Calvinism in particular has from its start emphasized "two books" of revelation: the Bible and a natural world whose orderliness and beauty exhibit hallmarks of their Creator. A recent, excellent treatment of this notion and its role in American cultural history and environmentalism is Mark Stoll, *Inherit the Holy Mountain: Religion and the Rise of American Environmentalism* (New York: Oxford University Press, 2015). Another, and even more prominent, current to a high estimate of the meaningfulness of the natural world and human experience of it lies in American literature. For a general treatment, see John Gatta, ed., *Making Nature Sacred: Literature, Religion, and Environment in America from the Puritans to the Present* (London: Oxford University Press, 2004), and Roger Lundin, ed., *There before Us: Literature, Religion, and Culture from Emerson to Wendell Berry* (Grand Rapids: Eerdmans, 2007).

modern American literary giants as T. S. Eliot, Theodore Roethke, John Updike, Wendell Berry, Richard Wilbur, Annie Dillard, and Marilynne Robinson, to name but a few. For this array of writers, the world is at times transfigured with an ineffable majesty that elicits awe and profound gratitude for simple being. This cognitive possibility urges the notion that even amid the grim inevitability of death and all of nature's violence, humankind nonetheless comes upon varieties of insights, predominantly aesthetic and relational, that press the notion that some sort of loving, transcendent presence "shines" within the darkness.

Malick dramatizes the possibility of a path through and beyond the riddles of a predatory natural world to some transcendent Something Else and more both within and beyond nature's enveloping horrors and unrelenting death. In Malick's imagination, these disparate questions intertwine in a complex, intricate web wherein they inform and refine one another, as a sort of interactive critique. On the one hand, that other power in nature, death, is the inevitable culmination of the omnivorousness that dominates nature and all life within it. On the other, Malick counters with the possibility of some sort of, one, perceptible divine presence within all of nature, people and landscape included, and, two, "immortality" for the individual self. These are finally not separate strands of thought but very much intimately related, the notion of an afterlife very much an existential expansion of the goodness of a plenitude of beauty and delight in the natural world. Having posed in the prologue the collision between violence and beauty, fear and delight, Malick proceeds immediately to take up the very personal encounter and subsequent wrestle with the same, particularly the unlikely prospect of personal survival beyond physical death. Malick's dialogic narrative and cinematic structures restlessly recast and assay this conflict in multiple formulations throughout his film, though nowhere more so than the experience and ruminations of central character Witt.

Witt and the Meaning of Death

From the brief dialogic opening, the story proper begins with Private Witt's experience while AWOL in a Melanesian coastal village, a sojourn that features two crucial recognitions that shape the rest of his story and the film as a whole. A quiet and diffident young man, Witt has already been in the army six years, though he is still only a private, the apparent result of regular disciplinary infractions. From the "lyrical" prologue of crocodile and sun-lit glade, this second sequence, roughly ten minutes in length, continues Malick's exploration of the nature of nature and, in an intricately related matter, explores the possibilities of immortality. All this Malick treats with his signature polyphonic style, now in full bloom as he begins to construct nuanced "responses" to the questions posed in the prologue, responses that the long war story that follows will elaborate and test.

As the quietly rapturous music of Fauré's "Im Paradisum" continues to play, gently melodious and exultant, the scene shifts to a setting that seems a universe away from combat, and it too is deeply embedded in the natural world. What viewers witness seems the very antipode of war: as the music plays, indigenous children swim and play. Music and images meld further in two minutes of wordless montage of Solomon Island village life, a setting that seems not only beautiful but also tranquil beyond measure, idyllic if not wholly Edenic. Paradise, indeed. And here again, in conjuring a response to his own questions, Malick simply shows far more than he tells, though here too he will provide spare but amply sufficient verbal comment.

AWOL, Witt clearly relishes this seaside realm amid his own surprise and wonder, happily swimming and playing with the village children, even though his military identity seems a trespass upon the tranquillity of the village's common life. Throughout, as in the film's beginning, Malick's camera simply watches, just as soldier Witt watches, seeing what soldier Witt sees and, in his facial expressions, what he feels in response—in effect, allowing the viewer to experience Witt's experience, behind his eyes and in his skin, so to speak, striving to make fresh and immediate Witt's sense of the beguiling world in which he has taken refuge. Two eminent critics, Leo Bersani and Ulysse Dutoit, in their *Forms of Being*, deem this soldier's "look" a crucial marker for the core of Malick's view of human experience and meaning.[15] And there, in the recurrent expressiveness in this "look" at the world before him, we observe persistent wonder and pleasure, for within this inviting world Witt happens upon sufficient extraordinary surprise and delight, if not ecstasy, to revise radically his heretofore dark estimate of what characterizes all of life. Witt seems to spend his days in quiet exultation

15. Leo Bersani and Ulysse Dutoit, *Forms of Being: Cinema, Aesthetics, Subjectivity* (London: BFI, 2004), 18.

at the beauty of the landscape and the amiable lives of those who live within it; the two seem to have become contiguous to him. Whatever pleasure he imbibes during his village sojourn—indeed, elation and enchantment, made clearer still by Malick's musical choices—seems now to occasion Witt's recurring reflections on the immanence of beauty and goodness within the natural world, its splendor and luminescence arguing for a transcendent origin because it is so radically "other" not only from the mundane quotidian facticity of ordinary life but especially from the omnivorousness of war.

Witt's wonder and delight in all he experiences seem to cue the subsequent exploration of immortality, the second of Malick's central concerns. This is a crucial pivot wherein Witt seems to glimpse, even more perhaps than in his recognition of transfixing beauty, "another world," as he later asserts to the thoroughly skeptical Welsh (13:14). The crucial event in this transit, one rarely mentioned by Malick scholars, occurs as Witt observes a pastoral scene of village women bathing children in a pond. Surprisingly, the scene does not recall for Witt, as one might expect, pleasant memories of similar tenderness from his own childhood and his mother's care. Instead, as he watches the village women, Witt remembers his mother's death, a mordant recollection that clearly pains and haunts, and in his voice-over we gather some of the backstory that inspired that opening question about the war in nature. Witt explains that at the deathbed of his mother, "all shrunk up and gray," he feared to "touch the death I seen in her," and while she did not fear death, Witt admits that he "couldn't find anything beautiful or uplifting about her going back to God," tingeing the last phrase with a bit of scorn. In fact, he tells a buddy, if there is immortality, "I ain't seen it" (4:52).

Then, in a flashback, or in what at first seems like a flashback, Malick ventures into rich but ambiguous and highly contested cognitive territory. With Witt sitting head in hand, lost in thought, a troubled look upon his face, viewers see what is in effect Witt's "retake" amid a sort of reverie, a personal reenvisioning, of his mother's death experience. In other words, viewers witness Witt's imaginative recasting (or is it some sort of vision, or both?) of his mother's death. Or perhaps Witt sees now what he earlier overlooked. The sequence begins realistically enough, the camera in close watching Witt's bedridden mother caress her son's hand, and then, as the camera pulls back and slowly turns, we seem, remarkably, to leave realism behind to witness surreal events that end up supplanting Witt's notion of physical death as the final annihilation of self. The camera moves from Witt's mother to, by her bedside, a small teenaged girl dressed in a lacy white chemise who with arms outstretched in welcome summons Witt's mother in the moment of her death (the sound of heartbeats on the soundtrack fade to silence) to rise from her bed to enter the smiling girl's ardent embrace. The young woman enigmatically touches the mother's sternum and then lays her head on the woman's chest, holding her fiercely, a euphoric smile upon her face.

What exactly happens here and what it amounts to loom over the entire story, though few critics venture to even mention it, and those that do are clearly flummoxed by what to make of it. Whether this is Witt's sister, as two different scholars have suggested; Witt's imaginative revisioning of his mother's experience of death, amounting to a kind of wish fulfillment; his mother's actual experience; or something else, we simply do not know. It is likely that Malick here simply deploys traditional popular Christian iconography of angels welcoming the deceased, and this one seems to have all but the wings. Here though, to be sure, viewers find a fresh, vivid rendition of that possibility, specifically the deeply mysterious exit from mortal life to a realm of blessed, joyous intimacy within the reality of divine care. Most importantly, though, what Witt sees makes sense for Witt, modestly educated and very likely steeped, given his grammar and distinctly Southern accent, in Bible Belt Christianity, as the language he later uses also suggests.

On the other hand, how much Malick the writer-director affirms Witt's beatific vision depends on the measure of trust the film comes to bestow on Witt as a character. At this point we know very little of him, and any final judgment awaits the tale itself and, as well it should, the film's end. Along the way, however, as Carl Plantinga has pointed out in considerable detail, Malick's camera privileges and even exalts Witt among all the other characters in the film.[16] The camera pays close heed to Witt's "look" at the world, and regularly places him visually and narratively in a central and superior position. And it is safe to say, in addition, that in the moment of his own death, Witt experiences a similarly joyous sort of well-come.

In this re-envisioning of his mother's death, quite apart from what follows, it becomes clear that the sequence has enormous consequence for Witt. After all, the vision or dream, or whatever it is, conjures an

16. Plantinga, "Affective Incongruity," 96.

ideal rendering of the way death should be amid humankind's inveterate yearning for some sort of "more"—in this case, for a smooth, exultant transit into the embrace of light, warmth, and, from the look and feel of it, "pure, sweet love" ("Wings of a Dove," used memorably in Bruce Beresford's *Tender Mercies* [1983]). A similar but fuller rendition of the same sort of vision appears in the last sequence of *The Tree of Life*, Jack O'Brien's personal vision of a domain of intense, pure light consisting of reconciliation and love, a segment overlaid by the Agnus Dei of Berlioz's *Requiem*. For Witt, no matter its uncertain verifiability, this new portrait of his mother's death proves revelatory, a wild, rapturous hope at least or intimation of a postdeath, loving welcome and survival that entirely transforms death itself. To be sure, such might well reshape one's view of death and immortality, and so it is with Witt.

In addition to its importance for Witt, Malick seems to imbue the sequence with considerable weight, especially in making sure that it achieves ample affective clout for his viewers. First, the movement of the deathbed scene rather precisely repeats the mood and dramatic structure of symbolic movement in Fauré's "Im Paradisum," which perhaps functions as the central thematic leitmotif for the film as a whole—namely, the movement of the soul from death to life. Recall that that section of the choral Mass plays as the casket of the deceased leaves the church, a movement that symbolically parallels the soul's entrance into heaven, a kingdom of light and love, as the mood of the piece amply displays. That in effect is exactly what transpires within Witt's vision of his mother's death. She too makes the transit from mortality to beatific welcome, though Witt's vision is strikingly more Protestant than Fauré's Roman Catholic liturgical flourish. A fitting coda for the substance of Witt's vision and mood follows upon the culmination of Witt's reflection on calm. Immediately following his ruminations on death, as Witt stands on the beach looking about, a faint smile upon his face, a buoyant and playful Melanesian hymn begins to play as the camera watches children comb the beach and, in the next shot, a close-up of clasped hands that we later understand to be part of a procession toward worship (Melanesia was Christianized in the late nineteenth century). The music seems to function doxologically, a postlude to Witt's vision that in its lilt and exuberance suggests the substance and texture of Witt's psycho-spiritual state of gladness and gratitude for his newly acquired vision of immortality.

In this effort, more than simply watching Witt watch, Malick suggests the content of Witt's interior world with music, an element that has gone largely unexplored in the many discussions of Malick's films. A number of commentators have written at length about the role of sound in the film, especially of waves and wind, as they contribute to the cultivation of embodied perception, but oddly, the role of music, a far more conspicuous and dominant element in the viewer's experience of Witt's experience, has received scant attention. One commentator has even argued that because we do not understand the words of a song sung in Melanesian, the music lacks significance, which is to diminish, if not dismiss, the significant affective register of the music virtually all films deploy to narrate, to intensify experience, and sometimes, as with Malick, to supply still another "voice" beside the visual and verbal within the narrative.[17] In any case, music plays through almost the entirety of what viewers see of Witt's village life, implying how much Witt relishes that world. As is typical of film music, there is some ambiguity whether the music is meant to represent or convey, in rough equivalency, what Witt himself feels (he is not himself humming a tune), or Malick's interpolation of Witt's interior world, a musical equivalency or evocation of Witt's interior state. In the end, regardless of the director's intention, the music does work to embellish the subjective mood of Witt's interior apprehension of the world in which he finds himself, and goes a long way to impart his (or Malick's) sense of the experiential texture of that world to viewers.

That same music provides the "commentary" for his walks through the village. The music of that Melanesian hymn, particularly joyous and melodic, mounts and swells, and viewers can understand that to indicate not only the music Witt hears within the village but also, as suggested, as an apt expressive interpolation of the mood or texture of Witt's own inward "calm," or at least the beginnings of it. The music does seem, at least for the viewer, to clarify and comment on Witt's experience, and Malick at one point near the end shows Witt in the background listening attentively to the music as a small parade of villagers sing on the way to worship. That same music has played earlier during Witt's conversation after his beach reverie on his mother's death and during the talk with the young mother in which he remarks, "Kids here never fight" (7:12). Clearly, his sense is—judged on his facial expressions, the music, and his question to the young Melanesian

17. Chion, *The Thin Red Line*, 29.

mother—that he has fallen into a kind of Eden, pristine, idyllic, not only devoid of violence and ugliness but also infused with peace and joyousness. Regardless of lyrical content, the exultant mood of the music echoes and displays intense relish for the simple goodness of living and ample cause for joy, and it will thereafter recur at pivotal moments in the story.

As Witt and the mother end their conversation, music again mounts, this time Hans Zimmer's lilting symphonic variation on the earlier hymn tune, and that strain then overlays a wordless montage summary of Witt's days in the village: learning to thatch roofs, playing with children, and simply watching and thinking, as is his habit. In one brief shot he swims, treading water as he looks back at the shore, a look of smiling, deeply happy wonder and gratitude upon his face (one must be cautious about reading too much into any "look"; what it is not, though, is what we see a number of times in the film—the chilling, reductive "look of death," in Emily Dickinson's words).[18] And all the while the exultant music plays, so much so that the film suggests that Witt becomes, or at least joins, the deeply arresting music, or that its mood in large measure expresses the substance of his perception of the place and people. Perhaps, following T. S. Eliot's description of his quasi-mystical "distraction fit," Witt becomes "the music while the music lasts."[19]

In any case, the centrality of the music and what it inspires culminate when Witt, standing in the background, watches that procession of village people clapping and singing an exultant hymn as they proceed to worship, following a leader who prominently carries a large Bible under his arm. The point is that Witt very early in the film already glimpses bright flashes or "shining" of "the light," as he later refers to it, a notion and image that is in just about every way, from script to cinematography and music, central to the film as a whole. Whatever its lyrics, the music seems to exult both mind and soul.

Nor does Malick let go of the consequence of the vision, visually arresting and musically amplified, for it shapes the remainder of Witt's

---

18. "There's a Certain Slant of Light." This is one of Dickinson's more famous and more chilling and cryptic poems, especially in locating specific referents for some of her descriptors. What is clear is the mordant, and even dire, estimate of the "Heavenly Hurt" that the prospect of death elicits.

19. T. S. Eliot, *The Complete Poems and Plays, 1909–1950* (New York: Harcourt, Brace, and World, 1962), 119.

village sojourn, his time in combat, and his own death. In fact, through the whole length of the film, Malick strives to make Witt's sense of the world a felt reality that becomes more palpable and probable to Witt (and viewers) by embodying it in Witt's immediate experience. Importantly, that rhetorical project begins in Witt's remaining time in the village. Malick at once clarifies and emphasizes the significance of Witt's epiphanic re-vision of his mother's death, for what he finds in the life of the village is indeed a sort of salient, validating extension, socially manifested, of the sort of "calm" or tranquillity with which his mother met her death. The village's remarkable social texture stands diametrically opposed to a Darwinian world of war, and on the hideous nature of war the film will emphatically insist. Following his brooding questions about death and immortality, Witt seems ever more taken with this seeming paradise, as if it were a palpable manifestation of the embrace and restoration at the core of his mother's "well-come." Witt seems to conclude, especially when all the discrete elements and registers of the prologue are taken together, that the very welcome that animates and illumines the deathbed death-to-life sequence informs the landscape and life of the village. In short, here is tangible, living confirmation of what in his re-vision of death may have been delusory, a possibility he soon thereafter concedes to Welsh in their shipboard brig conversation (13:22).

Throughout this sequence, Malick's filmmaking strives to induct viewers into the same texture of being that informs his montage of Witt's days in village life. Viewers observe Witt's increasing calm and indeed delight, as clearly seen in his facial expression, as he, treading water offshore, smilingly imbibes this seemingly pacific landscape and people. For Witt, relish and contemplation go hand in hand, and this comports with the gist of that deathbed vision of loving embrace and cosmic welcome. All these elements seem consonant with one another, collaborating to evoke, for the viewer, as for Witt, the likely prospect of some sort of transcendent "shining" that at times flames incandescent within ordinary mundane experience. To his immense good fortune Witt has come to apprehend the world with, as Marilynne Robinson's dying minister in *Gilead* puts it, "a sort of ecstatic fire that takes things down to essentials."[20] Here, for Witt, as for British Jesuit poet Gerard Manley Hopkins, the world does, for a while at least, seem "charged

20. Robinson, *Gilead*, 197.

with the grandeur of God," and on occasion that grandeur does indeed, in natural beauty and in mystical promptings, "flame out like shining from shook foil."[21] Malick labors to convey what plays in Witt's soul as his newly exultant eyes and ears absorb pristine nature and pacific Melanesian islanders.

By the end of his island sojourn, Witt in multiple ways has come to sense the possibility that mysteriously inhering deep within reality itself is such a thing as Love, a presence palpable, pervasive, and profound that infuses and wells up in the luminousness of the most rudimentary foundations of this world, such as water, shore, light, birdsong, and people, elements that Malick dwells on in all his films. For Witt, given the range of his experience from combat to days AWOL, it seems akin to a cosmic embrace, such as the one that greeted his mother upon her death. Here, what seems a transcendent measure of love is manifest in natural and human splendor, and this luminescence presses upon souls whose eyes see and whose flesh feels. Much in the film suggests that Witt feels ample surprise that there is anything at all—matter, consciousness, soul, whatever. Throughout the film, Malick features Witt alone, swimming or walking, wide-eyed and meditative before what he encounters (and it is an encounter, something far more central and profound than "just seeing" or observing). Beyond that even, at times Witt seems startled, and elated within a beguiling, resplendent efflorescence, whether in the physical splendor of nature and people or in the commonweal of Melanesian social harmony. For Witt, as the rest of the film makes clear, these are all facets of a persistent, profound wonderment at the startling measure of beauty that seems to inhere in the fabric of the world, albeit simultaneously coexistent with the enmity of conflict and death. This "shining" something—for he can barely name it—both abides and on occasion seems, in Hopkins's words, to "flame out" to elicit from Witt a posture of awe followed by gratitude, meaning a persistent reverence and profound care, no matter how grim the setting in which it transpires, whether nature or war.

Witt's wonderments gather quietly, incrementally, to the point where language runs out, at least language of the propositional sort, and poetry and freestyle ruminative meditation become the dominant mode of his verbal discourse. Indeed, many of Witt's subsequent voice-

21. Gerard Manley Hopkins, "God's Grandeur," Poetry Foundation, accessed September 7, 2016, https://www.poetryfoundation.org/poems-and-poets/poems/detail/44395.

overs play as a sort of quizzical, meditative pondering of the world. Moreover, the visual splendor of the film speaks its own nonverbal or supraverbal language. After all, there are countless instances of experience and images that lie beyond words—Witt swimming and smiling in the Melanesian sea and waterfalls, Witt tending the wounded beside running streams, Witt beside still water, soldiers savoring small flowers, splendorous birds, windblown grass on hillsides, Witt's own startling death experience, Welsh at Witt's grave, the Melanesian people with whom Witt sojourns, the green palm on the beach, light pouring down through the jungle canopy, candles and flames in darkness, light glistening on running water—all beyond the capacities of language or, for that matter, the capacities of images, no matter Malick's visual inventiveness and persistence. For Witt, and one suspects for Malick as well, the manifold beauty of this world in nature and in people is such, telling and cogent, that it removes Witt's fear of death, echoing and affirming the "calm" that he recognizes in his mother's death. Finally, then, Witt, and Malick as well, conclude that in the "shining" of the world lies an exultant splendor that beckons all to intimacy, a "shalom" that lies at the heart of the Judeo-Christian apprehension of both creation and revelation, arguing that the wellspring and ether of reality are relational and loving.

The remainder of the film tracks Witt's new vision to put it to the test, so to speak, making *The Thin Red Line* not only meditative but also rhetorical. Witt never stops earnest questioning of the nature of ultimate reality, and much of his experience—and that of the viewers—probes and assesses the varieties of hope he carries away from his time AWOL. In fact, the gist of many of his regular voice-over ruminations throughout the film comes as questions about central philosophical riddles initiated there. That does not, however, diminish the significance of his pivotal experience of insight, a nonrational, subjective seeing into the heart of things that informs and shapes, as does his relish of natural beauty, his sense of "the beautiful Light," as Welsh later mockingly calls it, the divine "smiling" through in the "all things shining" he cites in his postmortem voice-over (2:22:27; 2:43:00). The remainder of the film delineates and simultaneously interrogates the adequacy of what has dawned on Witt in this obscure part of the world, one that has since become known as an infamous site of some of the fiercest combat in either theater of World War II.

Evil and Beauty: The Dialogic Crucible

Within *The Thin Red Line*, however, it is a long trip to Witt's end and the film's end, for much of the film is devoted to dramatizing the multiple domains within which Malick develops his dialogical thematic, namely, that "war in the heart of nature." That a sizable war rages in nature is no surprise to anyone, though it is a reality that most smoothly but unwisely glide over. To this end, Malick gives viewers repeated memorable shots of predators and death, including enormous snakes, limbless bodies, and dogs feasting on human carrion, and these reside always within the seemingly beauteous, tranquil heart of the natural world that Witt comes to apprehend.

Tragically, this does not stop with the animal world. Late in the film, for example, there is a second crocodile, another huge specimen, lashed to the rear of a truck, this one captured for the amusement of the GIs (2:11:22). This brief insertion, which serves no particular narrative purpose and proves more than a little ironic, suggests that the crocodile, for all of its fearsome size, guile, and look, is not the worst of predators, especially as the soldiers prod and poke it in much the same manner as some have already taunted and abused their Japanese captives. And so it will go, inescapably, relentlessly. On the one hand, humankind inhabits a predatory natural world, itself the game, but on the other, the species is no less grievously susceptible to preying on all that is. How fractured and combative this world is, is hard to convey and grasp amid Witt's raptures. Melville perhaps caught the dissonance best in one brief sentence in *Moby-Dick*: "Though . . . this visible world seems formed in love, the invisible spheres were formed in fright."[22] Brokenness soaks the globe, hounding and inescapable, though allure and rapture of beauty counter, a balm for which humankind yearns enormously and perpetually. Indeed, it is this "lack" that the nihilistic Welsh laments in the film's closing minutes, especially as one who has come, through Witt, to acknowledge the claims of beauty (2:39:13). Insofar as humankind is part of nature's rapacity, something upon which Malick insists, it partakes of, if it does not amplify, all the ferocity of the nonhuman natural world. With Swiftian penetration, Malick suggests that much of the human species' vaunted brainpower goes to making

22. Melville, *Moby-Dick*, 164.

it still more vicious and lethal.[23] To this end, Malick artfully constructs multiple sites of conflict between this predatoriness and what it is that Witt apprehends in that press of an elusive beauty that elicits from him wonder, delight, and, as viewers will see, large measures of selflessness.

Foremost among these capacities for savagery and predation is war itself. Obviously, at horrific costs, societies and cultures clash, and the war in which all in the film find themselves provides the chief case in point. Its terrors replay over and over in scene after scene and character after character, especially in the mounting terror of the American soldiers, as they ready to go ashore on Guadalcanal, and then repeatedly as they make their way inland. Bluntly put, dread and horror have their toll, withering and consuming, and troops implode under their obscene weight, as is the case of multiple soldiers, most notably Sergeant Mc-Cron (John Savage) and Corporal Fife (Adrien Brody).

Whatever fear the troops suffer seems more than justified, given what they encounter in combat—sudden and capricious violence and death, pain and terror that become agonistic, as Malick shows at length in the caprice of Sergeant Keck's (Woody Harrelson) death, the agony of Captain Staros's (Elias Koteas) desperate prayer, the screams of the dying soldier for whom Welsh risks death to deliver morphine, and the poignancy of the death of the sweet-tempered Private Beade (Nick Stahl), a remarkably boyish, even angelic-looking, soldier. What the Americans suffer at the hands of the Japanese, the Japanese in turn suffer at the hands of the Americans, who by and large seem no more moral than their enemies, and in one instance notably less so when Private Dale (Arie Verveen) taunts and extracts teeth from the dead. Both sides seem equally inclined to inflict as much suffering and death as possible, and some soldiers seem to actually like the opportunity, though exactly why is not explained. One of Welsh's early comments seems to get to the apparent futility of warfare, a view that Malick dramatizes repeatedly in often wrenching detail. As Welsh puts it, "We're living in a world that's blowing itself to hell as fast as everybody can

23. There remains no better analysis of Western cultural hubris than book 4, "A Voyage to the Country of the Houyhnhnms," of Jonathan Swift's *Gulliver's Travels* (1726). Gulliver's master interrupts Gulliver's detailed, and very gory, account of warfare as practiced by Europeans, telling him that he can bear no more and concluding that instead of possessing reason, humankind possessed only enough reason to "increase our natural vices" in discovering ever more inventive ways of making warfare more lethal. *Gulliver's Travels* (New York: Barnes and Noble, 2003), 246.

arrange it" (13:33). With very few exceptions, war seems to eviscerate whatever measure of common decency and restraint humankind possesses. The Japanese fire desperately on the attacking American troops, and the GIs in turn are more than eager to overrun their encampment at whatever cost to the enemy. And some more than enjoy taunting and torturing, though they seem later to repent of their deeds. By no measure is the picture pretty.

Nor does Malick pretty any of this up in a stir of patriotic self-sacrifice for others, as does Spielberg in *Saving Private Ryan*, a film released a few months before *The Thin Red Line*. As many have noted, Malick's version of *The Thin Red Line* lacks any appeals to patriotic nobility, and any self-giving or noble talk is of an entirely different sort than sacrifice for country. This absence of high motives for war is markedly aggravated by the conspicuously crass, amply dark reasons for which war is often fought, specifically for the rank self-interest (pun intended) of officers, the higher the guiltier. After all, war offers a good opportunity for professional advancement, and that fuels the thinking and motivation of ruthless commanders, as with both Brigadier General Quintard (John Travolta) and the notably older Lieutenant Colonel Tall (Nick Nolte), a West Point graduate repeatedly passed over for promotion. In the shipboard conversation prior to landing, Quintard self-consciously patronizes Tall, if only to stoke his resentment in order to fuel his determination to win promotion at any cost. All this is dressed up in talk of battle objectives, but the subtext of personal benefit looms large, however unspoken, although sometimes the real goals become painfully clear. Quintard pointedly asks Tall at one point, "How much do you want it?" Tall's response is equally blunt: "As much as I have to, sir" (18:23). Both know well enough that the "it" refers to victory in order to secure promotion, and they also know well enough what achieving "it" will cost in others' pain and lives.

Any doubt about what is at stake here is dispelled by Tall's voice-over rumination as Quintard cajoles, patronizes, and threatens, using every trick in the book to get his inept commander to succeed. At this point in his career, Tall seethes in resentment and remorse, bitterly complaining about the human costs of his military career, especially to his family: "All they sacrificed for me, poured out like water on the ground" (18:38). More than that, looking gaunt and desperate, Tall regrets the waste of his passion and idealism within the political wrangling and sham of the promotion game. He laments what he would have expended for nation and family, for Tall is not at all, whatever his current mournful moral stature, insensible to virtue and nobility. He undertook a military vocation and his classical education at West Point with great seriousness, and he still references Caesar—appropriately, "The closer to Caesar, the greater the fear" (19:56)—and quotes Homer on the loveliness of the dawn (in the Greek, no less). In short, once upon a time, back at West Point, his altruism bought the heroic fantasy. He recalls now, in one of the film's more memorable lines, both his enthusiasm and his folly, lamenting, "What I might have given for love's sake" (18:52), though now, for him, it is "Too late, dying, slow as a tree" (19:09).

At least the struggle within Tall still echoes, though hereafter, given his thirst for promotion and self-justification, virtue and idealism thoroughly capitulate. Perhaps a bit like George Patton, or at least the movie version of him, Tall is a warrior displaced, far removed from the Greek codes of heroic combat and thrust now into the ambiguities of impersonal, mass warfare. Tall can invoke Homer's "rosy-fingered dawn" all he wants, but that will not transfigure his circumstance or change what he has to do to succeed, which is more like rampant bloodletting than like self-sacrifice for love's sake. The dire answer to the debate in Tall has long since come, but the debate itself echoes still in conscience and soul. Only the disapproval of others he esteems, especially of subordinate Captain John Gaff (John Cusack), a kind of surrogate son to Tall, restrains his impulse to expend his troops in a still more reckless fashion. A case in point is the first time Staros[24] brings up the matter of water for the men, who are passing out from thirst even before the assault on the hill. Tall responds with a contempt that pretty much informs his actions: "The only time you worry about a soldier is when he stops bitching" (38:34). So much for soldiers. And here Tall arrives at a condition that very much resembles Ahab's "madness maddened," and especially so in his disregard for the fate of his crew.[25]

The effect is that at this late, mournful stage of Tall's career, every-

---

24. A recent self-published book by Paul Maher Jr. and Caitlin Stuart, *Love That Loves Us: Reflections on the Films of Terrence Malick* (2015), contends that the name Staros alludes to the Greek word for the Christian cross, *stavros* (56). This seems a plausible reading, especially given Staros's agonized private prayers that display his intense concern for the well-being of his men. The staging and lighting of those scenes also seem to allude to traditional Christian paintings of Jesus alone in the Garden of Gethsemane immediately prior to his arrest and crucifixion.

25. Melville, *Moby-Dick*, 143.

thing military, including the war itself, has become a self-perpetuating game in which his men are simply pawns, and for their deaths, as in the proposed frontal assault, or for their suffering, as in the plea for more water that he dismisses, he really does not give a damn. The meaninglessness of the entire military system is more than clear to him in his dismissal (and cynical promotion) of Staros, whom he will ship stateside and amply and falsely decorate, mostly to ensure his silence. Whatever burns in Tall's soul now shows as plain evil, made all the worse by his self-awareness and calculation. It is for him all gainful farce, and he wants only gain, no matter the farce. His vengeful troops may be blithe in their cruelty to their captives; the same cannot be said for Tall, who resembles E. E. Cummings's fierce indictment in "I Sing of Olaf Glad and Big" of American militarism: a "trig westpointer . . . a yearning nation's blueeyed pride,"[26] who willingly lets his men torture and murder a pacifist in their ranks. Tall knows morality, self-doubt, and remorse well enough, but now, here, in this war and in this battle, with his last chance for promotion, he intentionally puts those aside. However, tragically, that conscious rejection does not keep him from hauling those fancy notions out as rationale to excuse his actions or look noble in the eyes of others.

Happily, Malick offers counterforces to Tall's recklessness. A complete foil to Tall's callous disregard is Penn's Sergeant Welsh, whose blunt cynicism sees war as largely a matter of real estate, the mortal tussle over who gets what, whether land or rank, and morality or rightness has little or nothing to do with it. Blunt and plainspoken, Welsh brandishes in demeanor and conversation Darwinian realism on the indifference of the universe. Though in this regard his official creed mirrors Tall's ruthlessness, he in fact contrasts with Tall, for Welsh, despite all his protestations of cynicism, does in fact care. He broods over his soldiers like an anxious hen, and he will risk his life to save them or ease their pain. Near the end Welsh admits as much to Sergeant Storm (John C. Reilly), a soldier who recently achieved the much-desired state of numbness, a condition in part gained by imbibing colossal quantities of alcohol. For Welsh, throughout the story, high-sounding language about honor and patriotism, whether coming from Tall or Captain Bosche (George Clooney), whose name amply clarifies the moral sta-

26. E. E. Cummings, "I Sing of Olaf Glad and Big," Poets.org, accessed September 7, 2016, https://www.poets.org/poetsorg/poem/i-sing-olaf-glad-and-big.

tus of everything he says, only cloaks the bitter reality in which GIs become disposable.

The most conspicuous foil to Tall comes in Staros, a name that does not exist in Jones's novel, and he perhaps is the man Tall once was. As several critics have pointed out, Malick's name echoes Starbuck from Melville's *Moby-Dick*, that tale of a monomaniacal whaling captain who seeks revenge on the enormous and canny white whale that chomped off his leg. To protect both his own family and the ship's crew, First Mate Starbuck opposes his captain's revenge. In *The Thin Red Line*, Malick amplifies Starbuck to an intensely caring "father" to his troops—in fact, he plays the role Ahab should have. If Quintard represents one pole of the debate in Tall, the man Tall now chooses to placate, then Staros is the other "better angel," who will risk all to hoard the life of his troops, his "own sons," as he will call them before his forced departure from Charlie Company and the war. No dreamer, Staros knows he will lose troops, but he refuses to commit them to costly assaults that have little chance of success. This means refusing a direct order from Tall to undertake a frontal attack on the well-defended Japanese machine gun emplacement on the top of the hill. A lawyer in civilian life, Staros well knows that refusal might end in court-martial and ignominy.

So passionate is Staros, the dialogic foil to Tall, that Tall might indeed have a point in relieving him of his command. At times, Staros seems close to paralysis in making battlefield decisions, though in the end he seems to make the right ones. And when his men suffer wounds and death, he himself quietly sheds tears. Throughout, Staros displays the sort of tender love for others shown by just two others in the film, Welsh and Witt. At one point, on the night before their assault on the hill, the audience sees him in the candlelight of his tent, wracked in agonizing petitionary prayer, staring at the candle as if its light were the Light, and praying, "Let me not betray You, let me not betray my men. In You I place my trust" (40:39). Nothing in his approach to the divine suggests the least iota of self-concern. Here the chiaroscuro lighting and palette recall Rembrandt, especially his images of the petitionary Jesus; more than that, though, the staging of the scene, visually and verbally, alludes to numerous prominent biblical images that emphasize central elements of the incarnation, such as the opening chapters of the Gospel of John and in Jesus's kenotic self-reference as "the Light of the world" that shines still amid an overwhelming darkness that strives to obliterate all mercy and justice. Staros will again resort to this posture later in the film, after the first assault, praying as he eats beneath a full moon ("You are my Light, my guide," he says [1:26:10]). Staros's petitionary compassion echoes Jesus's pleas to God in Gethsemane prior to his crucifixion that the waiting cup of suffering be removed. In fact, Staros goes further still, for his prayer is not at all about his own survival but simply to lead his soldiers wisely.

To push the contrast between Tall and Staros even further, as if to emphasize that Tall sees a very different sort of light, the scene cuts from Staros and his candle to Tall observing the first rays of the "rosy-fingered dawn." While he witnesses the first light of day, his sense of light does not begin to approach Staros's sense of Light as a transcendent wellspring of compassion. Indeed, Tall belongs in the warrior code of Homer's *Iliad*, a realm where triumph as a warrior counts above everything else. The juxtaposition of the two appeals suggests the enormous distance between two very different notions of light. For Tall, it is achievement and the physical dawn, impressive, to be sure, and worth noting; for Staros, light signals a traditional Christian conception of transcendent Light that weeps for the suffering of the world.

Nor does Malick's dialogism stop with simple character contrast and conflict, which is the basic stuff of drama. The same sort of dialogic structure that informs these initial conflicts between and within characters over belief and morality also shapes the very core of the combat action that occupies much of the long middle portion of the film. One of Malick's remarkable accomplishments, cited by many critics, lies in the extent to which he sustains, even amid the so-called action midsection of the film, the philosophic and moral questions that inform its opening sections. The narrative often seems disjointed or digressive, and it is to some extent, because the story often moves from one character to another with no particular logic, but despite this, or because of it, the film's dialogic thematic coherence never dissipates. Malick seems far more interested in the impact of war upon people than simply the means by which people triumph or die. One example of this refocus is that viewers see the aftermath of an event without seeing the event itself, such as in the injuries of Keck and Beade. With this Malick straightforwardly denies that the "means" of combat and fatal wounds have more interest than how the characters themselves manage death. Rather, the random perils of combat bring surprise upon surprise, the strong and the innocent alike dying by horrific means, whether by malice or by accident.

Much of the force of the film lies in the visceral impact that Malick achieves by regularly smashing narrative conventions with unexpected death and a variety of wrenching departures from both genre conventions and moral existence. For example, he disposes of some of his superstar cast, the most notable being Woody Harrelson, whose role in the film is little more than a cameo. Keck could, in fact, be anybody, for if the heroic expectations that Harrelson brings with him can disappoint, then anybody can expire. Within the film as a whole, in fact, instead of featuring individualistic heroism, Malick intentionally pushes toward impersonality, a kind of everyman quality, filling his cast with largely unknown look-alike actors whom we see only episodically, whose identities blur, and whose names either blend (Doll, Dale, and Bell, for example) or remain mysterious, if they are even supplied in the story. The same blurring recurs in the train of voice-overs, most of which not only sound alike but often could come from just about anyone in the film. This lack of heroic individuation yields an everyman quality; identities and fates are interchangeable but for random luck. All this unconventionality is to good effect, however, especially in Malick's goal of generalizing the horror and stupidity of war in order to subvert the much-vaunted satisfactions of heroism and patriotic glory. War, on the other hand, in its dire reality, is indiscriminate, impersonal, inescapably vicious, final, and very, very often deadly.

A sequence of four scenes, somewhat arbitrarily chosen, demonstrates the extent to which Malick, even amid the long account of combat, sustains and deepens his dialogic "ruminations" amid the violent swirl of war and personal suffering and profound individual longing. In the first of these, immediately following Staros's first assault on the hill and his subsequent refusal to obey Tall's order for a frontal attack, and as if to make a point about the toll of Tall's driving disregard, Malick depicts the death of Beade, played by Nick Stahl, who looks a delicate and boyish fifteen and the very picture of gentle innocence. In this sequence, Malick pointedly slows action, seemingly to dwell on the immediate, very specific costs of war in general and Tall's command in particular. In a signal departure from the conventions of the war film, Malick forgoes the usual information about how and where Beade was wounded, and viewers simply see him in the last minutes of his life. For Malick, the important question is how one dies as opposed to what means bring about death. Beade's friend Fife (Adrien Brody) is there, for whom Beade has asked, and there is a distraught Staros, visibly up-

243

set, trying to ease the distress of one of his "sons," and by the scene's end Staros is shedding tears.

Through the course of the film, many soldiers bother to tend the dying, from Witt tending to Keck (Harrelson) and Welsh (Penn) risking his life to rescue the wounded Ash (Thomas Jane). With Beade, however, as if having made that point, Malick further complicates death by assuming the point of view of the dying soldier himself. Here Beade's last minutes seem to echo Witt's own experience, Beade also apprehending an intense natural beauty that seems to efface the press of surrounding combat and his own impending death. As Beade lies on the ground, Malick uses a subjective, first-person point of view in another instance of embodied perception, and the audience sees what Beade sees: the sun and sunlight shining directly down, first through a sparse canopy, and then, in a shot following seconds later, through the holes in a single leaf (1:10:18).

On the one hand, this is the peculiar sort of thing Beade notices, as an earlier scene shows him, in the midst of battle, bothering to appreciate the delicate symmetry of a weed leaf (52:18; similar shots focusing on the minutiae of nature abound throughout both *The New World* [2005] and *The Tree of Life* [2011]). The sequence reprises the experience of Witt, viewers encountering through Beade still another luminous world, albeit one clouded with the smoke of battle and grass fires. For Beade, light shines through the physical haze and the looming darkness of approaching death, and as Beade breathes his last, broken light filters through to shine on his face.

Malick is quick, however, to prevent any facile leap to sentiment or beatific vision by subverting the scene with two very brief intercuts of different soldiers in the midst of combat, one simply falling over dead and the other obviously driven insane by the horror of combat. These two, surely, know nothing of the serene departure of Beade. Still, Malick pushes that serenity even further with the pronounced manipulation of sound. The noise of battle recedes as swelling symphonic string music rises, over which sounds the occasional tolling of bells, perhaps denoting the surety that in time death reaps all creatures. Here, regardless of how one finally interprets the scene, Malick poignantly drives home the palpable immediacy and pertinence of his moral and epistemological wrestles. For some come random, sudden, and speedy death, and for others, like Beade, bells tolling and virtual choirs of angels. One would be inclined to make little of this sequence if Malick did not so obviously make so much of it by complex orchestration of his visual and aural ingredients.

From the beatific scene of Beade's death, Malick moves by dissolve to Tall walking through a smoky, devastated battlefield, a stroll intercut with a brief shot of a soldier holding a dead friend, a helpful visual bridge from the poignancy and price of Beade's death. Again, Malick draws a link between death and Tall's doing. Given this, and the general carnage everywhere, it is no wonder that Tall laments in voice-over that he feels "shut up in a tomb, can't lift the lid, play the role I never conceived"; to be sure, the tomb is one Tall himself has constructed, and it contains his own dead humanity (1:11:36). Still, despite this apparent despair, or surprise at his feelings and what he has become, Tall does not relent from his win-at-any-cost posture. He soon belittles and chastises GIs for so much as having a shirt off, and with Staros he rants, informing everyone that they will take the ridge by nightfall, another of his spectacular judgments that will prove conspicuously wrong. Tall screams, helmet to helmet, straight into Staros's face, "Alright, g——, we're gonna do things my way" (1:12:35). To his credit, Staros does not cower but forthrightly reports that "the ridge is quite aways from being reduced, sir." Like Gaff later in the assault, Staros regards Tall with unconcealed incredulity, hardly grasping the measure of derangement manifest in his commanding officer, a figure who increasingly resembles the mad Ahab risking all for personal vengeance.

Then, as if to make the point that not all insanity is delusional or hysterical, Malick cuts to one whose experience of battle has plainly unhinged him. Platoon leader Sergeant McCron lost all twelve of his men in the first moments of the attack on the hill, and that reality has undone his psyche, for, in another nod to Melville (or Shakespeare), he roams the battlefield as a mad prophet of horror and doom. In contrast to self-aware and callous Tall, who is "madness maddened," as Melville's Ahab labeled himself, McCron seems the sane and sensible one, seeing the war and soldiers within it as they in fact are. Earlier he tears up grass—"That's us . . . just dirt"—to throw in the air to support his assertion, echoing many biblical complaints, that human life is much like grass that withers and dies (1:01:37). In this scene he walks aimlessly through the battlefield, asking God, much as did Job, to "Show me how to see things the way You do" (1:12:55), a request Malick later puts at the center of *The Tree of Life*. Of course, to that request there is no route to knowledge or answer, for that is shrouded by a dark glass, or the smoke of battle. Mysteries abound, especially amid clouds of smoke and gunfire.

On the other hand, that we are not dirt or blown grass emerges in the next long sequence in which Private Bell (Ben Chaplin) leads a reconnaissance party of six to the top of the ridge to determine the extent of Japanese firepower and battlements. Almost there, Bell chooses to go the rest of the way by himself, crawling through the grass, all the while recalling his wife and the richness of their erotic intimacy; it is a full minute's worth of vivid recollection pointedly disrupting and countering the terror of the slow crawl to a perilous vantage point (1:16:14–1:17:12). In this and many similar sequences of recollection prompted by longing and present horror, Malick's emphasis is not so much on passion per se or sexual culmination; it is almost exclusively on the surprise and delight of sensuality as a domain of beauty and a path to intimacy, or at least that's Bell's read of it and one that Malick at least partially endorses. It is that memory and promise of return that sustains Bell through the demands of war, though in the end this means to his particular kind of "calm" will prove brutally fickle, for his wife, weary of waiting for his return, later writes to request a divorce so she can marry a flyer. Given the length and frequency of Bell's "meditations," it is clear that Malick certainly exalts sensual delight as a dimension of and conduit into the deep goodness of living, though its fragility does at the same time signal that romantic love rather too much resembles "grass" that withers and dies, as McCron puts it. That tricky thematic lies at the heart of Malick's 2012 *To the Wonder*.

In Malick's imaginative world, all these ambient worlds collide, swirling up against and through one another, hauling viewers into the immense variability of individual perception and experience. The result is a constant and complexly thick dialogic description of people amid war. After one tour through the diverse ordeals of this combat zone, Malick is at it again: Tall reasserting his authority over Staros, who clearly holds Tall in contempt; Welsh telling Witt to guard himself against this war because, given who Witt is, it will kill him (1:21:50); Witt looking contentedly (and calmly) back at Welsh and then at palm trees waving in the breeze in a moonlit sky, as if imbibing an antidote to Welsh's fatalism; McCron roaming and raving on, his voice overlaying a shot of dogs feeding on the dead, about the inscrutability of human suffering, like Lear on the heath ("Who decides who's going to live, who decides who's going to die? . . . Why? . . . How come they all had to die?" [1:23:24]); Bell again, awakening to dream of lost intimacy; and last, Staros, looking at the bright moon that recalls the light of his candle, again agonizing, beseeching divine aid, praying, "You are my Light, my Guide" (1:26:08). Then follows the long assault on the hill. How to make sense of all these juxtaposed elements, all consorting, interrogating one another, in search of a handhold on the real Real?

The Matter of Witt

To that question, Malick brings the experience of Private Witt, the one viewers know best, who assumes the unpromising role of pilgrim in a combat zone. No character in the film receives as much focus as Witt, from the first scenes to the last voice-over, though there are long stretches where he plays no significant role, seemingly disappearing as a motive force or even an interest in the film. With this, Malick diverges from the usual focus in almost all war movies upon whether and how two or three "heroes" survive or accomplish an objective. Rather, a good part of his attention fixes on how humanity endures battle, what it does to an interior world, even among the "good guys," not to mention the Japanese, those "little brown brothers" Tall references. War becomes a cauldron, and its perils press upon the interior structures of being, especially strategies of self-understanding and a search for some sort of meaning that will sustain the self in what seems this worst of all possible worlds.

Those concerns display in a host of soldiers, from Tall to Bell, Mc-Cron, Staros, Welsh, and, of course, Witt. Needless to say, all these characters differ greatly as they individually thrash toward some sort of resolution of the "big questions." In these varied points of view within just a small sliver of humanity, Malick delivers a small sample of enormous variety among American soldiers in war in the mid-twentieth century. And despite obvious differences in rank and background, many are also very much alike, wrestling with big choices as they question the meaning of war and life—and death.

The exigent circumstances of war preclude thoroughgoing revaluation of what they thought they knew prior to their immersion in war's horrors. Most continue doing what they have done. Tall, for example, seems to damn his own choice to pursue career even as he labors to advance it. Seemingly without other resources, such as Staros or Witt, Bell fixes exclusively on the very real but nonetheless untrustworthy delights of erotic relationship; these prove beguiling and consoling but, tragically, given their fleshly frailty, remarkably unreliable. Staros holds fast to his Christian belief in the "Light" that informs, or at least rationalizes, his passionate care for his men. And Welsh labors resolutely to enact a posture of cynical indifference, something he cannot quite pull off, no matter how hard he tries, as he himself confesses to Storm late in the film. For all his efforts, war has not yet numbed his susceptibility to sorrow and compassion.

Clearly, Witt, more than any of these soldiers, asks the big perennial metaphysical questions about the nature of reality and this world, and he is also the most open and sustained in his search for conclusions. Welsh, by the end, arrives at thinking as openly as Witt, but that is a very late arrival at a new posture, one instigated, it seems, by his grief for Witt. As for Witt, even after his revelatory village sojourn, he continues to ponder and question, recycling prior questions as circumstances work to pose variations or extensions of his initial ruminations on evil and death. Indeed, he mulls, recasts, broods, meditates, and tests whatever hunches have come his way amid the puzzlements of being alive deep within the dire muddle of war. Through his long presence in the film, amply influenced by his time in the village, Witt amid his pondering seems quietly self-confident and tranquil, even as he repeatedly volunteers for dangerous assignments such as storming the hilltop gun emplacement and reconnaissance of Japanese troops, a venture that gets him killed, just as Welsh predicts that something in him will somewhere get him killed, for selflessness has a price. Nor is there any self-dramatizing in Witt's demeanor, either in action or in what he says to anyone. With Witt, it seems, what we see is what we get, utter transparency, and Malick very much relies on Witt's credibility to make him a reliable index to what seem to be Malick's own queries and responses.

The measure of Malick's liking and trust of Witt shows clearly, as discussed earlier, in Malick's manner of filming Witt, usually shooting upward to place Witt against the sky or trees. This strategy not only elevates Witt, quite literally, but also identifies him with the purity of beauty in nature that Malick himself seems to venerate. In addition, then, to that fetching "look" of attendance to the world, Malick not only singles him out for particular attention but also regularly visually exalts his status and role within the film.

Ill-educated though Witt is, as is obvious in his lack of conventional grammar and syntax, he nonetheless possesses a quizzical intelligence and proves perceptive and articulate in his film-long wrestle with the contingent mysteries that envelop him. Unlike many of the others, whose words mean little, Witt seems to value words as meditative instruments that limn the contours of his experience, no matter how extraordinary. And what Witt—or anyone else, for that matter—cannot articulate, Malick attempts to show, and nowhere more so than in Witt's own death. In short, Witt is indeed unique and pivotal, and Malick takes enormous care in constructing the portraiture of this untutored southern soldier, not only by periodically providing further ruminations but also in visual presentation and in the behavioral consequences of his choices. Words and rumination only go so far, particularly in cinema, as Malick certainly knows, and thus at most every opportunity throughout the film, Malick fully deploys in Witt's behalf multiple registers of cognition and understanding for Witt and, by extension, the audience.

Witt carries throughout the film that weighty, pivotal experience in the seaside village. That has left him attuned to the beauty of the natural world, an affect that prods him to see quotidian materiality as, to quote Hopkins, "charged" with a resplendence that at times "will flame out" like "shining from shook foil"[27] (and there is, too, in Witt much of American poet Walt Whitman). In addition, Witt takes away from his time AWOL a clear sense of what a harmonious, beatific world might look like. He may indeed see village life as an instance of Edenic mutuality and delight. Whatever Witt does see Malick seems to confirm with the exultant music produced by villagers processing to worship, a choral overlay that regularly reappears amid Witt's recollections. And there is, of course, his vision of his mother's death. Importantly, this peculiar "vision" of divine welcome reinforces Witt's sense that even amid death there courses a benign, loving agency in this world, one that is transcendent but that still intimately pervades multiple domains of life, aesthetic and social, and even death itself (here Malick seems to conjure a panentheistic divinity, one that is simultaneously immanent and transcendent). All these individually and together bespeak a luminous, loving presence, however intermittently recognized amid the violent chaos people stage, that makes itself known within the palpable immediacy of daily life, even on a battlefield.

All this has lodged in Witt's mind and soul. But just because he has glimpsed the probable reality of "another world," as he describes it to Welsh, does not mean that Witt rests comfortably. Instead, the same bent for reflection that brought him to ponder the negation of his mother's death soon brings him to probe and assay the limits, character, and effability of that "beautiful Light," as philosophical foil Welsh will late in the film term the object of Witt's belief. Always thoughtful and meditative, Witt continues to try to figure it all out, experimenting with various formulations, mulling and ruminating, conjecturing as best he can with what words he has. In this regard, Witt seems intellectually in his metaphysical questions very much an experimental pragmatist and, for that matter, much like Malick in his project in *The Thin Red Line*, looking for a new and more satisfying way of couching the questions and, tellingly, responses (something so emphatic as a clear-cut, indisputable "answer" seems beyond Malick's intent). So Witt asserts to Welsh that he has indeed "seen another world." That claim comes in response to Welsh's assertion of his own self-protective individualism in an essentially demonic "world that's blowing itself to hell as fast as everybody can arrange it." After all, argues Welsh, "In this world, a man, himself, is nothing, and there ain't no world but this one"

27. Hopkins, "God's Grandeur."

(12:48). Bemused with Welsh till now, Witt's face assumes a distant, haunted look as he counters, "You're wrong there, Top. I seen another world. Sometimes I think it was just my imagination" (12:59). And so it will go between the two throughout their long war-zone contest over the nature of the world. Lodged in his brig cell, though, and seemingly striving to recapture or recall somehow that other world he has seen, Witt, after talking with Welsh, sits alone striking match after match, examining closely the flame of its brief light. In the midst of one such burning, a scene from childhood, in which he is playing in the wind on a hay wagon, appears briefly on the screen. One obvious read associates his experience while AWOL with the transparent joy of that childhood experience, especially as it compares with Witt's pleasure in playing with the village children. In sum, Witt seems to spend his days in quiet exultation at the beauty of the landscape and the amiable lives of those who live within it. It seems for him that the two have proven contiguous. Or, at the very least, the recollection supplies a brief glimpse of how Witt himself assesses the world as a place of beauty and delight quite apart from Welsh's grim analysis of humankind's plight.

We next hear Witt in long, slow monologue in voice-over, wondering and questioning, as Charlie Company moves inland on Guadalcanal. The sequence does not make much narrative sense because by now Witt has for punishment for going AWOL been removed from Charlie Company to serve a disciplinary stint in a company of stretcher-bearers, and as a later sequence suggests, he is physically in a different part of the island. Nonetheless, Malick layers Witt's wondering voice over natural sounds of the jungle and background music of quiet but quick percussion as the camera watches troops make their slow, guarded way through grasslands, bamboo forest, and a gnarled, horrific-looking swamp. As the camera at one point, just as it did at the film's beginning, looks straight up at the sun-laced jungle canopy, Witt's voice starts with a question, "Who are You who live in all these many forms?" (30:48). The camera then cuts to take in the dazzle of bright, multicolored parrots, and then it moves to the top of a stand of bamboo, slowly tilting down to see the troops walking through as Witt pointedly asks in reference to the soldiers, "Your death that captures all?" In good dialogic fashion, Witt then counters his own description of the inclusiveness of death with a contrary, seemingly paradoxical assertion about the character of the "You" he addresses: "You too are the source of all that's going to be born" (31:25). The indefiniteness and ambiguity of this "You" remain through the length of the film, including in its very last words. Malick himself seems reluctant to name this nebulous "You," in fear of making whatever he has to convey seem either trite or doctrinaire. Indeed, the indefiniteness seems intended to engage the viewers in the task of figuring the matter out for themselves.

To this vexing paradox of life and death within the same force, amplifying mystery still more, Witt ventures a response, seemingly answering, however tentatively, his own question, describing this Mystery in a way that excludes from it the sway of death. This he ekes out word by slow word over forty seconds, a quiet but fervent freestyle litany of praise for the benign agency that is the "You": "Your glory . . . mercy . . . peace . . . truth . . . you give calm of spirit, understanding, courage, the contented heart" (32:02). Here Witt articulates, as best he can, in a sequence usually disregarded by academic interpreters, aspects of the character of the benign mystery with which he contends. More than that, the sequence, in substance and form, echoes Saint Paul's singular formulations in his New Testament letters that by simple enumeration of attributes try to encompass the nature of a particular sort of divine manifestation. For example, Paul's letter to the Galatians recounts fruits of the indwelling of the Holy Spirit: "love, joy, peace, patience, kindness, goodness, faithfulness, gentleness, self-control" (5:22–23). Witt's recitation seems to echo both form and, as best he can from memory, substance, much of which, even though rephrased, is strikingly congruent with the biblical source (see also another of Paul's letters, Colossians 3:12–13). Within many traditional Christian communities, Witt's allusion would be more than clear, and especially so amid the southern, down-home America from which Witt hails.

Whatever religious or metaphysical certainty Witt seems to embrace finds more than enough trial in his stint in the rescue unit. As Charlie Company makes its way inland, they come across the decaying body of a legless soldier, and later they deal with the death of Sergeant Keck (Harrelson) after he is mortally wounded in mishandling a grenade. The scenes are taxing visually and emotionally. Indeed, for Witt and just about everyone else, the horrors of war are more than adequate as a test case of hopes for kindness in a violent, fear-soaked universe. Still a part of a stretcher company now in the rear of the operation, Witt is seen from above walking shirtless amid the severely wounded against a sunny blue sky (again juxtaposition), and then from below as he tends to a soldier whose face we never see, offering him water as he sits by the side of a running stream on which sunlight glistens (this seems to echo another central biblical passage in Matthew 25 where Jesus identifies himself with the thirsty and afflicted in need of care by others).

No wonder, then, observing and pondering, as is his wont, that Witt speculates in voice-over, "Maybe all men got one big soul that everybody's a part of, all faces of the same man, one big self. Everyone looking for salvation by himself, he's like a coal thrown from the fire," the fire denoting human origins in the Light itself (36:28). Scholar critics have latched on the quotation to suggest that Malick embraces the notion of an Emersonian Oversoul, though the film does not return to that idea, if indeed Malick is serious about it all. In a more likely reading, Malick here seems to suggest the commonality of human struggle for knowledge and, as Witt says, "salvation." Individualism, indeed, seems to doom any hope of access to the "fire," something that Witt himself seems to realize as he tends the soldier, giving water and comfort, a gesture Witt will later repeatedly undertake in his willingness to sacrifice himself for others. There indeed, perhaps, lies a good portion of the "fire" of the "beautiful Light," especially as its loving-kindness opposes the self-protective nihilism of Welsh and, not far from him, the brutal, self-aggrandizing Tall. The statement seems as likely to emphasize human solidarity as it does Transcendentalism, especially since it comes in the context of Witt caring for the anonymous wounded. Here, too, in still more dialogic construction, despite the suffering all about, the sun shines on the blood-filled water (with ample reference to biblical motifs of water and blood, soldiers bleed and are bathed in water, and another medic washes blood from a canvas stretcher).

Malick repeats instances and images of water and bathing through the length of the film, and these images carry considerable emotional clout, though they do not necessarily assume emphatic symbolic specificity. Rather, they carry a kind of diffuse cultural resonance, especially of Christian notions of baptism (rebirth), cleansing, and healing. Critics with a heavy religious bent might hasten to see baptism in all of this, but that measure of specificity seems, here at least, a considerable stretch. A sounder read, in support of the solidarity notion, comes in the echo from Bell's ruminations on his erotic bond with his wife, another prominent strand in the film that emphasizes embodiedness, the same that shapes much of Witt's rumination. Indeed, Bell's words carry the same images of water, flowing, and drinking that Malick makes central in the streamside ministrations of Witt: "We, we together, one being, flow together like water, till I can't tell you from me. I drink you, now, now" (1:24:40). Or, for that matter, the sort of counsel that comes in the New Testament where God identifies and tends to, as in Matthew 25, those most battered by the malice of this world, whether the thirsty, the hungry, the imprisoned, the orphaned, and the list goes on.

From this point in the film till its very end, Witt remains on the periphery of the action. He is one of those who volunteers, along with Bell, under the command of Captain Gaff (Cusack), to assault the hilltop. And when Charlie Company stands down for a week of R&R, a solitary Witt roams the countryside and, instead of drinking himself into oblivion as his compatriots do, revisits the village of his days AWOL. At one point he talks briefly with the solitary Welsh, who sits alone on the porch of a roofless, decaying country house. Nor does he say very much to anyone, though the audience does hear the occasional voice-over rumination that replays and, to some extent, recasts his wrestle, chastened as he seems to be by the toll of evil manifest in war and people.

However, several internal debates do become critical, in content and narrative placement, for understanding Malick's destination in the film and the importance of Witt's meditations. As important as words remain, Malick frequently pushes cinematic resources to convey or go beyond, if he can, what the words denote. Frequently, the audience simply watches Witt watch, Malick letting viewers derive what meaning and significance they can in simply seeing his reactions and seeing what he does, his "look" shaping and testing their own as they try to understand what they see in relation to how Witt sees the same. By this means, Malick implicates viewers, viscerally and intellectually, in the action itself. Witt, after all, is both an inviting and a cryptic character, and Caviezel artfully keeps a balance between Witt's winsomeness and his interiority.

To be sure, Malick is not all hope and happy talk. While Charlie Company does take the emplacement and then overruns Japanese forces encamped on the long ridge, giving Tall his yearned-for singular accomplishment, victory itself proves hollow and costly. Here, to be sure, Malick seems to go out of his way to subvert the usual pleasures of military triumph that soldiers and viewers alike anticipate. Yes, victory, and war generally probably, has its necessities, but the costs remain incalculable. Violent, excruciating death, agony, and grief occupy just about every frame, especially in shots of the conquered. And Witt will brood amply on this sort of malign reality, a darkness that threatens to swallow light. In voice-over as the camera surveys the process of "victory" wrought by the "good guys," Witt recoils and questions, echoing both Job and Melville: "This great evil, where's it come from? How'd it steal into the world? What seed, what root did it grow from? Who's doing this, who's killing us, robbing us of life and light, mocking us with the sight of what we might have known? Does our ruin benefit the earth? Does it help the grass to grow, the sun to shine? Is this darkness in you too? Have you passed through this night?" (1:50:25). Witt's somber recognition is that "this great evil" does indeed seem to be everywhere and in everyone, especially in the likes of Tall, on whom Malick has let the camera dwell, and who has damned himself mightily with his own special pleading to his mutely resistant subordinate Captain Gaff. After the battle, Malick dramatizes Witt's somber reflections with the conduct of some American troops, taunting and desecrating their captives, living and dead alike, as when Dale lolls on mounds of enemy dead and pulls teeth for war trophies.

In the first respite amid victory, Witt and others cool themselves in a muddy jungle pond, Witt pouring water over his head and watching water drain from large plant leaves onto which he has poured water. The falling water and the reflection of the canopy and blue sky above in the pond surface recall for Witt his days AWOL, first of bathing exultantly in a huge waterfall and then of pleasant village scenes of play and work. The strained music of the battle encounter is replaced with the exultant

hymn singing of the villagers, an efficient aural conjuring of the dialogic counters at the core of Witt's ruminations. On the one hand, this
visual and musical recollection seems to counter his earlier indictment
of the war and its voraciousness, an enterprise that robs "us of life and
light, mocking us with the sight of what we might have known." Clearly,
the real horrors of battle and violent death interrogate Witt's blissful
recollection of "what we might have known" if not for war. Whatever
hopefulness he might have felt for humankind's intrinsic goodness has
by now received a severe blow, and it is a daunting problem that he will
pursue, for if one cannot trust his early impressions of the potential
of delight and social harmony, what then of his village experience, especially his markedly subjective mystical recognitions? Can he or we
trust these as veritable and prescriptive? Staying true to his dialogic
disquisition, Malick takes Witt's apprehension with due seriousness.

Malick does give ample evidence for the rightness, or at least
reasonableness, of Witt's skepticism about human goodness and the
goodness of life itself. Immediately following, the newly empowered
Tall, for the most vainglorious, venal reasons, relieves Staros of his
command, and thereafter we glimpse, first, the self-satisfied Tall
sitting alone enjoying his triumph and, second, issuing imperial,
self-congratulatory proclamations to his weary, bedraggled troops.
The long battle sequence that forms the central action of the film
ends with shots of a solitary Tall thinking, interspersed with shots
of enemy and American dead, the latter with tags on their toes.
The last glimpses show flamethrowers in the night incinerating the
enemy encampment. As with previous scenes of fire and smoke,
the imagery is more than telling, Tall and others having seemingly
summoned hell itself, of which they are the chief sponsors, to rise
above ground.

Charlie Company's rest behind the lines allows for relaxation, mostly
by alcohol sedation. The troops swim, and Staros bids farewell to a small
group of his men lamenting his departure, though he tells them he'll
be glad to leave the war. Full of yearning, Bell writes his wife that he
will try to stay unchanged by the horrors of the war, wondering how
they will again "get to those blue hills" of oneness (2:08:21). In deft,
evocative writing, Bell wonders, "Love, where does it come from? Who
lit this flame in us? No war can put it out, conquer it. I was a prisoner,
you set me free" (2:08:34). As usual, Malick balances Bell's talk of flame
with the flames of a night attack on the base camp. And Bell's words

seem the flip side of Witt's pondering of the pervasiveness of evil. As ever in *The Thin Red Line*, the ever-nagging duality of experience will not relent. In any case, that looming question of the meanings of war weaves smoothly into the architecture of the sort of inquiry Malick stages throughout the film.

Throughout Malick makes sure that viewers recognize and feel negation, "feel what the wretches feel," as Lear puts it. Combat and the "spoils" are not an easy passage for anyone, and to make the point, Malick supplies a quick series of somber notes. Indeed, this war seems to eviscerate the soul, as is the case with Sergeant Storm (Reilly), who confesses to Welsh as they sit in the infirmary smoking and drinking, that he can "feel nothing . . . care about nothing" (2:09:50). Welsh envies him, despite his earlier claims of disinterest: "Sounds like bliss. I don't have that feeling yet" (2:10:03). Or nonfeeling. If there's any doubt as to why they feel as they do, the camera interrupts to cut to the dying and maimed (recalling a sequence in *The Deer Hunter* wherein the battle-blitzed, grief-ridden Nick [Christopher Walken] sobs as the camera shifts between him and a limbless soldier in a hospital ward). Malick's next scene, perhaps somewhat heavy-handedly, recalls the film's opening sequence, only in this instance staging a reversal that comments on humankind, just in case viewers have not yet gotten the point. An enormous crocodile lies bound on a truck bed for the soldiers' curiosity and amusement, though it is perhaps by this stage difficult to distinguish the two species, the reptile and the human, at least in terms of moral stature.

If all that were not bad enough, then follows Bell's letter from his wife asking for a divorce. The request subverts Bell's sustaining faith in erotic intimacy and "oneness" as an antidote to horror. Bell's purity of desire, to which he regularly attests, contrasts with her cupidity. Not all cruelty happens in war, and in Bell's case, longing and hopefulness prove no guide to truth or permanence, at least with regard to other people (the aching mysteries of attraction and alienation, both romantic and religious, form the core of *To the Wonder* [2012]).

Relational wholeness also proves elusive in Witt's return to the village of his AWOL excursion, a return that chastens his fondest recollections of pristine harmony. This time, however, in the wake of his battle lament on the "great evil," not all is paradisal, and Witt cannot avoid seeing flaws and limitations where he once saw perfection and bliss: children flee, women retreat at his approach, men quarrel, and children are covered with sores. Some of that aversion to him no doubt results in the fact that this time he comes in full combat gear and carrying his rifle. Some of what Witt sees, such as disease and strife, no doubt existed before, but he did not see it, just as he failed to see that children fought when they played, as one mother assured him they did. Such is the variability of perception within the course of experience, mood, and just living life. Still, he leaves mulling his first visit, though now markedly chastened and full of lament, eloquent and even psalmic: "We were a family. How'd it break up and come apart, so that now we're turned against each other, each standing in the other's light? How'd we lose the good that was given us, let it slip away, scattered, careless?" (2:17:00). Of human history, the rumination is a trenchant summation, especially of Jewish and Christian mythologies of a human Fall from sensuous delight and relational wholeness. From social accord and felicity humankind has turned to enmity and despair.

Despite this long catalogue of brokenness, Witt seems undeterred in hope and kindness. The hope continues in the sort of question he asks as he ponders the encompassing evil: on a hilltop on his slow walk to camp, he wonders, in a continuation of his village queries and as a forecast of his analysis of ways of understanding the ambiguities of the dying bird, "What's keeping us from reaching out, touching the glory?" (2:18:00). The horrors, in fact, might even have strengthened his resolve, though Malick does not haul viewers far enough into Witt's consciousness or actions to offer direct evidence of this. Witt does not reject the reality of all he encountered in his first visit to the seaside village, but he does question its lastingness, for things do seem to have changed, to have fallen apart, and this he mourns.

Nonetheless, on his trek back to the base, he runs across a cheerful, newly wounded soldier who's happy with the morphine the medic has given him and the prospect of leaving the war, something the wound in his knee has guaranteed. Witt makes sure the fellow prefers waiting for others, telling him that if he wants to return now to the camp he will help him along, and if not, he'll remind the bosses that a wounded soldier on the hilltop needs fetching. Reentering the camp, he quietly greets and shakes hands with many, ending up talking with Welsh. In a pivotal summative scene, Witt insists that he still sees in Welsh "a spark," a flicker of the "beautiful Light" Welsh ascribes to Witt's manner of seeing the world (2:22:53; 2:22:26). In response, Welsh insists that Witt is a "magician" in seeing a resplendent world, apparently by changing horror to light (2:22:42).

In this leisurely sequence, overlaid by Zimmer's score, a mix of gentle solemnity and hopefulness, Malick includes two prominent elements from Witt's re-visioning of his mother's death that make the referents of the conversation unmistakable. On the porch of the abandoned house hangs a birdcage, though it is now empty, unlike the one that hung by his mother's deathbed. As a traditional religious symbol for the body that holds the human soul, its presence here perhaps denotes the persistence of Witt's changed religious vision of the fate of the soul after death: the cage is there, but its occupant has left. The house lacks a roof, and Witt observes its absence in a movement that matches the camera movement and imagery that ended Witt's re-vision of his mother's death. Jelling with the empty cage, the absent roof and the shot of the clear blue sky suggest, as they did in Witt's vision of his mother's deathbed, limitlessness and infinitude. The sequence aptly foreshadows the final test of Witt's persistent affirmation amid the overwhelming woundedness of this world.

The very next scene, one that begins the conclusion of *The Thin Red Line*, finds Charlie Company back in the interior for more combat duty. It begins with one of Witt's voice-over conjectures, this one crisply distilling the epistemological joust at the philosophical and religious center of the film, reiterating one final time the dialogic poles of the philosophical and experiential riddle that courses through the center of its ever-arresting multifoliated cascade of images, action, music, and words. During a night encampment viewers see Welsh in the near dark roaming among his sleeping soldiers; strings provide a melodic but tense backdrop. Over this comes Witt's voice as the camera follows Welsh, thereby clearly identifying the "one man" of Witt's words with Welsh: "One man looks at a dying bird and thinks there's nothing but unanswered pain, that death's got the final word. It's laughing at him." Then, as a counter to Welsh's despair, the camera shifts, appropriately, to cloud-shrouded hills, and then to a sleeping Witt. His voice-over then offers an opposing view: "Another man sees that same bird and feels the glory, feels something smiling through it" (2:23:00). The scene ends with several soldiers stomping out sparks flying from the flaming embers of a campfire, perhaps foreshadowing the end of Witt's own "spark." Here again, Malick repeats a central motif in the film, one repeated prominently in *The Tree of Life*: a lengthy and central shot of light flickering in the darkness, whether in airborne embers or candle flame. Whatever the symbolism, the philosophical opposition is never clearer—absurdity and nothingness or "the glory . . . smiling through"—and with this statement Malick cues Witt's epistemological and existential posture in his confrontation with death. The visual and verbal texts inescapably allude to the famous, resonant opening of the New Testament's Gospel of John, a text that shapes a good deal of Western culture's iconography of being, from Shakespeare to *Star Wars*: "The light shines in the darkness, and the darkness has not overcome it" (John 1:5 RSV).

In its last sustained action sequence, the story then follows Witt's and Charlie Company's journey inland along a streambed, enemy artillery fire all around. In the absence of Staros, they have for a leader a new and very uncertain lieutenant who chooses two inept and fearful soldiers, Fife and Coons, to go into the jungle to scout the location of the enemy. Doubting the competence of the two, and of the lieutenant, Witt volunteers to join them "in case something bad happens," and it soon does (2:26:00). The trio slowly proceeds up the sunlit, fast-flowing stream, Malick cutting to look at an owl and sun-laced treetops, referencing perhaps two instances of abiding "glory" even as the soldiers venture ever further into peril. Soon thereafter Coons is seriously wounded in an exchange of gunfire with a Japanese platoon. Witt instructs Fife to return to the company with news of what they've found, Witt choosing to remain behind to tend to Coons—"My friend here doesn't have long," he tells Fife—knowing full well, from the look on his face and Malick's long take, that his choice will probably be his last (2:29:32). Witt then sends Coons floating down the stream to take him out of danger and, if he lives, down to the riverside base camp. In the meanwhile, Witt attempts to lead the large number of Japanese away from the vulnerable Charlie Company. To stage a convincing diversion, he charges noisily through the jungle whistling, shouting, and firing his rife in order to make the Japanese think that he is a larger force.

And then the end, at least for Witt, and a remarkable, even spectacular one it is, both experientially, philosophically, and, when understood, cinematically. After a considerable chase Witt emerges into a clearing to find himself surrounded by a large contingent of Japanese soldiers who clearly want him to throw down his weapon. Though speaking in Japanese (and without subtitles), their desires are more than clear. At first, as the officer continues to address Witt and closes in with his rifle raised and aimed, Witt's face is full of fear as he assesses his impossible predicament. From the approaching officer, the camera cuts backs to Witt, whose face, in a startling shift, has moved from fear to show rapt wonder as he stares, wide-eyed and open-mouthed, at something beyond and slightly above the encircling troops, transfixed by that which only he seems to see (2:34:11). Zimmer's gentle but lyrical orchestral music from Witt's AWOL days by the shore has already begun to play and swell (2:33:58). Witt's eyes only widen further as the camera dollies in to medium close-up, and then, as viewers hear the sound of a wave breaking upon the shore (2:34:35), Witt raises his gun, a gesture that he knows will kill him, and in the instant of his death, before his body hits the ground, the camera cuts to an up-looking ten-second shot of light cascading through a jungle canopy like water from a high fall (2:34:37–47). Here indeed, the glory seems to smile, or pour through, and the sequence suggests some sort of postdeath consciousness. Nor does Malick stop with that. He follows with a half minute of a delighted Witt swimming below a sunlit surface with the boys from the village. The sequence ends with a return to a massive jungle tree, the camera slowly tilting upward to take in its great height and its girth (the tree of life perhaps, here symbolic and perhaps a foreshadowing of the film to come). And through all, the quietly rapturous music continues, even as Witt lifts his weapon and dies.

There are two singular and surprising elements in the sequence: one lies in the manner of Witt's composure as he chooses death, for he does indeed seem, from the look and sound of it all, to meet death with "calm," as he put the matter at the very beginning of the film. The second notable, and even peculiar, ingredient lies in the apparent ecstasy he experiences after his body has fallen to the ground; the wave crashes and his mind (or soul) relishes and romps in a kind of exultant savor of the goodness of being. Philosophically, Malick seems here to push for some sort of postmortem consciousness, the survival of the self in an exultant realm of light and delight.

As enticing as this vision is, Malick imbues it with a still more radical vision of life and after-being by embedding within it another, though not contradictory, rendition of Witt's last seconds being alive. Here viewers see and experience the mood or state of mind with which Witt approaches and experiences death, imaginatively inhabiting the experience itself. Viewers have seen the same displayed on his face prior to lifting his weapon. In effect, Malick retells Witt's end by placing within the sound design of Witt's postmortem reverie the sound of a rifle firing. With this, Malick brings the viewer into Witt's subjective state *before*, *through*, and *beyond* his death. With this sleight of hand in sound design, Malick seems to double down on the significance of Witt's vision. The ecstatic vision that follows upon Witt's death (a bullet has clearly gone through his upper torso) in fact begins before the shooting, meaning that the viewer sees what the awed, wide-eyed Witt sees before his demise, rapt as he is in his recollection of beauty and delight (2:35:14). Roughly two-thirds through the sequence, amid the music and the waves, a gunshot is heard, presumably the one that kills Witt, and thus the sequence allows for an alternative vision of Witt's death (2:35:17). By such means, Malick allows the viewer to see what Witt sees in the seconds *before* and after his death. What Witt experiences postmortem *also* simultaneously contains the substance of what he perceives amid his last seconds of attention during his life, and it courses uninterruptedly through and beyond his physical death. In short, the sequence shows both what follows death *and* what precedes it. Before and after, continuous and apparently unending, Witt experiences the ecstatic perception of a rapturous "glory" abundantly shining and smiling in the physical world about him and in the depths of his soul. Here "calm" in awe and delight, Witt is anything but emotionless; rather there is only the resplendent, exultant "glory" of being alive, here both as foretaste and as realization. In the moment of his dying, himself now the dying bird, Witt himself, it seems, has been enveloped by "the glory . . . smiling through."

Hans Zimmer's enticing music carries far into the next scene, the burial of Witt, and then stops as the natural sounds of the forest fittingly take its place. In the whole long film, one in which death abounds, Witt is the only soldier buried by his fellows. In a glade by a pond, his body has been covered by gravel and his inverted rifle sticks in the ground at the head of the grave. Welsh crouches, first attaching Witt's dog tags to the gun and then carefully placing the helmet on the butt of the rifle. The camera surveys Witt's compatriots, from Bell to Doll, all sobered and mourning. As the others drift off, only Welsh remains, continuing to crouch at the foot of Witt's grave; thinking and brooding, he asks, "Where's your spark now?" (2:37:04). After that query, he grimaces and wipes his eyes at the loss of his friend. Malick then continues to insist on the full measure of the loss of Witt by immediately dissolving to Welsh listening to the insufferable banalities of his new captain (George Clooney), Staros's replacement, who babbles about being the new father and Welsh being the mother and the troops being the children. Welsh's voice-over response is more than just, and an apt summary of much of Malick's indictment of the apparatus of war: "Everything a lie. . . . They want you dead or in their lie" (2:37:17).

That, though, is not the end point for Welsh—or for Witt, for that matter. Welsh's voice-over soon approaches a major philosophical turn in the film and Malick's dialogism, namely, the movement of Welsh from cynicism to the possibility that Witt's spark might in fact have in it consequential light. He ruminates in voice-over as the troops march by a military cemetery on their way to the beach and departure from Guadalcanal, as Welsh first replays his protective individualism: "Only one thing a man can do—find something that's his [and] make an island for himself" (2:40:34). Then comes a fundamental change in what has heretofore been steely and cynical self-protectiveness, for Welsh comes to consider an additional and vastly different possibility, one constituting at least a nod toward the theistic "beautiful Light" notions of Witt. He forthrightly considers the possibility of a divine reality he cannot quite (yet?) bring himself to embrace, though he seems now to concede its reality: "If I never meet You in this life, let me feel the lack. A glance from Your eyes, and my life will be Yours" (2:39:12). Welsh seems now to have come to acknowledge the reality of the "beautiful Light" Witt professed but will not offer his assent until he himself sees the world as Witt sees it, until that Light, in other words, shows itself and embraces Welsh as it did Witt.

Closure

So we arrive at Witt's end, and a perplexing aftermath. Charlie Company boards a landing craft to return to a troop ship that will take what's left of it to fight another day on another island. Not so with Witt, whose words are the last we hear in the film. Though Malick has killed him off, Witt's voice continues in postmortem postscript. What Witt has to say brings viewers back to the very beginning and the dialogic queries he posed about the war in nature: "Darkness, light, strife and love, are they the workings of one mind, the features of the same face?" (2:40:49). The question sums up most of Witt's ruminations during his time on Guadalcanal, a place that has in multiple ways proven revelatory, hallowed ground for Witt: "Where is it that we were together? Who were you that I lived with, walked with? The brother, the friend," a query that ends, appropriately, with the camera on a solitary Welsh (2:41:09). From these immediate riddles, Witt's monologue slides into reflection on those persistent, exasperating metaphysical questions, ones that Witt mulled throughout and proved nearly impossible to tease apart and resolve. And so the film returns to where it began, pondering vexing oppositions between darkness and light and strife and love, the very ones that sketch the lineaments of Witt's imagination and soul. And to which Malick responds with predominantly visual and musical suggestions. The best answers seem not necessarily to be philosophical but depend on what and how one apprehends the plangent world all about, from birds to people and sounds.

And then, as is Witt's wont throughout, he slides into petition that ends in a free-form doxology. "O my soul [or Soul?], let me be in you [or You?] now. Look out through my eyes, look out at the things you [or You?] made, all things shining." These last words in the film are more than a little vexing, largely due to Witt's, and Malick's, penchant for the indefinite pronoun "you." The same is the case in Welsh's use of "Your" as he passes the GI cemetery, raising the question of just whom he addresses. Witt in the film's last words constructs a unique topography for the self, addressing his "soul," perhaps the spark within, as the distinct part of the self capable of apprehending metaphysical truth, at least of the sort Witt has come upon. So he bids his conscious self—including the intellect, for it has only gotten him to endless recycling imponderables—to forgo its vexations to enter the soul's apprehension of a world where all things shine in luminous transparency because behind all is divine love, the very thing that Witt at one point likens to the glory that smiles through the encompassing horror of warfare. Or, in fact, the soul he addresses is the divine soul, akin, as many have suggested, to Emerson's Oversoul. Whatever the case, what Witt labels the soul perceives this "glory" that for him, and maybe too for Welsh, trumps despair at the horror and apparent indifference of the natural world, a realm that includes humanity. Within Witt's experience, what starts in wonder ends in love; what the soul apprehends, then, is love smilingly "shining" in all that is, even amid that darkness, and it is to that liminal domain and depth of experience that Witt beckons his conscious, ratiocinating self to join. Indeed, constructing the experience of this sort of perceptual posture as a plausible, viable "felt reality" has been a major aim in the thickly "embodied" cinematic style of *The Thin Red Line*, and even more so in Malick's films since.

Witt's postmortem rumination, and the arc of his experience in the film as a whole, seems remarkably akin to the language and gist of one of the most celebrated (and demanding) passages in Augustine's *Confessions*, wherein Christendom's first major postapostolic theologian recounts his own progress in recognizing "those lovely things which you have made," all of which he comes to understand as a token of divine care, "beauty, so ancient and so new."[28] That light of recognition fell upon Augustine (and Witt, for that matter) when "you sent forth your beams and you shone upon me and chased away my blindness,"

28. Multiple translations of book 10, chapter 27 of Augustine's *Confessions* appear online. The book was published near the end of the fourth century and remains a towering work within the history of Christianity and Western culture. It would be easy to make the case that Witt is, in fact, a sort of poor man's Augustine, in both the tenor and shape of his rumination.

a transit that Malick deploys repeatedly in event, language, and visual and aural imagery throughout the film, all striving to "embody" at least a measure of palpable lived experience of perceptual depth and clarity. It is there, to be sure, in Witt's vision of his mother's death, in the comity and wonder of life in the Melanesian village, even in the midst of war, and it is there too in the "shining" splendor of the natural world, in repeated images of light pouring through enormous trees, of water and waterfalls, of flame in darkness, and all consort, even dance together, to conjure the prospect of a wholly different sort of reality than that prescribed by the horrors of war and, for that matter, the foreclosures of contemporary philosophical naturalism.[29]

29. Eliot's *Four Quartets* again serves as a helpful map to at least some of the path that Malick charts in *The Thin Red Line* and in his subsequent films. Indeed, it would be very easy to sculpt a reading of Malick's films in which Eliot's modern poetic masterpiece provides a bedrock topography of not only their religious landscape but also the paths into and through that terrain. A good deal of Eliot's view emerges from instances of arresting wonder and delight, moments that furnish "hints and guesses" that suggest paradoxical images of stillness, music, and dance, and his claim that "there is only the dance." Eliot, *Complete Poems and Plays*, 119.

FILMOGRAPHY

List of Referenced DVD Editions

American Gigolo. DVD. Directed by Paul Schrader. Paramount, 1980. Hollywood: Paramount, 2000.

The Apostle. DVD. Directed by Robert Duvall. Butcher's Run, 1997. Universal Collector's Edition. Los Angeles: Universal Studios, 2002.

The Color of Paradise. DVD. Directed by Majid Majidi. Varahonar Company, 1999. Culver City, CA: Sony Pictures, 2000.

Dead Man Walking. DVD. Directed by Tim Robbins. Polygram, Working Title/Havoc, 1995. Beverly Hills: MGM, 1995.

Heaven. DVD. Directed by Tom Tykwer. Miramax, 2002. La Crosse, WI: Echo Bridge, 2011.

Magnolia. DVD. Directed by Paul Thomas Anderson. New Line, 1999. Los Angeles: New Line Home Video, 2000.

The Shawshank Redemption. DVD. Directed by Frank Darabont. Castle Rock, 1994. Burbank, CA: Warner 10th Anniversary Edition, 2004.

The Thin Red Line. DVD. Directed by Terrence Malick. Fox 2000, Geisler-Roberdeau, and Phoenix, 1998. Los Angeles: 20th Century Fox, 2001.

Wide Awake. DVD. Directed by M. Night Shyamalan. Miramax, 1998. La Crosse, WI: Echo Bridge, 2011.

INDEX